THE AMERICAN HISTORY SERIES

RECONSTRUCTION AND THE CONSTITUTION

1866-1876

BY

JOHN W. BURGESS, PH.D., LL.D.

PROFESSOR OF POLITICAL SCIENCE AND CONSTITUTIONAL LAW, AND DEAN OF
THE FACULTY OF POLITICAL SCIENCE, IN COLUMBIA UNIVERSITY

NEW YORK
CHARLES SCRIBNER'S SONS
1902

COPYRIGHT, 1902, BY
CHARLES SCRIBNER'S SONS

TROW DIRECTORY
PRINTING AND BOOKBINDING COMPANY
NEW YORK

This scarce antiquarian book is included in our special *Legacy Reprint Series*. In the interest of creating a more extensive selection of rare historical book reprints, we have chosen to reproduce this title even though it may possibly have occasional imperfections such as missing and blurred pages, missing text, poor pictures, markings, dark backgrounds and other reproduction issues beyond our control. Because this work is culturally important, we have made it available as a part of our commitment to protecting, preserving and promoting the world's literature.

To the memory

of

RICHMOND MAYO-SMITH,

pupil, colleague, and life-long friend,

with grief too deep for words at his loss,

this volume

is affectionately inscribed

by the Author

PREFACE

In my preface to "The Middle Period" I wrote that the re-establishment of a real national brotherhood between the North and the South could be attained only on the basis of a sincere and genuine acknowledgment by the South that secession was an error as well as a failure. I come now to supplement this contention with the proposition that a corresponding acknowledgment on the part of the North in regard to Reconstruction between 1866 and 1876 is equally necessary.

In making this demand, I must not be understood as questioning in the slightest degree the sincerity of the North in the main purpose of the Reconstruction policy of that period. On the other hand, I maintain that that purpose was entirely praiseworthy. It was simply to secure the civil rights of the newly emancipated race, and to re-establish loyal Commonwealths in the South. But there is now little question that erroneous means were chosen.

Two ways were open for the attainment of the end sought. One was that which was followed, namely, placing the political power in the hands of the newly emancipated; and the other was the nationalization of civil liberty by placing it under the protection of the

Constitution and the national Judiciary, and holding the districts of the South under Territorial civil government until the white race in those districts should have sufficiently recovered from its temporary disloyalty to the Union to be intrusted again with the powers of Commonwealth local government.

There is no doubt in my own mind that the latter was the proper and correct course. And I have just as little doubt that it would have been found to be the truly practicable course. The people in the loyal Commonwealths were ready in 1866 to place civil liberty as a whole under national protection; and not half of the whites of the South entertained, at that moment, disloyal purposes or feelings. Even the solid Democratic South was yet to be made; and I doubt most seriously if it would ever have been made, except for the great mistakes of the Republican party in its choice of means and measures in Reconstruction.

I will not, however, enter upon the argument in reference to this question at this point. That belongs to the body of the book. I will only add that, in my opinion, the North has already yielded assent to this proposition, and has already made the required acknowledgment. The policy of Mr. Hayes's administration, and of all the administrations since his, can be explained and justified only upon this assumption. And now that the United States has embarked in imperial enterprises, under the direction of the Republican party, the great Northern party, the North is learning every day by valuable experiences that there are vast differences in political capacity between the races, and that it is the white man's mission, his duty and his right, to hold the reins of political power in his own hands for the civilization of the world and the welfare of mankind.

Let the South be equally ready, sincere, and manly in the consciousness and the acknowledgment of its share in past errors, and the reconciliation will be complete and permanent !

I have again to express my thanks to my friend and colleague, Dr. Cushing, for his aid in bringing this volume through the press. I desire also to acknowledge the courtesy of the New York *Independent* for allowing parts of my article on the Geneva Award, published some years ago in that esteemed journal, to be incorporated in the last chapter of this book.

JOHN W. BURGESS.

323 WEST 57TH ST., NEW YORK CITY,
    January 22d, 1902.

CONTENTS

CHAPTER I
THE THEORY OF RECONSTRUCTION 1

CHAPTER II
PRESIDENT LINCOLN'S VIEWS AND ACTS IN REGARD TO RECONSTRUCTION 8

CHAPTER III
PRESIDENT JOHNSON'S PLAN OF RECONSTRUCTION AND HIS PROCEEDINGS IN REALIZATION OF IT 31

CHAPTER IV
THE CONGRESSIONAL PLAN OF RECONSTRUCTION . . . 42

CHAPTER V
THE CONGRESSIONAL PLAN (*Continued*) 62

CHAPTER VI
THE CONGRESSIONAL PLAN (*Continued*) 84

CONTENTS

CHAPTER VII
The Congressional Plan (*Completed*) 107

CHAPTER VIII
The Execution of the Reconstruction Acts . . . 144

CHAPTER IX
The Attempt to Impeach the President 157

CHAPTER X
Reconstruction Resumed 195

CHAPTER XI
President Grant and Reconstruction 222

CHAPTER XII
"Carpet-Bag" and Negro Domination in the Southern States between 1868 and 1876 247

CHAPTER XIII
The Presidential Election of 1876 and its Consequences 280

CHAPTER XIV
International Relations of the United States between 1867 and 1877 299

INDEX 329

RECONSTRUCTION AND THE CONSTITUTION

RECONSTRUCTION

CHAPTER I

THE THEORY OF RECONSTRUCTION

The Conception of a "State" in a System of Federal Government—The Different Kinds of Local Government Provided for in the Constitution of the United States—Local Government Under the Constitution of the United States—"State" Destructibility in the Federal System of Government—The Effect on "State" Existence of the Renunciation of Allegiance to the Union—The Idea of "State" Perdurance—The Constitutional Results of Attempted Secession.

THE key to the solution of the question of Reconstruction is the proper conception of what a "State" is in a system of federal government. This is a conception which is not easy to acquire, and which, when acquired, is not easy to hold. The difficulty lies, chiefly, in the tendency to confound the idea of a "State" in such a system with a state pure and simple. Until the distinction between the two is clearly seen and firmly applied, no real progress can be made in the theory and practice of the federal system of government. Now the fundamental principle of a state pure and simple is sovereignty, the original, innate, and legally unlimited power to command and enforce obedience by the infliction of penalties for disobedience. On the other hand, the nature of a "State" in a system of federal gov-

The conception of a "State" in a system of federal government.

ernment is a very different thing. Such a "State" is a local self-government, under the supremacy of the general constitution, and possessed of residuary powers. In the federal system of the United States, it is a local self-government, under the supremacy of the Constitution of the United States, and of the laws and treaties of the central Government made in accordance with that Constitution, republican as to form, and possessed of residuary powers—that is, of all powers not vested by the Constitution of the United States exclusively in the central Government, or not denied by that Constitution to the "State."

It must be kept in mind that this is not the only kind of local government known in the constitutional law and practice of the United States. There is, and always has been, since the establishment of the federal system in 1789, for the larger part of the population which declared united independence of Great Britain in 1776, another kind of local government for a part of the United States, a local government which is not self-government, a local government which is but an agency of the central Government. In fact, there have been at times three kinds of local government in the political system of the United States, viz., local government by the executive department of the central Government—that is, local government by executive discretion, martial law—local government as an agency of the legislative department of the central Government—that is, Territorial government—and "State" government. That is to say, since 1789 the whole of the United States, territorially, has never been under the federal system of government, but has *always* been partly under federal government and partly under the exclusive government of Congress, and has *sometimes* been partly under federal government,

The different kinds of local government provided for in the Constitution of the United States.

partly under the exclusive government of Congress, and partly under the exclusive government of the President.

The Constitution of the United States recognizes and provides for all three of these species of local government, and vests in Congress the power of advancing the population of a district, the confines of which district shall be determined by Congress itself, from the lower to the higher forms of local government. While the Constitution does not expressly impose upon Congress the duty of making or permitting the change from one kind of local government to another, it impliedly indicates that Congress shall determine the kind of local government which the population of any particular district shall enjoy in accordance with the conditions prevailing, at any given moment, among them. If the maintenance of law and order requires the immediate exercise of military power, Congress may, and should, permit the continuance of the President's discretionary government. If, on the other hand, this is not necessary, Congress may, and should, confer civil government, under the Territorial form, and when the population of a Territory shall have become ripe for local self-government and capable of maintaining it, Congress may, and should, allow the Territory to become a "State" of the Union, a Commonwealth.

<small>Local government under the Constitution of the United States.</small>

Such being the nature of a "State" of the Union and such the method of its creation, what reason is there for speaking of the "States" in a system of federal government as indestructible? As they emerge from the status of Territories under the exclusive power of Congress, upon having attained certain conditions, why may they not revert to the status of Territories upon having lost these conditions of "State" existence; nay, why may

<small>"State" destructibility in the system of federal government.</small>

they not revert to the status of martial law by having lost all of the conditions of civil government? The dictum "once a State always a State" in a system of federal government has no sound reason in it. Under the Constitution of the United States, every "State" of the Union may through the process of amendment be made a province subject to the exclusive government of the central authorities; and when those who wield the powers of a "State" renounce the "State's" allegiance to the United States, renounce the supremacy of the Constitution of the United States and of the laws of the central Government made in accordance therewith, then from the point of view of political science it will become a state pure and simple, a sovereignty, if and when it permanently maintains, by its own power or by the assent of the United States, this attitude against the United States, but from the point of view of the constitutional law of the United States it simply destroys one of the fundamental conditions of local self-government, and gives, thus, warrant to the central Government to resume exclusive government in the district, and over the population which has become disorganized by refusing obedience to the supreme law of the land, as fixed by the Constitution of the United States. Whether the central Government has the physical power, at a given moment, to do this or not, is another question. It certainly has, at the outset, the legal right. The "State" is no longer a "State" of the Union, nor has it become a state out of the Union. It is simply nowhere. The land is there and the people are there, but the form of local government over it and them has been changed from local *self*-government to a Congressional or a Presidential agency, as the case may be.

The effect on "State" existence of the renunciation of allegiance to the Union.

Neither is there any reason for holding that the old

"State" organization perdures as an abstract something under the forms of Congressional or Presidential rule, and will emerge of itself when these are withdrawn. If the "State" form of local government should be established again over that same district and over the population inhabiting it, it would be an entirely new creation, even though it should recognize the forms and laws and obligations of the old "State." It must be, however, remembered that both the executive and judicial departments of the United States Government committed themselves fully to this theory of "State" perdurance as an abstract something unaffected by the loss of the conditions of the "State" form of local government through the rebellion of the "State" organization against the supremacy of the Constitution and laws of the United States, and that Congress did the same thing, at first, in some degree. It was this error which caused all of the confusion in the ideas and processes of Reconstruction, and we ought, therefore, to rid ourselves of it at the start, at the same time that we recognize its influence over the minds of those who engaged in the difficult work of the years between 1865 and 1876.

The idea of "State" perdurance.

The acceptance of this idea by the Government of the United States.

From the view which we take of the nature of a "State" in a system of federal government, and its possible destructibility, there is not much difficulty in determining the constitutional results of an attempt upon the part of such a "State" to break away from its connections in that system. What it does, stripped of all misconception and verbiage, is simply this : it forcibly resists the execution of the whole supreme law of the land, and destroys the prime condition of its own existence by making it necessary for the central Government to

The constitutional results of attempted secession.

assert exclusive power in the district where this happens. Naturally the executive department of the central Government must act first, and subdue by force the force which has been offered against the supremacy of the Constitution and laws of the United States. After that shall have been accomplished, the question as to how the population in the rebellious district shall be civilly organized anew, is one for the legislative department of the central Government exclusively. Congress may fashion the boundaries of the district at its own pleasure, and may establish therein such a Territorial organization of civil local government as it may see fit, and is limited in what it may do in this respect only by the constitutional immunities of the individual subject or citizen under every form of civil government provided or allowed by the Constitution of the United States. Congress may also enable the existing population of such a district, or such part of that population as it may designate, to organize the "State" form of local government, and may grant it participation in the powers of the central Government upon an equality with the other "States" in the federal system. These things are matters in which the President, as the executive power, cannot interfere. As participant in legislation, however, he may, at his own discretion, use his powers of recommendation and veto.

If rebellion against the supremacy of the Constitution and laws of the United States should not be committed by an existing "State" organization, but by a new organization claiming to be the "State" organization within the district concerned, the existing organization remaining loyal, but requiring the aid of the central Government to maintain its authority, then the withdrawal of that aid by the President after the accomplishment of its purpose would, of course, leave the old

"State" organization with restored authority, and Congress would have no function to perform in the re-establishment of civil government in such a district, or in the readmission of its population to participation in the central Government. This was the course followed in Missouri and Kentucky, and it was the course, which, at first, was attempted in the case of Virginia. In the first two cases it was entirely correct. In the last it had to be abandoned, for reasons, and on account of conditions, which will be explained later.

What we have, therefore, in the theory and history of Reconstruction is the case of existing "State" organizations forcibly resisting the execution of the supreme law of the land, and stricken down by the executive power of the central Government in the attempt, that power being exercised at its own motion and in its own way.

CHAPTER II

PRESIDENT LINCOLN'S VIEWS AND ACTS IN REGARD TO RECONSTRUCTION

Did Mr. Lincoln Have any Theory of Reconstruction?—Mr. Lincoln's Plan—Mr. Lincoln's Oath of Allegiance, and the Loyal Class to be Created by the Taking of this Oath—The Proviso in this Plan—Seward's Idea of Reconstruction and the Views of Congress and the Judiciary—Ten Per Centum "State" Governments—Reconstruction in Louisiana under Mr. Lincoln's Plan—The New Orleans Convention—The Election of a Governor—The Constitutional Convention of April, 1864, and the Constitution Framed by it and Adopted by the Voters—Reconstruction in Arkansas—The Beginning of Resistance in Congress to the President's Plans—The Wade-Davis Bill—Analysis of this Measure—The President's Attitude toward the Bill—The President's Proclamation of July 8th, 1864—The Wade-Davis Protest against the President's Proclamation—The President's Message of December 6th, 1864—The Threatened Schism in the Republican Party and the Presidential Election of 1864—The Refusal of Congress to Count the Electoral Vote from any "State" which had Passed the Secession Ordinance—Reconstruction in Tennessee—The Twenty-second Joint Rule—Reconstruction in Tennessee Continued—Civil Government Re-established in Tennessee—The Thirteenth Amendment to the Constitution of the United States—The Proposition of Amendment as it Came from the Judiciary Committee of the Senate—The Passage of the Proposition by the Senate—The House Draft—Rejection of the Senate's Draft in the House—Reconsideration of the Senate's Measure in the House, and its Final Passage.

SOME of the ardent admirers of Mr. Lincoln are disposed to dispute the proposition that he had any theory of Reconstruction. It seems, however, that they are unconsciously influenced in this by their desire to escape the conviction that Mr. Lincoln held an erroneous theory of Reconstruction. It does not seem that one can read impartially Mr. Lincoln's proclamation of December 8, 1863, without coming to the conclusion that Mr. Lincoln had a very decided notion on the subject. It is true that he said that it must not be understood that no other possible mode of Reconstruction than that proclaimed by him would be acceptable, but he laid down a very distinct mode, and he said it was the best he could suggest under existing impressions.

Did Mr. Lincoln have any theory of Reconstruction?

This plan recognized, in the first place, the continued existence of the "States" in rebellion as "States" of, and in, the Union. More exactly, it regarded the rebellion against the United States within these "States" as the act of combinations of disloyal persons, and not as the act of the "States" at all. These combinations had subverted the loyal governments within these "States," but the "States" themselves were not disloyal, because they could not be. They were impersonal entities, incapable of committing treason or any other wrong. According to this view the work of Reconstruction consisted simply in placing the loyal element in a "State" in possession of the government of the "State."

Mr. Lincoln's plan.

In the second place, therefore, Mr. Lincoln's plan contained the principle that the work of Reconstruction was an executive problem. It was the work of the Executive, through the power of pardon, to create a loyal class in a "State" which had been the scene of rebellion, and it was the work of the Executive to support that class by the military power in taking possession of, organizing, and operating, the "State" government.

Arkansas, Texas, Louisiana, Mississippi, Tennessee, Alabama, Georgia, Florida, South Carolina, and North Carolina, a number of persons, not less than one-tenth in number of the votes cast in such State at the Presidential election of the year A.D. 1860, each having taken the oath aforesaid, and not having since violated it, and being a qualified voter by the election law of the State existing immediately before the so-called act of secession, and excluding all others, shall re-establish a State government which shall be republican and nowise contravening said oath, such shall be recognized as the true government of the State, and the State shall receive thereunder the benefits of the constitutional provision which declares that 'the United States shall guarantee to every State in this Union a republican form of government and shall protect each of them against invasion, and, on application of the Legislature, or the executive (when the Legislature cannot be convened) against domestic violence.'"

It is true that Mr. Lincoln was careful to say in this proclamation that "whether members sent to Congress from any State shall be admitted to seats, constitutionally rests exclusively with the respective Houses, and not to any extent with the Executive," but it is plain that he did not think the Houses could constitutionally use their power of judging of the qualifications and elections of their members to keep members from "States" reconstructed upon his plan from taking their seats on the ground that these "States" had not been properly reconstructed.

The proviso in this plan.

And it is also true that there occurs in the proclamation another paragraph which appears to militate against the theory of the perdurance of a "State" through the period of its rebellion against the United States. It reads: "And it is suggested as not improper that in constructing a loyal State government in any State the name of the State, the boundary, the subdivisions, the constitution and the general code of laws as before the rebellion be maintained, subject only to the modifications made necessary by the conditions hereinbefore stated, and such others, if any, not contravening such conditions which may be deemed expedient by those framing the new State government."

It certainly may appear from this language that while Mr. Lincoln regarded it as convenient and desirable that the new "State" should be considered a continuation of the old "State," yet that he did not look upon it as absolutely necessary. Still, it seems more probable that this was only his cautious habit of leaving open a way of escape out of any position when necessity or prudence might require its abandonment than that he doubted the correctness of his idea of the indestructibility of the "States" in spite of the rebellion of a part of their population, or even of the whole of their population.

Mr. Lincoln was not alone in this view of the nature of the "States" of the Union and the problem of Reconstruction. His able Secretary of State certainly agreed with him; the resolutions and acts of Congress down to that time may be better explained upon this theory than upon any other; and so far as the Supreme Court had dealt with the question, its dicta, if not its exact decisions, had indicated the same trend of opinion. The President felt, therefore, no hesitation in applying his plan in the specific cases that were in a condition for its realization.

<small>Seward's idea of Reconstruction, and the views of Congress and the Court.</small>

Before treating of his reconstruction of Louisiana and Arkansas under this plan, however, there are two points of the proclamation which should be briefly noticed.

The first is the omission of Virginia from the names of the "States" to which the proclamation should apply. The reason for this is simple, and easily understood. The President had always recognized what was called the Pierpont Government at Alexandria as the true government of Virginia. Virginia, therefore, according to his view needed no reconstruction. It belonged in the class with Kentucky and Missouri.

Virginia not in need of Reconstruction according to President Lincoln's view.

The other point is the proposition to found "State" government upon ten per centum of the population of the "State." Now we know that "State" government in the federal system of the United States is local self-government. But local self-government cannot really exist where the part of the population holding the legal authority does not really possess the sinews of power; and where the conditions of the society are democratic, or anything like democratic, one-tenth of the population cannot really possess the sinews of power. The actual power to make their government valid, to enable their government to govern would have to come from the outside. While this may happen under certain temporary exigencies without destroying local self-government on the whole, yet it cannot be permitted as a principle upon which to build a local self-government, a "State" in a federal system. Provincial governments, Territorial governments may be sustained in that way, but the distinguishing principle of "State" government forbids it. It is simply not "State" government when holding in this way the power to govern, as the principle of its life, no matter what name we may give it. Upon this point, then, Mr. Lincoln's reasoning was crude and erroneous, and when applied was destined to result in mischievous error.

Ten per centum "State" governments.

As far back as the first week in December of 1862 General Shepley, then Military Governor of Louisiana, had, by permission from the President, ordered an election for members of Congress, in the districts over which his jurisdiction extended. The President had cautioned him against any choice of Northern men at the point of the bayonet, and had declared to him that such a procedure would be "disgraceful and outrageous." The General heeded the warning, and two old citizens of Louisiana, Messrs. Hahn and Flanders, were chosen, and were admitted by the House of Representatives to their seats. This happened in February of 1863, and it was certainly good evidence that the House of Representatives was, at that moment, resting on the theory of the perdurance of the "State" of Louisiana throughout the rebellion within its limits against the United States.

Reconstruction in Louisiana under Mr. Lincoln's plan.

The election of members of Congress.

Things went no further than this, however, during the year 1863, the military situation requiring the whole thought and activity of the Government. On the 8th of January, 1864, however, a convention was held at New Orleans for the purpose of advancing the work of reconstruction. This convention requested General Banks to appoint an election for officers of the "State" government. The General complied, naming the 22d day of February following for the election, and the 4th of March for the installation of the officers so chosen. Mr. Hahn was elected and duly installed Governor, and was soon after declared by the President to be "invested, until further orders, with the powers hitherto exercised by the Military Governor of Louisiana." The next step was for the new Governor to order an election of delegates to a constitutional convention and the assembly of

The New Orleans convention.

The election of a governor.

PRESIDENT LINCOLN'S VIEWS AND ACTS 15

the same in convention, for the purpose of so amending and revising the constitution as to make it fit the new conditions created by the war. This was done in March and April of 1864, and an anti-slavery constitution was established for Louisiana. The instrument drafted and proposed by the convention was adopted by the voters. Eight thousand four hundred and two votes were cast upon the question of adoption, about sixteen per centum of the vote cast at the Presidential election of 1860. This brought the action of the voters within the President's ten per centum rule. The vote was almost five to one in favor of adoption. The President's scheme was now put to the practical test, both in Louisiana and Arkansas, during the spring of 1864. *The constitutional convention of April, 1864, and the constitution framed by it and adopted by the voters.*

Congress was, however, by this time becoming convinced that Reconstruction was a legislative problem, that is, a problem to be solved by Congressional acts and constitutional amendment. This is evidenced not only by the fact that neither House would admit representatives from Arkansas elected under the new "State" organization to seats, but by the more pronounced attitude expressed in what is known as the Wade-Davis measure upon the direct question at issue. These gentlemen, Mr. Benjamin F. Wade and Mr. Henry Winter Davis, the former the chairman of the "Committee on the Rebellious States" in the Senate, and the latter the chairman of a committee having the same name and functions in the House, originated a bill and carried it through both Houses of Congress, which, for the first time, embodied the views of Congress on the subject of Reconstruction. This bill was finally passed on July 4, 1864, and it contained provisions of the following tenor: The eleven "States" which had passed *The beginning of resistance in Congress to the President's plan. The Wade-Davis bill.*

secession ordinances were all treated as rebellious communities, and the President was authorized to appoint a provisional governor for each. This governor should exercise all the powers of civil government in the community to which he might be appointed until "State" government should be recognized by Congress as restored therein. An oath of future allegiance to the Constitution of the United States was then prescribed, and the provisional governor in each "State" was ordered, whenever rebellion in his "State" should be suppressed, to direct the United States Marshal to enroll all the white male citizens of the United States, resident within the "State," in the respective counties of the "State," and give them the opportunity to take the oath of allegiance to the United States. The bill then directed that when a majority of such citizens should take this oath, they might be permitted to elect delegates to a convention, which convention might take action for the establishment of "State" government. The bill disqualified all persons who had held any office, civil or military, "State" or Confederate, in rebellion against the United States, or who had voluntarily borne arms against the United States, from voting for delegates, or from being elected as delegates, to the convention. The bill then provided that the convention thus elected and assembled might form a "State" constitution, but must insert in it clauses abolishing slavery, repudiating all debts, "State" or Confederate, created by, or under the sanction of, the usurping power, and disqualifying all persons who had held office civil or military, "State" or Confederate, under the usurping power, except civil offices merely ministerial, and military offices below the rank of colonel, from voting or being elected governor or members of the legislature. The bill then provided for the submission of the constitution so formed to the voters, and if ratified by a majority thereof, required the provisional governor to certify the same to the President. It then provided that the President, after obtaining the consent of Congress thereto, should proclaim the new "State" government as established, and as the constitutional government of the "State," after which Representatives and Senators in Congress, and electors of the President, might be chosen in said "State." Finally, the bill abolished slavery at once in all the rebellious "States" and imposed penalties upon all persons attempting thereafter to hold anyone in involuntary servitude; and declared all persons who should thereafter hold office civil or military, "State" or Confederate, in the rebel service, except an office purely ministerial or under the grade of colonel, not to be citizens of the United States.

A brief analysis of this bill will show that Congress was nearer to some doctrine on the subject of Reconstruction than was the President. In the first place, Congress claimed Reconstruction as a legislative problem. This was undoubtedly the true theory upon that point. In the second place, Congress required the loyalty to the United States of at least a majority of the white adult males as the basis of "State" government, local self-government. That also was undoubtedly true political theory as has been already explained. In the third place, Congress asserted the power to abolish slavery within the limits of those "States" whose legislatures or conventions had passed the ordinances of secession. That is, Congress dealt with these districts not as "States" of the Union, but as territories or districts subject to the exclusive authority of the central Government. Congress was here beginning, at least, to act upon the idea that the districts in rebellion did not perdure, as "States," through-

Analysis of this measure.

out the rebellion, but had lost thereby the forms, powers and functions of "State" governments, and were neither out of the Union nor in the Union as "States," but were under the central Government of the Union as territory inhabited by a population disorganized as to local government. This was also sound political science, and the President ought to have heeded its teachings.

But he did not. He did not, it is true, veto the bill. He simply allowed the session to expire without signing it. This having happened in less than ten days from the time it was submitted to him, the bill failed, as provided in such cases by the Constitution. He, however, issued on the 8th of July a proclamation in regard to the subject, in which he objected to the setting aside of the "free State constitutions and governments already adopted and installed in Arkansas and Louisiana;" doubted the competency of Congress to abolish slavery within the "States;" expressed the hope and expectation that this might be done for the whole country by constitutional amendment; declared his willingness to have the loyal people in any of the rebellious "States" reconstruct their governments upon the Congressional plan, if they should choose to do so; but declared also his unwillingness to commit himself inflexibly to any single plan of restoration; and virtually asked the voters to make the difference between himself and Congress upon the subject an issue in the coming Presidential election.

The President's attitude toward the bill.

The President's proclamation of July 8, 1864.

This was one of the boldest acts of Mr. Lincoln's career as President, and it is little wonder that men of so much intelligence, courage and tenacity as Messrs. Wade and Davis did not allow the proclamation to go unanswered. Congress had adjourned, as we have seen, before the appearance of the proclamation. There was,

PRESIDENT LINCOLN'S VIEWS AND ACTS 19

therefore, no way for Congress as a whole to make immediate answer. Messrs. Wade and Davis believed that the public interests would suffer if the answer should be postponed until the next meeting of Congress. They, therefore, issued a protest against the proclamation over their own names. The protest was printed in the New York *Tribune* of August 5, 1864. It was an intemperate arraignment of the President. It declared, among other things, that "a more studied outrage on the legislative authority of the people had never been perpetrated;" that the President had "greatly presumed on the forbearance which the supporters of his Administration" had "so long practised, in view of the arduous conflict in which" they were "engaged and the reckless ferocity of" their "political opponents;" that he must understand that their support was not of a man but of a cause; and that he must confine himself to his executive duties, and leave political reorganization to Congress.

<small>The Wade-Davis protest against the President's proclamation.</small>

Such denunciations of the President's purposes could have but one effect, viz., the strengthening of his hands by the support of the people, who so generally trusted him, in the election of 1864. It injured Mr. Davis so much that he failed of even a renomination for his seat in Congress.

The President, on the other hand, used his triumph with great tact and moderation. He made no reference, in his message of December 6, 1864, either to his proclamation or to the protest which had been so fiercely hurled against it. He simply informed Congress that important movements had occurred during the year "to the effect of molding society for durability in the Union;" and that "12,000 citizens in each of the States of Arkansas and Louisiana" had "organized loyal State

<small>The President's message of December 6, 1864.</small>

governments, with free constitutions, and" were "earnestly struggling to maintain and administer them." He also spoke of the gratifying situation and movements in Maryland, Kentucky, Missouri and Tennessee.

It may be that Mr. Lincoln did not interpret his great victory at the polls in November preceding as a specific approval of his Reconstruction policy. In the spring and early summer of 1864, the Republican party was threatened with schism largely upon the subject of Reconstruction. Eight days before the meeting of the regular nominating convention of the party, that is on the 31st of May, some three hundred and fifty men, representing, or professing to represent, the more radical element of the party, met in convention at Cleveland, Ohio. General John Cochrane of New York was made chairman of the body, and General John C. Frémont and General John Cochrane were nominated by it for the presidency and vice-presidency of the United States. The twelfth section of the platform provided, "that the reconstruction of the rebel States belongs to the people, through their representatives in Congress, and not to the Executive."

<small>The threatened schism in the Republican party and the Presidential election of 1864.</small>

The regular convention met June 7th at Baltimore, and adopted a platform which took no sides in regard to Reconstruction, but simply sought to rally all Union men around the President for the purpose of saving the Union and putting an end to the rebellion. Many war Democrats took part in it who favored Lincoln's ideas of Reconstruction, and many Republicans who did not. The Democratic convention met at Chicago August 27th and adopted a platform which virtually proclaimed the war a failure, and demanded a cessation of hostilities preparatory to a compromise with the Confederates. Their nominee, General McClellan, with whom was associated on the ticket Mr. George H. Pendleton of Ohio, repudiated the platform but accepted the nomination and made the race.

Under the condition of schism in the Republican ranks, his chances seemed at first fair. But on September 21st, Generals Frémont and Cochrane, the nominees of the radical Republicans, withdrew from the contest, and the reunion of the Republican party on the Baltimore platform was effected. It was thus a question whether the overwhelming electoral vote for Lincoln and Johnson, two hundred and twelve to twenty-one for McClellan and Pendleton, meant the approval of Lincoln's views and acts in Reconstruction, and it certainly behooved the President to exercise some caution in so interpreting it, especially as there was no such wide difference in the popular vote, the McClellan electors having received 1,835,985 votes to 2,330,552 for the Lincoln electors. There is no question, however, that the President still believed in the correctness of his method and was determined to pursue the course upon which he had entered.

Neither was there any sign manifested that Congress would desist from pressing its views of its own powers in the matter. Both Houses had refused to admit members from the reconstructed "States," and now they passed a joint resolution, on February 4th, 1865, which prohibited the counting of any electoral votes for President and Vice-President in the election of 1864, from "States" which had passed the secession ordinance. Elections had been held in Louisiana and also in Tennessee, and this resolution was intended to prevent the counting of the votes which the persons chosen electors for Louisiana and Tennessee should send in. The resolution was sent to the President for his signature. He

No change in the views of Congress caused by the Presidential election.

hesitated for several days, but approved it at last on the day that Congress counted the electoral votes, February 8th. In doing so, however, he addressed a message to Congress informing the two Houses that he had signed it out of deference to their views, and saying that "in his own view, however, the two Houses of Congress, convened under the twelfth article of the Constitution, have complete power to exclude from counting all electoral votes deemed by them to be illegal; and it is not competent for the Executive to defeat or obstruct that power by a veto, as would be the case if his action were at all essential in the matter. He disclaims all rights of the Executive to interfere in any way in the matter of canvassing or counting electoral votes, and he also disclaims that, by signing said resolution, he has expressed any opinion on the recitals of the preamble or any judgment of his own upon the subject of the resolution." The recitals of the preamble referred to read thus: "Whereas, the inhabitants and local authorities of the States of Virginia, North Carolina, South Carolina, Georgia, Florida, Alabama, Mississippi, Louisiana, Texas, Arkansas and Tennessee rebelled against the Government of the United States, and were in such condition on the 8th day of November, 1864, that no valid election for electors of President and Vice-President of the United States, according to the Constitution and Laws thereof, was held therein on said day, etc."

The refusal of Congress to count the electoral vote from any "State" which had passed the secession ordinance.

Louisiana, which had fulfilled the President's conditions of reconstruction, was thus included in this list, and also Tennessee, where by order of Governor Andrew Johnson, the candidate for Vice-President on the Lincoln ticket, an election of electors had been held. Tennessee had not, at the time of the counting of the electoral vote, completed any process of reconstruction. The convention, called at Governor Johnson's instigation to meet at Nashville for the purpose of nominating candidates for Presidential electors, had called a constitutional convention to meet in Nashville on December 19th, following the Presidential election, for the purpose of undertaking the work of reconstruction. Hood's advance upon Nashville delayed its meeting, however, until January 3d. This convention took the old constitution of Tennessee as its starting-point and subjected it to a pretty thorough revision in the direction of a "free State government." It also prescribed a rather stiff test oath for all persons offering to vote upon the adoption of the amendments, an oath which not only promised future loyalty to the Constitution of the United States, such as Lincoln had prescribed, but which also required the taker of it to swear that he was an active friend of the Government of the United States, and an enemy of the so-called Confederate States. The amended constitution had not, however, been submitted to the voters at the date when Congress counted the electoral vote, that is, before the 8th of February, 1865, and of course no "State" government had been elected under the amended constitution. The vote upon the constitution occurred on the 22d of February, and the election of the Governor and the members of the Legislature under it occurred on March 4th.

<small>Reconstruction in Tennessee.</small>

The case of Tennessee did not from this point of view appear as strong as that of Louisiana. But it is difficult to see how the Republicans could have consistently rejected the vote of Tennessee after having nominated and elected a citizen of Tennessee as Vice-President of the United States. It is certainly implied in the Constitution of the United States that no man is eligible to the office of Vice-President unless he be at the time of his election a citizen of a "State" of the Union. The Constitution implies that the Vice-President shall have the same qualifications as the President; and it distinctly says that in giving their vote, the electors in each "State" shall vote for two persons, "of whom one at least shall not be an inhabitant of the same State with themselves." If an inhabitant of Tennessee could be lawfully Vice-President of the United States, it does certainly seem implied that Tennessee was, at the time, a "State" of the Union in regular standing.

However this may have been, the President was certainly correct in saying that Congress was vested with full power over the count of the electoral vote, and that the Executive had no control over it whatsoever. It was a bit of harmless good humor that he signed the resolution as a perfunctory matter, and it was calculated to improve the temper of the somewhat irritated members of Congress.

Congress was not, however, formally notified of the fact that he had signed the measure until after the counting of the vote had been finished, and the two Houses met the exigency by the enactment of what was known as "the twenty-second joint rule," according to which the consent of both Houses was required to count the electoral vote from any "State" or any body or place professing to be a "State." As a matter of fact, the Vice-President, Mr. Hamlin, declared that he had in his possession returns from the "States" of Louisiana and Tennessee, but held it to be his duty not to present them, and he did not present them. He knew that the President had signed the joint resolution, although Congress had not been officially notified of it, and he acted under the res-

The twenty-second joint rule.

olution as law. The joint rule would have required the presentation of these votes to the joint meeting of the two Houses, and would have required the concurrence of the two Houses, acting separately, to have included them in the count. The joint rule was, therefore, not applied to the case for which it was enacted, but it remained unrepealed for more than ten years, and then showed itself a sort of Nemesis to its creators.

Tennessee pursued, however, the course of reconstruction upon which she had set out. Her test oath, as we have seen, required virtually that the basis of her reorganization should be the men who had *remained* loyal throughout the rebellion. It differed thus from Mr. Lincoln's oath, which rehabilitated those who would promise future loyalty. The vote in favor of the new constitution, which was the old constitution of the "State" amended by articles abolishing slavery, nullifying secession, and repudiating the debt created in aid of the rebellion, was more than twenty-five thousand, nearly twenty per centum of the vote for Presidential electors in 1860. This certainly much more than fulfilled all of Mr. Lincoln's conditions. Reconstruction in Tennessee continued.

Governor Johnson issued his proclamation on February 25th, 1865, declaring the adoption of the new constitution, and ordering the election of the Governor and legislative members under it for March 4th. W. G. Brownlow was chosen Governor. The newly elected legislature did not meet, however, until April 2d, and Mr. Brownlow was not inaugurated as civil Governor until April 7th. As Mr. Johnson was inaugurated Vice-President on March 4th, he had been obliged to lay down the military governorship on that date, in fact, a few days before, and Mr. Brownlow had been appointed Civil government re-established in Tennessee.

in his stead. Upon Brownlow's inauguration as civil Governor, the military régime in Tennessee was formally ended. Lincoln acquiesced certainly in this change.

It remained now for Congress to show its attitude, when the Senators and Representatives from Tennessee should present themselves for admission to seats in the two Houses. As this could not happen until the following December, the history of this point must be deferred until the events between March 4th and December 4th are related.

The experiences of the year 1863 with the slavery problem had convinced the President and the leaders of the Republican party in Congress that abolition must be effected by a constitutional amendment. The military acts of the President in this direction were, as all the purely military measures of the Executive, temporary, and with the re-establishment of peace would cease to have force; and it was by this time pretty clear that but few of the "States" would abolish slavery by their own act. Already on January 11, 1864, had the proposition for a constitutional amendment abolishing slavery throughout the length and breadth of the United States been presented in the Senate by Mr. John B. Henderson of Missouri, and referred to the Judiciary Committee of that body for consideration and report.

The Thirteenth Amendment to the Constitution of the United States.

The language of the first article of Mr. Henderson's proposition read: "Slavery or involuntary servitude, except as a punishment for crime, shall not exist in the United States." When it came back from the Judiciary Committee, as reported by Mr. Trumbull, it was called Article XIII., and read: "Sec. 1. Neither slavery nor involuntary servitude, except as a punishment for crime, whereof the party shall have been duly convicted, shall exist in the United States or any place subject to their jurisdiction. Sec. 2. Congress shall have power to enforce this article by appropriate legislation."

It will be advantageous in our further consideration of this article to recall briefly the reasons for these divergencies. The language used by the Judiciary Committee corresponds almost exactly with the wording of the ordinance of the Northwest Territory of 1787; and it is entirely evident that the Judiciary Committee had that act in mind when it reported the article. Mr. Henderson's proposition was that slavery or involuntary servitude should not exist in the *United States*. He well understood that it did not require a constitutional amendment to abolish slavery from those parts of the country where "States" had not been formed. He knew that Congress could do that. The Judiciary Committee, however, did not think it wise or necessary to "make two bites of a cherry." They preferred to make their prohibition apply to the whole country. They knew that the phrase *United States* was capable of being interpreted to mean only that part of the country where "States" existed, and they preferred and intended to make their prohibition of slavery extend to the whole country. From abundant caution they used the words United States, with the additional words "any place subject to their jurisdiction," in order to cover all territory over which the flag of the Union should fly in sovereign power.

<small>The proposition of amendment as it came from the Judiciary Committee of the Senate.</small>

The second section, giving to Congress special power to enforce this article, seems, at first, unnecessary, because according to the last paragraph of Section 8, Article I., of the Constitution, Congress is vested with the authority to make all laws necessary and proper to carry into execution all the powers vested by the Constitution in any department or officer of the Government. This abolition of slavery was, however, a restriction on the "States." It laid a new limitation upon their powers, and hence it was thought that Section 8 of Article I. might not apply in the execution of such a provision against the "States." But if we regard the provision from the point of view of the rights of an individual to his freedom against any "State" law to the contrary, then we must see that the amendment does invest the United States courts with the power to impose the restriction in behalf of the individual seeking deliverance from the attempt of a "State" to enslave him or to continue his enslavement. And once the power vested in the courts to do this the general provision of Article I., Section 8, will certainly apply. The resolution offered by the Judiciary Committee passed the Senate by the requisite majority on the 8th of April, 1864.

During this same period, Mr. William Windom, of Minnesota, offered in the House of Representatives a resolution upon the subject in the identical words of the Senate's resolution. It was referred to the Judiciary Committee of the House, February 15, 1864. While it lay in the room of the Committee, Mr. Stevens offered a substitute for it, which read: "Slavery and involuntary servitude, except as a punishment for crime, whereof the party shall have been duly convicted, is forever prohibited in the United States and all its Territories." This is another bit of evidence for the proposition that what was meant by the words "or any place subject to their jurisdiction" in Mr. Trumbull's resolution was all parts of the country not enjoying "State" government in local matters.

<small>The House draft.</small>

The Senate resolution was sent into the House on the

31st of May, and was there lost on June 15th, having received a large majority, indeed, in its favor, but not a two-thirds majority. Foreseeing the failure of the resolution at that juncture, Mr. J. M. Ashley, of Ohio, voted against the measure, although a stanch friend of it. His purpose was of course to be able to move, at some future and more propitious time, a reconsideration of the subject. He did not, however, feel that that time had arrived until after the election and the military victories of the autumn of 1864 had manifested the temper of the voters on the question of abolition and demonstrated the power of the Union to carry such a measure into execution. On the 31st of January, 1865, Mr. Ashley moved a reconsideration of the Senate resolution lost in the House on the 15th of the preceding June. Reconsideration was immediately voted, and the Senate resolution was then carried by the requisite two-thirds majority.

Rejection of the Senate's draft in the House.

Reconsideration of the Senate's measure in the House, and its final passage.

The proposed amendment was then sent to the President, who signed it, February 1st, 1865. Whereupon the Senate immediately passed another resolution, declaring that it was through an inadvertency that the measure had been sent to the President for his signature, that asking the President of the United States to sign a proposed constitutional amendment was an error, was without precedent in the practice of the Government, and that the President's approval should not be communicated to the House. A concurrent resolution was then passed by the two Houses authorizing the President to submit the proposed article of amendment to the "States" for ratification. The Secretary of State immediately sent it to the legislatures of all the "States" which could be reached by him, and during the summer and autumn to the legislatures of all the "States;"

and the new legislature of Tennessee ratified it on the 5th of April, 1865, that is, more than a week before Lincoln's death.

Such was the condition of things when the assassin's bullet ended the life of the great and good President and brought the Vice-President, Mr. Johnson, into the office.

CHAPTER III

PRESIDENT JOHNSON'S PLAN OF RECONSTRUCTION
AND HIS PROCEEDINGS IN REALIZATION OF IT

The Character of Mr. Johnson—The Radical Nature of Johnson's First Views on Reconstruction—The Retention of Lincoln's Cabinet by Mr. Johnson and the Modification of Johnson's Views by Mr. Seward's Arguments—Johnson's Amnesty Proclamation of May 29th, 1865—The Excepted Classes—The Effect of these Exceptions—The President's Plan—The Realization of it—The Administering of the Oath—Reconstruction in North Carolina—The Identity of Johnson's Plan with that of Lincoln—Reconstruction in Mississippi—Reconstruction in Georgia—Reconstruction in Alabama, South Carolina and Florida—Reconstruction in Virginia—Reconstruction in Louisiana, Arkansas and Tennessee—The Constitutional Conventions of 1865—The Form of the Work Done in these Conventions, and its Substance—The Erection of "State" Governments and the Election of Members of Congress—The Orders of the President Putting the Civil Government of the United States into Operation Everywhere—The President's First Annual Message.

MR. JOHNSON was a man who rose from very low estate through his own efforts. He was a man of considerable intellectual power and of great will power. He was somewhat vain of his success and somewhat piqued by the social neglect which he had suffered at the hands of the "old families." He was intensely loyal to the Union, and could regard secession and rebellion only as treason. Having suffered so much for his loyalty, he was somewhat moved by considerations of revenge. He was profoundly stirred by

The character of Mr. Johnson.

the assassination of Lincoln, and apparently believed it to have been planned by those high in authority in the Confederacy; and he was possessed with an intense desire to re-establish the Union on an enduring foundation.

With such a history behind him, and such a disposition impelling him, it is not to be wondered at that his policy in regard to Reconstruction should have been more stringent than that of Mr. Lincoln. In fact it was feared, even by the more radical Republicans, such, for instance, as Mr. Wade, that he would be bloody minded in the treatment of the rebel chiefs. He had, before his accession to the Presidency, declared so often, and so vehemently, that "traitors should be arrested, tried, convicted and hanged," that most men were expecting the strict application of the criminal law to the Confederate leaders.

The radical nature of Johnson's first views on Reconstruction.

Mr. Johnson retained Lincoln's Cabinet, and among them the conciliatory and persuasive Seward, who, in about six weeks from the night of the assassination, at which time he himself was seriously wounded, returned to his work in the State Department. There is no doubt that it was the influence of Seward which modified the views and purposes of Mr. Johnson. The compliant spirit manifested at this time by the Confederate chiefs helped strongly in the same direction. By the 1st of June, Seward had won Johnson completely for his plan of a rapid and forgiving reconstruction by the Executive. Congress was not in session, and the President was not inclined to call an extra session. The late rebel chieftains were pressing for the political rehabilitation of their section, and the President now fully believed that he had the power to proceed with the problem of Reconstruction, and was inclined to do so.

The retention of Lincoln's Cabinet by Mr. Johnson, and the modification of Johnson's views by Mr. Seward's arguments.

On the 29th of May, he issued his proclamation of amnesty and pardon to all persons who, having engaged in rebellion, had failed to take the benefits of Mr. Lincoln's proclamations of December 8, 1863, and March 26, 1864. To all such persons Mr. Johnson offered his pardon upon their taking an oath of the following tenor: "I — do solemnly swear (or affirm) in the presence of Almighty God, that I will henceforth faithfully support, protect, and defend the Constitution of the United States and the Union of the States thereunder, and that I will in like manner abide by and faithfully support all laws and proclamations which have been made during the existing rebellion with reference to the emancipation of slaves. So help me God." *Johnson's Amnesty Proclamation of May 29, 1865.*

He, however, excepted the following classes of persons from the benefits of the offer: 1st. Those who held or had held, under the pretended Confederate Government, civil or diplomatic office or agency, or military office above the rank of colonel in the army and lieutenant in the navy, or military or naval office of any grade, if educated by the United States Government in the Military Academy at West Point or the United States Naval Academy; and all those who held, or had held, the pretended office of Governor of a "State" in insurrection against the United States; *The excepted classes.*

2d. Those who had left seats in the Congress of the United States or judicial stations under the United States to aid in the rebellion against the United States, and those who had resigned or tendered resignations of their commissions in the army or navy of the United States to evade duty in resisting the rebellion;

3d. Those who had, in any way, treated persons found in the service of the United States, in any capacity, otherwise than lawfully as prisoners of war;

4th. Those who had been engaged in destroying the commerce of the United States on the high seas, or upon the lakes and rivers separating the British Provinces from the United States, or in making raids from Canada into the United States;

5th. Those who were, or had been, absent from the United States, or had left their homes within the jurisdiction of the United States, and passed beyond the military lines of the United States into the pretended Confederate States, for the purpose of aiding the rebellion;

6th. Those who, at the time they might seek to obtain the benefits of the proclamation by taking the oath, were prisoners of war, or under civil or criminal arrest, and those who had taken the oath of allegiance to the United States since December 8, 1863, and had failed to keep it;

And, finally, those who had voluntarily participated in any way in the rebellion and were the owners of taxable property to the value of more than twenty thousand dollars.

The effect of these exceptions. These exceptions would have shut out almost all of the leading men of most of the "States" that passed secession ordinances from the benefits of the proclamation, except for the subsequent provision in the proclamation, which ordained that special application might be made to the President for pardon by any person belonging to the excepted classes, and held out the promise that such clemency would be as liberally extended as might be consistent with the facts of the case and the peace and dignity of the United States.

The President's plan in a sentence. Briefly, the President proposed to pardon the rebel leaders, upon special personal application, as an act of high executive grace, and to amnesty every one else in a body; and upon the basis of

PRESIDENT JOHNSON'S PLAN

their re-established loyalty to use the old electorate of the South in reconstruction. How he succeeded we will now proceed to relate.

In the first place, the machinery for administering the cleansing oath was made very simple and accessible. Any commissioned officer, civil, military or naval, of the United States, and any officer, civil or military, of a loyal "State" qualified by the laws of the "State" to administer oaths, was declared by the President, through his Secretary of State, to be competent to administer this oath of loyalty, a copy of which should be given to the person taking it as his certificate of restored citizenship, and another copy sent to the State Department at Washington to be there deposited and kept in the archives of the Government. *The realization of it. The administering of the oath.*

In the second place, and by a second proclamation, issued on the same day, May 29th, the President appointed a Provisional Governor for North Carolina, and authorized and commanded him to cause the election of delegates to, and their assembly in, a constitutional convention of the "State" for the reconstruction of the "State," and its restoration to its constitutional relations to the United States. The electorate to be employed by the Provisional Governor should be those persons who were qualified to vote by the laws of North Carolina in force immediately before the 20th of May, 1861, and had taken the oath prescribed in the first proclamation. *Reconstruction in North Carolina.*

This second proclamation also commanded the heads of the departments of the United States Government to put the laws of the United States into operation in North Carolina, the United States judges to open the United States courts and proceed to business, and the military officers in the district to aid the Provisional

Governor in carrying the duties assigned to him into effect, and to abstain from hindering, impeding, or discouraging, in any manner, the organization of a "State" government as authorized by the proclamation.

It will thus be seen that Mr. Johnson's plan of Reconstruction was in substance the same as that of Mr. Lincoln. It rested upon the theory of the indestructibility of the "States," their perdurance as "States" throughout the period of rebellion, the commission of treason and rebellion by combinations of private persons, the right of the Executive to withdraw his military powers and put his civil powers in operation, whenever, in his judgment, the circumstances would warrant him in so doing, and his authority to recognize the old electorates of the "States" in which rebellion had existed as the respective constituent bodies of the "States," upon such terms and under such limitations as he might prescribe. He did not lay down any rule as to the numerical proportion which the modified electorates should bear to the old, in order to make their acts legitimate, as Mr. Lincoln did; and he did declare in his second proclamation that the North Carolina convention, when convened, or the legislature that might be thereafter assembled, should prescribe the qualification of electors, and the eligibility of persons to hold office under the constitution and laws of the "State," which Mr. Lincoln did not do in his proclamation. But there is no doubt that Mr. Lincoln would have indorsed this proposition. He could not have avoided it, while holding the theory that North Carolina was a "State" simply engaged in amending its constitution, the theory which his own proclamation apparently set up. In a word Johnson's policy and acts in reconstructing the "States" in which secession ordinances had been passed, and rebellion committed, were

The identity of Johnson's plan with that of Lincoln.

but a continuation of those of Mr. Lincoln. If Lincoln was right so was Johnson, and *vice versa*.

On the 13th of June, the President issued a proclamation of like tenor and containing similar orders for putting the laws of the United States into operation, and for putting similar machinery in motion for reconstruction, in Mississippi. He appointed William L. Sharkey Provisional Governor therein. On the 17th of June, similar steps were taken for the reconstruction of Georgia, with James Johnson as the Provisional Governor; on the 21st of June for the reconstruction of Alabama, with Lewis E. Parsons as Provisional Governor; on the 30th of June for the reconstruction of South Carolina, with Benjamin F. Perry as Provisional Governor; and on the 13th of July for the reconstruction of Florida, with William Marvin as Provisional Governor.

<small>Reconstruction in Mississippi, Georgia, Alabama, South Carolina and Florida.</small>

Already on May 9th, twenty days before the issue of his proclamation of amnesty, the President had issued an executive order putting the laws of the United States in operation in Virginia, and guaranteeing the support of the United States Government to Governor Francis H. Pierpont in all lawful measures for the extension and administration of the "State" government throughout the geographical limits of Virginia. This meant, of course, that the United States Government recognized the shadowy loyal "State" government, which had kept up at least a show of existence throughout the rebellion, as the true "State" government of Virginia, and that Virginia did not need reconstruction, but only the extension of the authority of this government throughout her territorial limits. This was, also, a simple continuation of Mr. Lincoln's policy, as we well know.

<small>Reconstruction in Virginia.</small>

Of course Mr. Johnson recognized the reconstruction of Louisiana, Arkansas and Tennessee as effected by Mr. Lincoln; so that by mid-summer of 1865 the reconstruction of all the "States" which had passed secession ordinances, except only Texas, had been completed, or had been put in course of completion.

<small>Reconstruction in Louisiana, Arkansas and Tennessee.</small>

During the summer, autumn and early winter of 1865, the Provisional Governors of Mississippi, Alabama, South Carolina, North Carolina, Georgia, and Florida ordered elections for the choosing of delegates to constitutional conventions, upon the basis of the old suffrage laws of the respective "States" once answering to these names, modified by the requirements of the Presidential pardon, received after taking the oath of allegiance; and these elections were held and these conventions assembled.

<small>The constitutional conventions of 1865.</small>

These bodies chose to do their work in the form of amendments to the old constitutions of the "States," whose constituent powers they assumed to hold, rather than in the form of new constitutions. Before the meeting of Congress on the first Monday of December, they had all passed ordinances, either repealing the secession ordinances of their respective "States," or pronouncing them null and void; had all voted amendments to the constitutions of their respective "States" abolishing slavery; and all, except Mississippi and South Carolina, had passed ordinances repudiating the debt incurred by their respective "States" in aid of rebellion against the United States.

<small>The form of the work done in these conventions, and its substance.</small>

Before the meeting of Congress also, elections of the members of the respective "State" legislatures and of "State" officers, and of the members of the House of Representatives in Congress, had been held by the Provisional Governors, under the direction of the respective conventions. And, finally, before the assembly of Congress, these Legislatures had, with the exception of that of Florida, met, organized, and elected United States Senators, and, with the exception of those of Florida and Mississippi, had adopted the Thirteenth Amendment to the Constitution. The legislature of Florida, not having met and organized, had not at that date been able to consider the Amendment. It met on December 18th and elected United States Senators, and adopted the Thirteenth Amendment on the 28th. The legislature of Mississippi, on the other hand, rejected the Thirteenth Amendment on the 27th of November.

<small>The erection of State governments and the election of Members of Congress.</small>

During the same period, the President had by his several proclamations and orders declared the cessation of armed resistance, the restoration of intercourse throughout the country, and the raising of the blockade and the opening of the ports, and had put the different branches of the civil Government of the United States into operation in all the "States" which had been the scene of the recent rebellion. He had not, however, restored the privilege of the writ of Habeas Corpus in these regions or in the District of Columbia, and he reserved the right to have recourse to military control therein in case of necessity. The Governors of South Carolina, Georgia, Mississippi and Florida under the Confederacy had, in the spring of 1865, assumed to summon the legislatures, chosen by these "States" while members, or pretended members, of the Confederacy, to meet together for reconstruction purposes. The President had, through his military officials, ignored and prevented all such movements. No farther resistance to his plan of Reconstruction had been attempted, but he saw

<small>The orders of the President putting the civil Government of the United States into operation everywhere.</small>

plainly that, without the United States military power to sustain the new "State" governments, there might be.

This was the situation when Congress met on the first Monday of December, and received President Johnson's first annual Message. This document contained a disquisition upon the political system of the United States, as "an indissoluble union of indestructible States," with the natural conclusion that by attempting secession, the "States" impaired, but did not extinguish, their vitality, suspended, but did not destroy, their functions. It then proceeded with a narration of the facts above stated, in which the President sought to establish, upon the basis of his power to pardon and withdraw military rule, and to guarantee a republican form of government to every "State," his authority to reconstruct "State" government, or at any rate to permit the pardoned citizens to do so under his direction.

The President's first annual Message.

Finally, this paper contained the official notice to Congress that the President had admitted the reconstructed "States"—and that would mean all that had passed the secession ordinance, except perhaps Texas, whose convention did not assemble until March of 1866—to participate in amending the Constitution of the United States. The President concluded his narration and argumentation upon this all-important subject in these words: "The amendment to the Constitution being adopted, it will remain for the States whose powers have been so long in abeyance to resume their places in the two branches of the National Legislature, and thereby complete the work of restoration. Here it is for you, fellow citizens of the Senate, and for you, fellow citizens of the House of Representatives, to judge, each of you for yourselves, of the elections, returns and qualifications of your own members."

It is entirely evident from all this that the President denied the power of the Houses of Congress, either separately or jointly, to prevent the Senators and Representatives from the reconstructed "States" from taking their seats upon any other grounds than defects in the election and return, or in the personal qualifications, of the particular persons under consideration.

CHAPTER IV

THE CONGRESSIONAL PLAN OF RECONSTRUCTION

The Stevens Resolution — Legislation of the Reconstructed "States" Concerning the Status of the Freedmen, and the Freedmen's Bureau—Vagrancy, Apprenticeship, and Civil Rights in the Reconstructed "States"—The View Taken of this Legislation by the Republicans—The Ratification of the Thirteenth Amendment to the Constitution—The Demand of the Senators and Representatives-elect from the Reconstructed "States" to be Admitted to Seats in Congress—The Joint Committee of the Two Houses of Congress on Reconstruction—Thaddeus Stevens's Idea of Reconstruction—Mr. Shellabarger's Theory of Reconstruction—Mr. Sumner's Theory of Reconstruction.

So soon as the House of Representatives had elected its Speaker, Mr. Colfax, and other officers, and before the reception of the President's Message, Mr. Thaddeus Stevens presented a resolution which proposed the selection of a joint committee of the House and Senate to inquire into the condition of the "States," which formed the so-called Confederate States, and to report by bill or otherwise, whether, in the judgment of the Committee, these "States," or any of them, were entitled to be represented in either House of Congress, and which provided that "until such report shall have been made and finally acted upon by Congress, no member shall be received into either House from any of the so-called Confederate

The Stevens resolution.

CONGRESSIONAL PLAN OF RECONSTRUCTION 43

States." The House passed this resolution by an overwhelming majority; and then adjourned without allowing a motion by Mr. Niblack of Indiana, to the effect that "pending the question as to the admission of persons claiming to have been elected representatives to the present Congress from the States lately in rebellion, such persons be entitled to the privileges of the floor of the House," the usual privilege accorded contestants, to come to a vote.

The view of the House was thus manifest from the start. It was that Reconstruction could not be effected by the Executive Department of the Government, but was a problem for Congress, and that this was a matter entirely separate from the power of each House to judge of the elections, returns and qualifications of its members, a matter to be decided by the whole Congress prior to the consideration of the question of the elections, returns, and qualifications of the members of each House. In a word, it was the question of the admission, or the readmission, of "States" into the Union, or more correctly the question of the establishment or re-establishment of the "State" system of local government upon territory of the United States under the exclusive power of the central Government.

The view of the House that Reconstruction could not be effected by the Executive.

There is no question that in sound political science the House was entirely correct in its theory, and that the objection of the Senate to that part of the Stevens resolution which provided that no member should be received into either House from any of the so-called Confederate States until the report of the Committee on Reconstruction should have been finally acted on by Congress, as trenching upon the exclusive power of the Senate to judge of the elections, returns and qualifications of its members, rested upon a confounding of the function of Congress to admit "States" into the Union with the power of each House to judge of the elections, returns and qualifications of those claiming to represent "States" or constituencies in "States" about whose position in the Union there was no question. The Senate finally swung into line, however, by passing this part of the House resolution as a concurrent resolution instead of as a joint resolution.

Passage of the Stevens resolution as a concurrent resolution.

There were two other considerations which moved the Republicans in Congress to assume this attitude in regard to Reconstruction. One was the legislation of the "States" reconstructed by the President concerning the status and the rights of the freedmen. On the 3d of March preceding, Congress had passed an act organizing a bureau in the War Department for the care of refugees and freedmen in the districts in rebellion or in the territory embraced in the operations of the army. This bureau was officered by a chief commissioner and assistant commissioners for each of the "States" declared to be in insurrection. These officers were authorized to take possession of the abandoned lands within these "States," and other lands belonging to the United States, and parcel them out to the loyal male refugees and freedmen, not more than forty acres to each, and protect them in the use and enjoyment of the same for the term of three years. They were also authorized to issue under the direction of the Secretary of War provisions, clothing and fuel to such loyal refugees and freedmen as were destitute.

Legislation of the reconstructed "States" concerning the status of the freedmen, and the Freedmen's Bureau.

There is no question that this was a most humane measure. It would have been a moral outrage for the Government of the United States to have taken the slaves away from the support and protection accorded

CONGRESSIONAL PLAN OF RECONSTRUCTION 45

them by their masters, and to have thrown them upon their own resources without any means of sustenance during the transition into the new status. But there is also no question that this measure was so administered as to do the race for whose benefit it was intended almost as much harm as good. When the Government began to furnish them with food, clothes, fuel and shelter gratis, they, like the children that they were, conceived of this, to them, very agreeable state of things as something that was to last forever, as the New Jerusalem. They gathered about the depots of the Freedmen's Bureau and could not be induced to go away in search of work or livelihood. The belief became quite general that the Government intended to give every man forty acres of land and a mule, and otherwise to support him permanently. The danger was that the newly emancipated would quit work altogether and throw themselves entirely upon the charity of the United States Government. Many did do so, and formed thus a sort of privileged class throughout the whole South under the special protection of the Government of the United States.
_{The administration of the Freedmen's Bureau.}

When, now, the newly reorganized "States" came to assume jurisdiction over matters concerning the freedmen, they found themselves driven to some legislation to prevent the whole negro race from becoming paupers and criminals. It was in the face of such a situation that the legislatures of these "States" passed laws concerning apprenticeship, vagrancy and civil rights, which were looked upon at the North as attempts to re-enslave the newly emancipated, and served to bring the new "State" governments at the South into deep reproach.
_{Vagrancy, apprenticeship and civil rights in the reconstructed "States."}

It must be remembered, however, that at the time of the passage of the Stevens resolution by the House of

Representatives, only two of Mr. Johnson's reconstructed "States" had passed any laws upon these subjects.

<small>Examination of these vagrancy acts, etc.</small> These two were Mississippi and South Carolina; and a close examination of the text of these enactments will hardly justify the interpretations placed upon them by the radical Republicans. The South Carolina Preliminary Act came first in the order of time. It provided that "all free negroes, mulattoes, and mestizos, all freedwomen, and all descendants through either sex of any of these persons, shall be known as *persons of color*, except that every such descendant, who may have of Caucasian blood seven-eighths, or more, shall be deemed a white person; that the statutes and regulations concerning slaves are now inapplicable to persons of color; and although such persons are not entitled to social or political equality with white persons, they shall have the right to acquire, own, and dispose of property, to make contracts, to enjoy the fruits of their labor, to sue and be sued, and to receive protection under the law in their persons and property"; and "that all rights and remedies respecting persons or property, and all duties and liabilities under laws civil and criminal, which apply to white persons, are extended to persons of color, subject to the modifications made by this act and the other acts hereinbefore mentioned."

The acts to which this one was preliminary were not passed until the latter half of December, and could not have served, except by prevision, as grounds for the Stevens resolution. Moreover there was little in this Act which was really calculated to arouse any pronounced hostility at the North. It evidently recognized the emancipation of the former slaves, and the prohibition of future slavery, as fixed facts, and provided for substantial equality in civil rights between persons of color and white persons. The discriminations which it referred to, rather than made, were those of a social and political nature, matters which to that time had been controlled, if controlled at all, wholly by the "States," except of course in those parts of the country in which "States" had not been erected.

The Mississippi acts were all passed in November. They were the acts which were before the view of Congress and the country in the beginning of December, 1865, and, with the exception of the South Carolina Preliminary Act just commented on, the only ones. They require, therefore, a somewhat fuller treatment. They consist of "An Act to regulate the relation of master and apprentice relative to Freedmen, Free Negroes, and Mulattoes, passed November 22, 1865"; the "Vagrant Act of November 24, 1865"; an "Act to Confer Civil Rights on Freedmen and for other purposes," passed November 25, 1865; a supplementary Act to this, passed November 29, 1865; and another supplementary Act, passed December 2, 1865.

The Mississippi Acts.

The first Act provided that freedmen, free negroes, and mulattoes under the age of eighteen years, being orphans, or the children of parents who could not, or would not, support them, should be apprenticed by the clerk of the Probate court in the county where found to competent and suitable persons, and on such terms as the court should direct; under the restrictions, that the former owner of the minor should be selected by the court as the master or mistress if, in the judgment of the court, he or she were competent and suitable; that the terms fixed by the court should have the interest of the minor particularly in view; and that the apprentice should be bound by indenture, to run, in the case of males, until the completion of the twenty-first year, and, in the case of females, until the completion of the eighteenth year.

This Act further provided that in the management and control of apprentices, the master or mistress should "have power to inflict such moderate corporal chastisement as a father or guardian is allowed to inflict on his or her child or ward at common law," but that in no case should "cruel or inhuman punishment be inflicted."

It furthermore provided, that in case of desertion by the apprentice, he might be apprehended and brought before a justice of the peace, who might remand him to his master or mistress, and might, on the refusal of the apprentice to return, commit him to jail, on failure to give bond, until the next term of the County court, which court should inquire into the matter, and determine whether the apprentice had left the service to which he was bound without good cause or not, and should, in the one case, compel the return to service by ordering the infliction of the necessary penalties, and in the other, should order the discharge of the apprentice, and enter "judgment against the master or mistress for not more than one hundred dollars, for the use and benefit of the apprentice."

The second Act provided, that "all free negroes and freedmen in the State, over the age of eighteen years, found on the second Monday in January, 1866, or thereafter, with no lawful employment or business, or found unlawfully assembling themselves together, either in the day or night time, and all white persons so assembling with freedmen, free negroes, or mulattoes, or usually associating with freedmen, free negroes, or mulattoes on terms of equality, or living in adultery or fornication with a freedwoman, free negro or mulatto, shall be deemed vagrants, and on conviction thereof, shall be

CONGRESSIONAL PLAN OF RECONSTRUCTION 49

fined in the sum of not exceeding, in the case of a freedman, free negro or mulatto, fifty dollars, and in the case of a white man, two hundred dollars, and imprisoned, at the discretion of the court, the free negro not exceeding ten days, and the white man not exceeding six months."

It further provided, that in case the freedman, free negro or mulatto should not pay the fine within five days from the time of its infliction, the sheriff of the proper county should hire him or her out to any person who would for the shortest period of service pay the fine and all costs, giving the preference, however, to the employer of the freedman, negro or mulatto, if there should be any, and, if no person would hire the same, should hold him or her to be dealt with as a pauper. It also provided that the freedman, free negro, or mulatto refusing or failing to pay a tax should be dealt with by the sheriff in the same manner.

And it provided, finally, that the same duties and liabilities existing among white persons in the "State" to support indigent whites should attach to freedmen, free negroes and mulattoes in regard to the support of colored paupers, and that in order to carry out the same a poll tax, not exceeding one dollar a head, should be levied on every freedman, free negro, and mulatto, between the ages of eighteen and sixty years, and should be collected and paid into the hands of the treasurers of the counties to be used in the support of colored paupers.

The third Act provided, that freedmen, free negroes and mulattoes might acquire, hold, and dispose of, personal property in the same manner and to the same extent as white persons, and might sue and be sued in all the courts of the "State" as white persons, but that they should not rent or lease lands or tenements except in incorporated towns or cities, and under the control of the corporate authorities.

It provided, further, for the intermarriage of freedmen, free negroes and mulattoes, and for the legalization of all previous and existing cohabitations between them, and the legitimation of the issue therefrom; but it forbade intermarriage between them and white persons, under penalty of life imprisonment, and it defined freedmen, free negroes and mulattoes as comprehending all of pure negro blood, and all descended from negroes to the third generation inclusive, although one parent in each generation should have been white.

It provided, further, that freedmen, free negroes and mulattoes should be competent as witnesses in all civil cases, in which they themselves or other freedmen, free negroes and mulattoes were parties or a party to the suit, and in criminal cases where the crime charged was alleged to have been committed by a white person or persons upon or against the person or property of a freedman, free negro, or mulatto.

It provided, further, that every freedman, free negro and mulatto should have a lawful home and employment, and should have written evidence thereof in the form of a license from the police authorities to do irregular or job work, or in the form of a written contract for labor. It required that all contracts made with freedmen, free negroes and mulattoes for labor for a longer period than one month should be in writing, a copy of which should be furnished to each party, and that if the laborer should quit the service of the employer before the expiration of the term fixed in the contract, he should forfeit his wages for that year up to the time of quitting.

It provided, further, for the arrest of any freedman, free negro, or mulatto quitting the service of an employer, and for the determination of the question whether the quitting was for good cause or not, and for the disposition to be made of the deserter.

It provided, further, that enticing or persuading freedmen, free negroes or mulattoes to desert from their legal employment, or employing deserters from contract labor knowingly, or giving or selling them food, raiment or other thing knowingly, should be a misdemeanor punishable by fine, or by imprisonment in case the fine should not be paid.

It provided, further, that no freedman, free negro or mulatto, unless in the military service of the United States, or licensed thereto by the police authorities, should keep or carry arms, ammunition or murderous weapons, and that every civil and military officer should arrest any such person found in possession of such articles, and commit him for trial.

It provided, further, that "any freedman, free negro, or mulatto committing riots, affrays, trespasses, malicious mischief and cruel treatment to animals, seditious speeches, insulting gestures, language or acts, or assaults on any person, disturbance of the peace, or exercising the functions of a minister of the gospel without a license from some regularly organized church, or selling spirituous or intoxicating liquors, or committing any other misdemeanor," should be fined or imprisoned, and, upon failure to pay the fine in five days' time after conviction, should be publicly hired out to the person who would pay the fine and costs for the shortest term of labor from the convict.

And it provided, finally, that "all the penal and criminal laws now in force in this State, defining offences, and prescribing the mode of punishment for crimes and misdemeanors committed by slaves, free negroes or mulattoes, be and the same are hereby re-enacted, and declared to be in full force and effect, against freedmen, free negroes and mulattoes, except so far as the mode and manner of trial and punishment have been changed or altered by law."

This is a fair sample of the legislation subsequently passed by all the "States" reconstructed under President Johnson's plan. In fact, in the legislatures of several of them, bills containing substantially these provisions were under consideration when Congress met, and it was fair to suppose that they would be enacted. Congress had thus in the first week of December, 1865, substantially before it what the reconstructed "States" proposed to do in reference to the status and rights of the former slaves, and in reference to the relations between the negro and the white man in the future.

The Mississippi legislation a fair sample of the subsequent legislation in other "States."

As yet, we must remember, the Thirteenth Amendment had not been proclaimed as adopted, in fact had not been adopted, on the basis of the calculations of Mr. Seward, the Secretary of State, the officer who alone could proclaim adoption; and the abolition of slavery rested upon the military power of the President, and on the acts of the "States" themselves, the first of which is temporary as to its effects, and the second of which might be reversed by the "States" at pleasure.

The Northern Republicans professed to see in this new legislation at the South the virtual re-enslavement of the negroes. This was an extreme view of it, although it certainly did not give the negro equal civil right with the white man, or anything approaching that, to say nothing of failing to offer him any prospects of ever participating in political functions. Of course it would be an abstract assumption to say that the negro ought, at the moment of his emancipation, to have had equal civil right with the white man. Civilized man can be safely

The view taken of this legislation by the Republicans.

CONGRESSIONAL PLAN OF RECONSTRUCTION 53

intrusted with a much larger civil liberty than the barbarian or the semi-barbarian. There is no question also that much severer penalties for the commission of the same crime are necessary among a barbarous race or class than among a civilized race or class. From these points of view this Mississippi legislation does not appear as far from what was natural and even necessary as Mr. Stevens and his followers made it out. The law of apprenticeship was not severe, and, if justly and sincerely executed, it would probably have been beneficial to the young negroes, deprived of the care given them up to that time by master or mistress, and now thrown upon themselves without a cent of money or a particle of property, most of them knowing no parent except a mother as poor as themselves, and entirely unacquainted with the new conditions of life now confronting them.

<small>This legislation from the point of view of natural justice.</small>

The law of vagrancy was severer. But it is easy to see that a reasonable execution of that law had as much help as harm in it for the former slave. It would have preserved him against idleness, drunkenness, and thievery, although it did curtail largely his liberty of action. It was, undeniably, the third act, which came so near to the re-enactment of the old slave code in regard to crimes and misdemeanors committed by negroes, that gave the greatest offence. Almost every act, word, or gesture of the negro, not consonant with good taste and good manners, as well as good morals, was made a crime or misdemeanor, for which he could first be fined by the magistrates, and then consigned to a condition almost of slavery for an indefinite time, if he could not pay the fine. There is no question that the "States" of the Union had at that moment the power under the Constitution of the United States to do these things. At that time the determination of the criminal law, both as to the definition of crime, the fixing of penalties, and the fashioning of procedure, was almost entirely a function of the "States," and there was no provision in the Constitution of the United States which required the "States" to treat their own inhabitants with equality in regard to their civil rights and obligations.

Under these circumstances it is not at all surprising that the Republicans of the North strongly felt that the freedom of the negro had not yet been sufficiently guaranteed to render the acknowledgment of the resumption of "State"-powers by the communities so lately in rebellion against the United States for the upholding of negro slavery safe and wise.

It was certainly natural, and it was just and right, that the party in power in Congress should have considered it their duty to so amend the Constitution of the United States, before according "State"-powers to the communities lately in rebellion, as to reap the just fruits of their triumph over secession and slavery. It was certainly their duty to the country to secure the adoption of the Thirteenth Amendment, and any further amendment, necessary to accomplish this result, before putting the recently rebellious communities in a position to defeat the same. And it is certainly not strange that the Republicans should have feared that the Democrats of the North in Congress would soon be found fraternizing with the Senators and Representatives from the reconstructed "States," and that it was their duty to secure "perpetual ascendancy to the party of the Union," before admitting the Senators and Representatives from these "States" to participation in public power. Properly interpreted this only meant that loyal men must govern the country. But it did not follow that only Republicans were loyal men, and that the loyal Democrats of the North would follow

Correctness of the Republican position.

CONGRESSIONAL PLAN OF RECONSTRUCTION 55

the recently disloyal Democrats of the South in legislating upon the issues of the war. Republicans were likely to commit this fallacy in their reasoning. Many of them did commit it. And the result of it was to intensify partisanship at the expense of statesmanship.

Just two weeks after the passage of the Stevens resolution by the House of Representatives, Mr. Seward announced the adoption of the Thirteenth Amendment to the Constitution of the United States. In making this announcement, he declared that there were thirty-six "States" in the Union, and that the legislatures of twenty-seven "States," just three-fourths, the necessary number, had voted its adoption; and among those voting to adopt, he counted the legislatures of Virginia, Louisiana, Arkansas, Tennessee, North Carolina, South Carolina, Georgia and Alabama. *The ratification of the Thirteenth Amendment to the Constitution.*

It is to be remarked, however, that had he counted none of the "States" that had passed secession ordinances, either in the whole number, or in the three-quarters necessary to adopt, the Amendment would in that case also have been adopted. There would have been, in that case, twenty-five "States" in the Union, and of these nineteen had adopted the Amendment. And if any controversy had arisen over the use of fractions in making nineteen three-fourths of twenty-five, this would have been quickly overcome by the fact that the legislatures of four more of the loyal "States" adopted the Amendment soon after Mr. Seward's declaration, making twenty-three out of twenty-five. It will not, of course, be disputed that, if the "States" that passed secession ordinances should have been counted in arriving at the whole number of "States" in the Union, those of them adopting the Amendment should also have been counted in making out the three-fourths majority necessary to adoption, and that if, on the other hand, they should have been excluded in arriving at the whole number, they should also have been excluded in making up the three-fourths majority. In other words, it does not matter from which point of view we regard the subject, the Amendment was regularly and lawfully adopted. It must be admitted, however, that Mr. Seward followed in this most solemn procedure, the amending of the Constitution, the Presidential plan of Reconstruction, and gave great encouragement to the Senators- and Representatives-elect from these reconstructed "States" to expect that they would have the aid and influence both of the Democrats in Congress, and of the Administration, in securing their seats.

They had gone to Washington and, bearing themselves confidently from the first, they now became defiant in demanding their rights. Many of them were men who, less than twelve months before, had been in arms against the United States, and one of them was the person who was the Vice-President of the Confederacy at the moment of its downfall, Mr. Alexander H. Stephens. Such an attitude on his part and their part roused again great bitterness of feeling among the Republicans, many of whom conscientiously thought that the real deserts of such persons were the penalties of treason. Moreover, the legislatures of some of the other "States" reconstructed under the President's plan enacted, during December, January and February, measures concerning the status and rights of the emancipated slaves similar to those passed by the legislature of Mississippi, and in some respects even more illiberal than those passed by that body; and it was evident that all of them would finally stand upon the same general ground in regard to this subject.

The demand of the Senators- and Representatives-elect from the reconstructed "States" to be admitted to seats in Congress.

CONGRESSIONAL PLAN OF RECONSTRUCTION 57

This was the situation in the last week of February, 1866, when the Senate passed a resolution, concurrent with the Stevens resolution in the House, denying seats to any of the claimants from the "States" lately in insurrection until the report of the Joint Committee on Reconstruction should be made and finally acted upon. Four of the Republican Senators, Messrs. Cowan, Doolittle, Dixon and Norton went against their party associates in this question, but there was still a two-thirds majority in both Houses resolute and resolved to combat the Presidential plan of Reconstruction and to construct and enforce a Congressional plan.

As we have already seen, the Senate had concurred with the House in regard to that part of the Stevens resolution which provided for the appointment of a Joint Committee on Reconstruction, at the time it was passed by the House. The members of the Committee were chosen soon after the passage of this part of the Stevens resolution by the Senate. They were, from the Senate, Messrs. Fessenden, Grimes, Harris, Howard, Johnson and Williams, all Republicans except Mr. Reverdy Johnson of Maryland, and from the House, Messrs. Bingham, Blow, Boutwell, Conkling, Grider, Morrill, Rogers, Stevens and Washburn, all Republicans except Grider of Kentucky and Rogers of New Jersey. The Republicans had given themselves a larger representation on the Committee than their numerical relation to the Democrats warranted, but there is no reason to think that the report of the majority would have been in any respect different, if that relation had been more strictly observed.

<small>The Joint Committee of the two houses of Congress on Reconstruction.</small>

This Committee sat for about six months before making its final report. During this period, however, several propositions issued from it, and two great measures of statute law were passed by Congress, all of which must be more nearly considered in order to keep the thread of the narrative of Reconstruction. Moreover the debate upon the subject of Reconstruction was at the same time in progress and the view of the subject held by the leading Republicans was becoming more clear and fixed.

The activity of Congress in the interim between the appointment of the Committee on Reconstruction and the Report of the Committee.

Mr. Stevens opened this debate in the House on the 18th of December (1865). In a powerful speech, he developed anew his doctrine that the territory once covered by the "States," which had seceded from the Union, was nothing now but a conquered district, whose future condition depended upon the will of the conqueror. If "States" should ever be erected there again, it must be accomplished, he contended, by virtue of that provision in the Constitution which declares that "new States may be admitted by Congress into this Union." This theory involved the admission that secession had been temporarily successful. This Mr. Stevens frankly acknowledged. He said: "Unless the law of nations is a dead letter, the late war between the two acknowledged belligerents severed their original contracts, and broke all the ties that bound them together."

Thaddeus Stevens's ideas on Reconstruction.

This was the extreme doctrine on the one side. It was in blunt contradiction to the doctrine upon which the Administration was acting, the doctrine that the attempt at secession was entirely abortive, and that the "States" where it was attempted were still in the Union *as "States,"* and had never been anywhere else or anything else, in fact could not be; that the rebellion was the work of private individuals combined as truly against the real "States" in which it existed as against the

Contradiction between Stevens's view and the view of the Administration.

CONGRESSIONAL PLAN OF RECONSTRUCTION 59

United States; and that, therefore, the overthrow of these combinations and the cessation of the military rule of the President must be followed by the resumption on the part of the "States" concerned of all their rights and powers of local self-government and of participation in the United States Government, as guaranteed by the Constitution of the United States, unimpaired, and without any action whatever on the part of Congress. Mr. Raymond represented this view on the floor of the House of Representatives. He was a Republican of the Seward school, and sympathized entirely with his patron upon this subject. It was a great embarrassment to him that the Democrats immediately gave in their adherence to this view. It helped to prevent him from gaining any following at all for it among the Republicans.

But while the Republicans of the House repudiated entirely Mr. Raymond's principles, the great mass of them were not able to accept Mr. Stevens's view of the temporary validity of secession, and the temporary existence of the Southern Confederacy as a foreign power. Their feelings and instincts required a principle of reconstruction which, at the same time that it did not recognize secession as having any validity for the shortest moment, yet regarded the "States" in which it was attempted, as having thereby become something other than "States" of the Union, and as requiring the assent of Congress to the rightful resumption of that status.

It was Mr. Shellabarger, of Ohio, who did more than anybody else to give the proper logical interpretation to these feelings and invent the theory of Reconstruction on which the Republicans could plant themselves. Briefly stated that theory was that, while secession was a nullity legally from the beginning, and could not take the territory

Mr. Shellabarger's theory of Reconstruction.

occupied by the "States" attempting it, or the people inhabiting that territory, out of the Union, or from under the rightful jurisdiction of the United States Government and Constitution for one instant, yet it worked the loss of the "State" status in the Union, and from a legal point of view left this territory and the inhabitants of it subject exclusively to the jurisdiction of the United States Government, a status from which they could be relieved only by the erection of "States" anew upon such territory, an operation which could be effected, under the Constitution of the United States, only by the co-operation of Congress with the loyal inhabitants of such territory.

This was sound political science and correct constitutional law. It could not fail to command the assent of the great majority of the Republicans in the House and in the country. This same doctrine was, at the same time, developed in the Senate by Mr. Sumner, Mr. Fessenden and Mr. Wilson, and it was easy to see that it had become the theory of the Republican party in Congress long before the final report of the Committee on Reconstruction promulgated it. Even Stevens and his radical followers were in line with it in so far as practical results were concerned. That is, the Republicans all stood together on the principle that Reconstruction could only be effected by Congressional acts, since it was tantamount to a conferring, or reconferring, of the "State" status upon a population at the moment subject to the exclusive jurisdiction of the Government of the United States. This meant that the entire Republican party in Congress, with the exception of the four members of the Senate already named, and of Mr. Raymond and one other in the House (and this constituted a majority of two-thirds in each House) would antagonize the plan of Executive Reconstruction

Mr. Sumner's theory of Reconstruction.

devised by Lincoln and Seward and persisted in by Johnson and, to that moment, by his cabinet. How far the Republicans in Congress would go in the attempt to set aside Executive Reconstruction depended chiefly upon the moderation of the President, and the sincerity of the people in the South. It depended also in some degree, to say the least, upon what would be necessary to keep the Republican party, which conceived itself to be the only really loyal party to the Union, in power. {The Republicans in Congress almost unanimously in favor of the Shellabarger-Sumner plan.}

There is no doubt that the Sumner-Shellabarger theory of Reconstruction was correct. The only question was how exacting Congress would be in realizing it. Under such a situation it behooved the President to act with great caution and moderation, and to do nothing to provoke a conflict in which he was certain to be worsted. And it also behooved the people of the South to make no opposition to the bestowal of a large measure of civil liberty upon the freedmen, nor to such an adjustment of the basis of political representation as would not necessitate negro suffrage, and not to insist upon sending to Congress, at the outset, the men who had made themselves particularly obnoxious to loyal feeling. How both the President and the persons in authority at the South disregarded these considerations of prudence, and how the position assumed by them upon these subjects drove Congress into more and more radical lines, is the further subject of the next three chapters.

CHAPTER V

THE CONGRESSIONAL PLAN (*Continued*)

The Freedmen Codes in the South—The Reports of Grant and Schurz in Regard to the Status in the South—The Freedmen's Bureau Bill of 1866—The President's 22d of February Speech—The Civil Rights Bill—The Veto of the Bill—The Veto Overridden—The Fourteenth Amendment—The Discussion of the Proposition in Congress—The President's Attitude toward the Proposed Amendment—Mr. Seward's Acts in Regard to Ratification—The Requirement that the Ratification of the Proposed Amendment should be the Condition of the Admission of the Senators and Representatives-elect to Seats in Congress—The Tennessee Precedent.

WE have reviewed the acts of the new legislature of Mississippi concerning the civil status of the freedmen.

The Freedmen codes in the South. It is sufficient to say that during the winter of 1865–66, the other reconstructed legislatures followed the example of the legislature of Mississippi. These movements forced upon the Republican party in Congress the conviction that the civil rights of the freedmen must be secured by national law. As yet there existed only the Thirteenth Amendment to the Constitution upon which to base Congressional statutes, and this, as we know, simply abolished and prohibited slavery and involuntary servitude, and empowered Congress to pass appropriate laws for the execution of the Amendment. By virtue of the war powers still exercised by the Administration several of the Union Generals, as we shall see, had set aside this legislation in

CONGRESSIONAL PLAN OF RECONSTRUCTION

some of these reconstructed "States." But, of course, it was well understood that this was only a temporary remedy. During the month of January, 1866, the Republicans in Congress became convinced that the newly organized "States," with the exception of Tennessee, were consciously developing freedmen's codes which would not differ greatly from their old slave codes.

The President had sent General Grant and General Carl Schurz on tours of inspection and inquiry through the South, during the late summer and autumn of 1865; and Congress now asked the President to impart to it the information thus gathered. The two reports were quite contradictory. *The reports of Grant and Schurz in regard to the status in the South.* General Grant said that he drew the conclusion from his observations that "the mass of thinking men of the South accept the present situation of affairs in good faith." He also indicated that the officers of the Freedmen's Bureau were a useless set of men, dangerous to the peace and prosperity of the South, and recommended that the military officers in the different districts should be put in charge of the bureau.

Mr. Schurz, on the other hand, reported that his conclusions from his observations were that there was no loyalty among the leaders and the mass of the people in the South, except such as consisted in submission to necessity; that they were consciously attempting in their new legislation to establish a new form of slavery, distinct only from the old chattel slavery; and that this could be prevented only by national law and national control, at least for many years to come.

General Grant's visit had been a flying one, and his inquiries upon the subject were secondary only to his other business. On the other hand, General Schurz had journeyed deliberately, and his inquiries were the chief, if not the sole, purpose of his visit. Moreover, General Schurz was a keener observer in regard to such matters than General Grant, and a much better reasoner.

Despite, therefore, the great popularity and influence of General Grant, Congress was inclined to place more credence in the report of General Schurz. While its Committee on Reconstruction was deliberating, it, therefore, most naturally set itself about doing what it could, under the Thirteenth Amendment, and also under its still existing war powers, in behalf of the civil rights of the freedmen.

The attitude of Congress toward the reports.

The first measure it attempted was one to enlarge the powers of the Freedmen's Bureau. This supplementary project originated with the Judiciary Committee of the Senate, and was presented in the Senate on the 12th of January, 1866. The new bill proposed to increase the personnel of the bureau and expand the powers vested in it as provided in the law of March 3d, 1865, in the following most important respects:

The Freedmen's Bureau bill of 1866.

First, While the law of March 3d, 1865, provided for the appointment of a commissioner and ten assistants as the entire personnel of the Bureau, the new bill authorized the appointment of a commissioner, twelve assistant commissioners, and the appointment or detail of an agent for each county or parish throughout the section where the Bureau might operate.

Second, While in the law of March 3d, 1865, the Bureau rather appeared to be under the civil administration of the President, the new bill placed it distinctly under the military administration of the President, and authorized the President to extend "military jurisdiction and protection over all of the officers, agents, and employees of the Bureau."

Third, While the law of March 3d, 1865, confined the powers of the Bureau to the giving of aid to refugees and freedmen and the distribution of abandoned and confiscated lands among them, the new bill proposed, in addition to this, to vest in the Bureau the power to build school houses and asylums for the freedmen, and the most wide-reaching jurisdiction over all civil and criminal cases where equality in civil rights and status, and in the application of penalties, was denied, or the denial thereof attempted, on account of race, color, or previous condition of servitude; and it authorized military protection in all such cases to be extended to the suffering party. In a single sentence, this bill provided a sort of palatine jurisdiction over the freedmen in the section lately the scene of rebellion.

It was a stiff measure even for the transition period from war to peace. It cannot be justified constitutionally as anything but a war measure. It is true that the Thirteenth Amendment, just adopted, could be interpreted as giving Congress the power to prohibit inequalities in civil rights and in criminal punishments, as the incidents of slavery or involuntary servitude, and to extend the ordinary jurisdiction of the constitutional courts of the United States over all cases where the attempt to apply such inequalities should be made. But it certainly did not give Congress the power, under any ordinary circumstances, to create a new system of courts, subject to the Executive, officered by military men, and armed directly with military power to enforce decisions. It was, as has been said, a war measure, and nothing else. The question was reduced simply to this: Ought the Congress of the United States to enact a new war measure, after armed resistance had ceased everywhere, except perhaps in some parts of Texas? Was it sound policy, was it good morals, to do so, when the people in the sections lately in rebellion were settling down into the pursuits of peace, even though Congress might legally have the right to do so? The bill was debated long and carefully in the Senate by all of the leading members, and the opinion finally prevailed among them that it was a measure necessary to preserve and protect the freedom of the newly enfranchised. It passed the Senate by a vote of 37 to 10, and the House by a vote of 136 to 33.

The passage of the bill.

On the 10th of February (1866) it was sent to the President for his signature. In a Message, dated the 19th of February, the President put his veto upon this bill. The document was a strong and sound presentation of reasons for his dissent. He said he could not approve of a war measure, with an indefinite term, when the authority of the United States was not disputed in any part of the country, when the rebellion was at an end, and when the country had returned, or was returning, to the pursuits of peace. He referred to the fact that the law of March 3d, 1865, was still in operation, and claimed that it furnished him with all the extraordinary powers necessary to protect the freedmen. He called attention to the army of officials which this proposed law would create, and to the enormous expense which it would entail. And he denied the constitutional power of the Government of the United States to assume functions for negroes which it had never been authorized to assume for white men. There is little question now that the President was correct about this matter, and that the Congress was both reckless and aggressive, not to say vindictive. But it is questionable whether the President did not himself lessen unnecessarily his influence with his party in Congress, by his unqualified opposition to any strengthening of the measure of 1865. He might have returned the bill with the suggestion that it should have a definite limit as to the time it should run, and have ex-

The veto upon it.

CONGRESSIONAL PLAN OF RECONSTRUCTION 67

pressed his willingness to sign a bill which should be so limited. Johnson was blunt in his honesty. But Seward was his adviser, and Seward was, above everything, politic. It would seem that he either failed to advise with his usual sagacity in this case, or that his advice was unheeded.

For this once the President's arguments convinced enough of the Senators to deprive the bill of the support of the necessary majority to carry it over his veto, even so stanch a Republican as ex-Governor Morgan of New York voting against the bill after its return. The Republican majority was deeply chagrined, not to say discouraged, and the President was injuriously encouraged to enter upon the struggle with Congress over the question of Reconstruction. *The veto effective.*

On the evening of the 22d of February, three days after his successful veto, the President made a most important speech from the steps of the White House to a large popular meeting assembled to congratulate him upon his victory. He was betrayed by his elation and warmth into an abusive denunciation of his enemies, once, and only a few months before, his best friends. He went so far as to declare that Stevens and Sumner and Phillips and others like them were, in his opinion, laboring as assiduously to destroy the fundamental principles of the government as were the leaders of the rebellion. After such an open challenge, the contest was nearly unavoidable. It was not avoided, whatever might have been the possibilities of re-establishing harmony. And it cannot be denied that, from this moment, personal rancor against the President filled the heart of Stevens, at least, if not of the others. The President's utterances were, indeed, highly exasperating, and it would have required a very large measure of public virtue to have ignored them. *The President's 22d of February speech.*

As a part of the same plan for securing the civil rights of the freedmen against the hostile legislation of the President's reconstructed "States," the Judiciary Committee of the Senate reported a Civil Rights bill to the Senate one day before it reported the Freedmen's Bureau bill, that is, on the 11th of January. The right of way, so to speak, was, however, given to the latter bill, and Congress was nearly two months longer in perfecting the former than the latter. This Civil Rights bill certainly avoided many of the most serious objections which could be truthfully made against the Freedmen's Bureau bill. It was not a war measure in a time of peace. It did not provide a privileged jurisdiction for any class, and it did not create an army of new officials to drain the Treasury and increase the patronage of the President.

<small>The Civil Rights Bill.</small>

The purpose of it was simply to establish equality in the enjoyment of civil rights for all citizens of the country and to make all persons born in the country and not subject to any foreign power citizens. The substantial part of the bill, as perfected, read: "All persons born in the United States and not subject to any foreign power, excluding Indians not taxed, are hereby declared to be citizens of the United States; and such citizens of every race and color, without regard to any previous condition of slavery or involuntary servitude, except as a punishment for crime whereof the party shall have been duly convicted, shall have the same right, in every State and Territory in the United States, to make and enforce contracts, to sue, be parties, and give evidence, to inherit, purchase, lease, sell, hold, and convey real and personal property, and to the full and equal benefit of all laws and proceedings for the security of person and property, as is enjoyed by white citizens, and shall be subject to like punishment, pains and penalties, and to none other, any law, statute, ordinance, regulation or custom, to the contrary notwithstanding."

This is simply equality for all before the law. It conferred no political privilege and no social equality. It was fairly within the power of Congress to pass such a measure, by interpreting broadly the Thirteenth Amendment, without having any recourse to the idea of war powers. Slavery was nothing but extreme inequality in civil rights between master and servant. The prohibition of slavery and involuntary servitude could, therefore, most certainly be held to be the prohibition of all of these incidents.

The remaining provisions of the bill did nothing more than fix penalties for violating, or attempting to violate, civil equality as thus defined, designate the officers charged with the duty of prosecuting the offenders, and establish the jurisdiction for the trial of such cases.

The penalties were somewhat grave. They might be as severe as a fine of one thousand dollars, or imprisonment for a year, or both, in the discretion of the courts. But they were not cruel or unusual, and were, therefore, within the power of Congress to prescribe. The officers authorized and required to institute proceedings against violators of the law were the district attorneys, marshals and deputy marshals of the United States courts, the commissioners appointed by the Circuit and Territorial courts of the United States, the officers and agents of the Freedmen's Bureau, and every other officer whom the President might see fit to empower thereto. And the jurisdiction established for the trial of such cases was that of the United States courts, upon which was conferred original and exclusive jurisdiction in any case under the law, and to which any case touching these subjects commenced in a "State" court could be removed on motion of the defendant. But all these things were authorized by a liberal construction of the Thirteenth Amendment, which expressly vests in Congress the power to make all laws necessary and proper to enforce the prohibition of slavery throughout the whole country.

It was, indeed, a great change in the system of the jurisprudence of the United States that the central Government should define and protect civil equality within the States. But it was a change which history had forced upon the country, and the sovereign power of the nation had deliberately legalized it. There is no question now that it was sound political science, too, and that it was required by public morality. Real civil liberty is always national. Its concepts and principles spring out of the national consciousness of rights and wrongs. And civil equality is the first principle of modern justice, the most pressing behest of the public morality of the age. Moreover, this measure did not militate against the President's plan of Reconstruction. He could have accepted it without compromising that plan in the slightest, and it was a monumental blunder on his part that he did not do so.

The measure sound from the points of view of modern jurisprudence and modern political science.

On the 27th of March, he sent his veto of the bill into the Senate. It was a weak argument throughout. He objected to making the freedmen citizens by an act of Congress, while eleven of the thirty-six "States" were unrepresented in Congress, and made out that it was a discrimination in favor of the ignorant negro against the intelligent foreigner not yet naturalized. He objected to the extension of the powers of the central Government in behalf of civil equality within the "States" as destructive of the federal system of government, and as degrading to the

The veto of the bill.

CONGRESSIONAL PLAN OF RECONSTRUCTION 71

legislators and officials of the "States." He did not deny that the proposed measure might be sustained as constitutional under the Thirteenth Amendment, but maintained that it was unnecessary for the execution of the provisions of the Amendment. He objected, further, to the number of officers and agents authorized to institute proceedings under the measure, to the fee which they should receive, and to the power of the President to order the courts of the United States to migrate from one place to another when necessary for the prompt administration of justice. And he objected, finally, to the power vested in the President to use the land and naval forces and the militia to prevent the violation, and enforce the due execution, of the measure.

Now all this was easily answered from the point of view which Congress and the North had now firmly taken, viz.: that the eleven former "States" in which rebellion had for so long prevailed were not "States," although the territory formerly occupied by them, and the population formerly inhabiting them, were within the United States and were subject to the jurisdiction of the central Government; that the rebellion had demonstrated that the central Government must be intrusted with a large increase of powers in protecting civil equality and civil liberty; and that the sovereign Nation had willed this in the enactment and adoption of the Thirteenth Amendment to the Constitution.

Really there was but one thing in the bill susceptible of successful criticism, and that could be explained so as to avoid it. It was the ninth section, which authorized the President to use military power in execution of the law. The language would permit the President to use the military before bringing the matter before the courts and securing a decision. It would permit the President to use the military as the

Criticism of the bill.

primal, instead of the final, agency for executing the law. It appeared to be in this respect a real force bill, that is a bill in which the Executive is empowered to use the military, not for the enforcement of judicial decision in aid of the marshals, deputies, constables, and their posses, which is the customary order in time of peace, but for the execution of the law in the first instance, before decision rendered or trial had. But it was entirely clear that what was meant in this section of the bill was that, when combinations too powerful to be dealt with by the courts and their officers should undertake to prevent the execution of the law, the President might use the military to overcome them. Under such an interpretation, this provision was justifiable and proper, certainly so in a transition period from a condition of general rebellion against the laws of the United States to that of gradual, and only gradual, acquiescence in their enforcement.

The President most decidedly lost his chance of rehabilitating himself with his party, and leading it in the work of Reconstruction, by not signing this bill. He sinned against the Southerners themselves in not doing so. His veto of it made them believe that they could count upon the Administration, the Administration Republicans, and the whole Democratic party of the North, in denying equal civil rights to the freedmen, and that such a combination must eventually triumph. They, therefore, persisted in their course of exceptional legislation against the freedmen in the South, and in their arrogant demands for the immediate admission to seats in Congress of the very men who had led the rebellion for four years against the sovereignty and Government of the United States. It is amazing that they did not see that the large Republican majority in Congress would

The President's blunder.

CONGRESSIONAL PLAN OF RECONSTRUCTION 73

be driven to the alternative of seeing the work of four years of terrible sacrifice undone or of securing its permanence by making such changes in the organic law as would effect it, while yet they had the power. On the 6th of April, the Senate overrode the President's veto of the Civil Rights bill, and on the 9th the House did likewise.

The veto overridden.

While, as we have seen, the President did not exactly deny the constitutionality of the bill, the Democrats in Congress, and the Southerners seeking seats in Congress, did. There was, therefore, but one course left open to the Republican majority, and that was to make what they considered to be the incidents of the Thirteenth Amendment express provisions of the Constitution. There were also several other things which had become clear in the course of the debates in the Civil Rights bill and the Freedmen's Bureau bill.

The Fourteenth Amendment.

In the first place, it was seen that the emancipation of the slaves would increase the representation in Congress and in the Presidential electoral college from the old slave "States" by two-fifths whenever the Southern communities should be recognized as "States" again, and that too without the admission of the emancipated persons to the exercise of political suffrage. It was certainly to be apprehended that, with such increased representation, the Southern members and the Northern Democrats would constitute a majority in Congress and in the electoral college, and might proceed not only to repeal the Civil Rights Act, and all acts in behalf of the freedmen, but also to throw the Confederate debt or a part of it upon the United States, or establish pensions for Confederate soldiers, or even repudiate the debt of the Union made in defence of its own life. While the danger of these things was, probably, somewhat exaggerated, still it would not have been becoming for men of prudence and patriotism to have failed to provide against them. Really there was but one thing to do, and that was to enact, and secure the adoption of, another amendment to the Constitution covering these points, while the power to do so still existed.

It would be an agreeable thing to the writer of this period of American history, were he able to record that the principal matter which occupied the thought and attention of the Committee on Reconstruction was how to secure the necessary civil rights of the freedmen. But in the interest of exact truth he is compelled to forego this pleasure. The first thing which that Committee considered and recommended to the Houses of Congress was the political matter of a redistribution of the representation in the House of Representatives and in the Presidential electoral college. On the 22d of January (1866) the Committee reported to the two Houses the following proposition as an amendment to the Constitution of the United States : " Representatives and direct taxes shall be apportioned among the several States which may be included within this Union according to their respective numbers, counting the whole number of persons in each State—excluding Indians not taxed—provided, that whenever the elective franchise shall be denied or abridged in any State on account of race or color, all persons of such race or color shall be excluded from the basis of representation." For nearly six weeks both the Committee and Congress were occupied in the discussion of this proposition. In a slightly modified form it was adopted in the House, but, at last, on the 9th of March, it came to vote in the Senate, and not having received the necessary two-thirds majority, it was abandoned as a separate measure, and

[Sidenote: The political provision in the proposed Fourteenth Amendment.]

CONGRESSIONAL PLAN OF RECONSTRUCTION

merged into the general article containing the regulations of all the points to which reference was made above.

It was Monday, April 30th, before the Committee was ready to report the entire article, which took the name of the Fourteenth Amendment to the Constitution. The article as presented to the Houses of Congress by the Joint Committee on that day read as follows:

"Sect. 1. No State shall make or enforce any law which shall abridge the privileges or immunities of citizens of the United States; nor shall any State deprive any person of life, liberty or property without due process of law; nor deny to any person within its jurisdiction the equal protection of the laws.

"Sect. 2. Representatives shall be apportioned among the several States which may be included within this Union according to their respective numbers, counting the whole number of persons in each State, excluding Indians not taxed. But whenever in any State the elective franchise shall be denied to any portion of its male citizens not less than twenty-one years of age, or in any way abridged, except for participation in rebellion or other crime, the basis of representation in such State shall be reduced in the proportion which the number of such male citizens shall bear to the whole number of male citizens not less than twenty-one years of age.

"Sect. 3. Until the 4th day of July in the year 1870, all persons who voluntarily adhered to the late insurrection, giving it aid and comfort, shall be excluded from the right to vote for Representatives in Congress and for electors for President and Vice-President of the United States.

"Sect. 4. Neither the United States nor any State shall assume or pay any debt or obligation already incurred, or which may hereafter be incurred, in aid of insurrection or war against the United States, or any claim for compensation for loss of involuntary service or labor.

"Sect. 5. The Congress shall have power to enforce, by appropriate legislation, the provisions of this Article."

The chief difficulties with these provisions were, first, that they did not define who were the citizens of the United States; second, that while they disfranchised for two or three years all who had voluntarily taken part in the rebellion, they did not disqualify anybody from holding office or legislative mandate on account of such conduct; and third, that while they forbade the payment of any debt or obligation incurred in aid of rebellion, they did not guarantee those incurred in the suppression of such rebellion.

Defects in the first draft of the Amendment.

The discussion in Congress upon these provisions lasted through the month of May and well into June. At last in the second week of June, the two Houses arrived at an agreement upon the modifications which seemed proper and necessary, and the Article as thus perfected was adopted by the necessary two-thirds vote in each branch.

The discussion of the propositions in Congress.

The first section had been modified by the incorporation into it of a sentence which defined citizenship of the United States. It reads: "All persons born or naturalized in the United States, and subject to the jurisdiction thereof, are citizens of the United States and of the State wherein they reside." This cleared up all difficulties in determining who the persons were, whose privileges and immunities were to be protected against "State" action. It also settled the question, forever, as to whether citizenship of the United States or citizenship of the "State" is primary. There is no doubt that in that clause of the original Con-

The final draft agreed on.

CONGRESSIONAL PLAN OF RECONSTRUCTION

stitution which declares that the Constitution of the United States, and the laws of Congress made in accordance therewith, and the treaties made under the authority thereof, are the supreme law of the land, no matter what may be found in "State" constitutions or laws to the contrary, primary allegiance of all citizens and persons to the United States was established and required, but the advocates of "State" sovereignty always contended that, because there was no express clause in the Constitution defining citizenship, and declaring the citizenship of the United States primary, citizenship was primarily of the "State," and, hence, allegiance was due primarily to the "State" by all its inhabitants. It was very proper and very desirable that this contention should be set at rest.

The language of the second section had been revised so as to make its meaning more clear, but it had not been changed at all as to its meaning. It reads in its perfected form: "Representatives shall be apportioned among the several States according to their respective numbers, counting the whole number of persons in each State, excluding Indians not taxed. But when the right to vote at any election for the choice of electors for President and Vice-President of the United States, Representatives in Congress, the executive and judicial officers of a State, or the members of the legislature thereof, is denied to any of the male inhabitants of such State, being twenty-one years of age, *and citizens of the United States*, or in any way abridged, except for participation in rebellion or other crime, the basis of representation therein shall be reduced in the proportion which the number of such male citizens shall bear to the whole number of male citizens twenty-one years of age in such State."

For section third, denying suffrage until 1870 to all

persons who had given aid voluntarily to the rebellion, Congress had substituted an entirely new resolution, which rendered the Confederate chieftains ineligible to office instead of disqualifying the rank and file for suffrage. It reads as follows : "No person shall be a senator or Representative in Congress, or elector of President and Vice-President, or hold any office, civil or military, under the United States, or under any State, who having previously taken an oath, as a member of Congress, or as an officer of the United States, or as a member of any State legislature, or as an executive or judicial officer of any State, to support the Constitution of the United States, shall have engaged in insurrection or rebellion against the same, or given aid or comfort to the enemies thereof. But Congress may, by a vote of two-thirds of each House, remove such disability."

This was certainly a wise change. It certainly could not be contended that disqualifications for holding office and legislative mandate violated any so-called natural right. It was better that whatever punishments of a political nature might fall upon the Confederates should strike the leaders, rather than the followers. And it was not a severe punishment which required that, for a time at least, the people inhabiting the communities lately in rebellion should choose as their representatives to the National legislature and to the Presidential electoral college, and as their "State" officers, men not identified with the rebellion so closely as to have been among its leaders. It is difficult to see how the Confederate leaders could have been required to suffer less, and have been rebuked at all for their acts.

Finally, section four was supplemented by a sentence which declared that "the validity of the public debt of the United States, authorized by law, including debts incurred for payment of pensions and bounties for services in suppressing insurrection or rebellion, shall not be questioned." The last words of the section were also somewhat modified in the direction of greater emphasis, but the meaning remained the same. As thus perfected, the section declared the validity of all the existing obligations of the United States, and repudiated all obligations whatsoever assumed in aid of rebellion, and all claims for the loss or emancipation of any slave. This covered the ground completely in regard to the security of the public obligations of the United States both from the positive and negative side, and it prevented both Congress and the "States" from ever recognizing, in the future, the claim for any relief from the natural consequences of unsuccessful rebellion, and the right to any compensation for deprivation of property in man.

As Congress passed these propositions by the necessary two-thirds majority they were not submitted to the President at all, it being considered that his disapproval, if given, would avail nothing against such a majority. This has been the custom from the first in Congressional propositions of amendment, and it is now too late to dispute its regularity. But it is easy to see that the President might support a veto of such propositions by such reasoning as to make it at least possible that sufficient votes might be changed from affirmative to negative upon them, to finally defeat them; and it is certainly true that the Constitution requires that every bill, order, resolution, or vote to which the concurrence of the Senate and House of Representatives may be necessary (except on a question of adjournment) shall be presented to the President and is subject to his approval or veto, no matter by what majority it may have been passed.

However, President Johnson had no opportunity to express himself officially or make himself officially felt in regard to this Amendment. It was pretty well understood that he did not view it with favor while it was pending, and it soon became manifest that he was advising its rejection by the "States."

The President's attitude toward the proposed amendment.

Mr. Seward issued his notification of the passage of the amendment by Congress to the "State" legislatures for their ratificatory action on the 16th of June. He sent the same to the legislatures of all the "States," that is, to the legislatures of those bodies claiming to be "States" under the President's plan of Reconstruction, as well as to the legislatures of those "States" which had never pretended to secede from the Union. This was, again, certainly a recognition of all these bodies as "States" of the Union by the executive branch of the Government, at least.

Mr. Seward acts in regard to ratification.

On the other hand, the Reconstruction Committee of Congress had reported a bill along with the Article of Amendment, which virtually proposed to make the ratification of the proposed Amendment by the respective legislatures of the reconstructed Southern communities the condition of the admission of the Senators and Representatives-elect from them to seats in Congress. That is, it was proposed that Congress should make its recognition of the reconstructed bodies as "States" conditional upon their ratification of the Article of Amendment. Or perhaps some of those supporting this proposition would have preferred the statement that it was proposed that Congress should make its recognition of the reconstructed governments of the "States" in which secession had

The requirement that the ratification of the proposed Amendment should be the condition of the admission of the Senators and Representatives-elect to seats in Congress.

CONGRESSIONAL PLAN OF RECONSTRUCTION 81

been attempted conditional upon the ratification of the Amendment by the legislative departments of these reconstructed governments respectively.

No matter how it might have been stated, it was an absurdity. The true theory on this point was that held by Mr. Stevens, viz., to consider only those "States" which had never attempted secession, those "States" which had never been members of the Southern Confederacy, as constituting the "States" of the Union at that moment, and all other territory and people subject to the jurisdiction of the United States as being under the exclusive government of the central Government; to amend the Constitution by a three-fourths majority of these loyal "States"; and then to admit these reconstructed communities as new "States" into the Union with its amended Constitution. The absurdity of the condition.

The amended Constitution would then have the same power over them as if the Amendment had been ratified by them. In fact, their petition for admission or recognition as "States" of the Union with the amended Constitution would imply their assent to the Amendment as well as to every other part of the Constitution. The more moderate Republicans feared that the Southern communities would not feel obligated by a Constitution amended in this way. It is difficult to see why they should not. The Southern statesmen knew that Congress had no power under the Constitution to require of new "States" obedience to anything as a condition of their admission to the Union, but the Constitution as it was at the moment of their admission. Looked at from the point of view of the present, it would certainly appear that the exaction of such an unlawful promise, imposing such a degrading discrimination, would have been far more exasperating than anything else which could have been invented or imagined.

Enough of them saw this to prevent Congress from enacting the bill proposed by the Reconstruction Committee into a law, and when the proposed Amendment went to the legislatures of the "States," there was no requirement attending it which appeared to deprive any legislature, or body claiming to be a legislature, of its discretion in dealing with the subject.

As a matter of fact, however, the legislature of Tennessee ratified the proposed Amendment within about a month after receiving the Article from Secretary Seward, and Congress thereupon passed the following joint resolution and sent it to the President for his signature: "Whereas in the year 1861 the government of the State of Tennessee was seized upon and taken possession of by persons in hostility to the United States, and the inhabitants of said State, in pursuance of an act of Congress, were declared to be in a state of insurrection against the United States; and whereas said State government can only be restored to its former political relations in the Union by consent of the lawmaking power of the United States; and whereas the people of said State did, on the 22d of February, 1865, by a large popular vote, adopt and ratify a constitution of government whereby slavery was abolished and all ordinances and laws of secession and debts contracted under the same were declared void; and whereas a State government has been organized under said constitution which has ratified the amendment to the constitution abolishing slavery, also the amendment proposed by the thirty-ninth Congress" (the Fourteenth Amendment) "and has done other acts proclaiming and denoting loyalty: Therefore, *Be it resolved by the Senate and House of Representatives in Congress assembled,* That the State of Tennessee is hereby restored to her former practical relations to the

The precedent set by Tennessee.

CONGRESSIONAL PLAN OF RECONSTRUCTION

Union, and is again entitled to be represented by Senators and Representatives in Congress."

These proceedings made it certain that, while Congress had failed to pass any formal act making the acceptance of the proposed Fourteenth Amendment a condition precedent to the readmission of the other "States" which had been in rebellion, Congress would not readmit any of them which did not do this. Tennessee, it was thought, had sinned the least of all, and, therefore, should be readmitted on lightest terms. More might be righteously required of the others, but not less. *The Tennessee precedent.*

The President signed the resolution, but accompanied the same with a short message in which he made a rather telling criticism upon the procedure of submitting proposed constitutional amendments to bodies not already "States" in the Union, and warned Congress against construing his approval as committing him to all of the statements of fact contained in the preamble to the resolution, or to the doctrine that Congress had any right "to pass laws preliminary to the admission of duly qualified Representatives from any of the States." These latter words manifest the fact that the President was still holding on to the idea that the whole function of Congress in Reconstruction consisted in the power of each House to judge of the election and qualifications of its members. *The President's message in regard to the rehabilitation of Tennessee.*

CHAPTER VI

THE CONGRESSIONAL PLAN (*Continued*)

The Reports of the Committee on Reconstruction—The Idea of a New Electorate as the Basis and Condition of Reconstruction—The Freedmen's Bureau Act of July 16th, 1866—The Disaffection in the Cabinet—The New Orleans Riot—The Issue of Reconstruction in the Campaign of 1866—The Congressional Election of 1866—The President's Final Proclamation Declaring the Civil War Ended—The October Elections—The President's Message of December 3d, 1866—Rejection of the Proposed Fourteenth Amendment by the legislatures of the Reconstructed " States."

Two days after the transmission of the Fourteenth Amendment to the "State" legislatures, the Joint Committee of Congress on Reconstruction made its final report, or rather reports, since there were two of them, one being signed by all the Republican members of the Committee, and the other by all the Democratic members.

The reports of the Committee on Reconstruction.

The majority report was an able defence of the view, that by rebellion and attempted secession the eleven "States" in which these things happened had lost their "Statehood" and had become disorganized communities, but that while they could and had destroyed "State" government, and placed themselves outside of the Union so far as exercising the powers and privileges of "State" local government was concerned, they could not, and had not, escaped the obligations of the Constitution and the authority of the

The majority report.

central Government. The exact language of the report on this point was: "The Constitution, it will be observed, does not act upon States, as such, but upon the people; while, therefore, the people cannot escape its authority, the States may, through the act of their people, cease to exist in an organized form, and thus dissolve their political relations with the United States." The doctrine is here more clearly expressed than in other places, but even here there is a confusing modification contained in the words "in an organized form." It would have been much clearer if they had been entirely omitted. The framers of the report were evidently haunted by that spectre of an abstract, unorganized "State," which has played such havoc with good sense in some of the subsequent decisions of the Supreme Court, and which is nothing more than a Platonic idea.

Based upon this doctrine, the majority report naturally vindicated the exclusive right of Congress in the work of Reconstruction, which work was virtually the admission of new "States" into the Union. It, furthermore, demonstrated that the situation in these disorganized sections was one largely of exhausted disloyalty only, and that all that the inhabitants of them had done under the President's Reconstruction policy was directed toward putting the same men in power who had led in the rebellion and toward denying civil, to say nothing of political, rights to the freedmen.

And its final conclusion was, "that Congress would not be justified in admitting such communities to a participation in the government of the country without first providing such constitutional or other guarantees as would tend to secure the civil rights of all citizens of the Republic; a just equality of representation; protection against claims founded in rebellion and crime; a temporary restoration of the right of suffrage to those who have not actively participated in the efforts to destroy the Union and overthrow the Government; and the exclusion from positions of public trust of at least a portion of those whose crimes have proved them to be the enemies of the Union, and unworthy of public confidence."

As we have seen, the proposed Fourteenth Article of Amendment had provided for all of these things, except the direct conferring of suffrage on anybody. With this exception, it had gone even further, in its provision declaratory of citizenship, and in its protection of the public debt of the Union.

The report of the minority, that is of the three Democrats, was written by Mr. Reverdy Johnson, of Maryland. It was, as a lawyer's brief, an able presentation of the view that a "State" of the Union can never become anything else than a "State," no matter what may be the character, deeds, attempts or disposition of the people who inhabit it, and is at all times entitled to the same powers, rights and privileges, under the Constitution of the United States. It was, however, the veriest dry bones of legal reasoning, the veriest sophistry of juristic abstraction. There was no political science in it, no common sense in it, and it ended with an unfortunate and irritating defence of President Johnson's personal loyalty, which had not been in the slightest degree impugned by the majority.

The minority report.

The majority report indicated, at least, that Congress might require something more than adoption of the Fourteenth Amendment by the communities lately in rebellion before they would be recognized as having been restored to their proper relations in the Union as "States," and entitled to representation in Congress. At the moment, however, it is probable that a prompt adoption of

The idea of a new electorate as the basis and condition of Reconstruction.

the proposed Amendment by any of the reconstructed legislatures would have been followed by a joint resolution on the part of Congress similar to that enacted in the case of Tennessee. There is no doubt that many of the more radical members of Congress had been long considering the question of creating an entirely new electorate in the South as the only proper basis for reconstruction, and that some of the conservatives, from being opponents of this idea at the beginning of the year, had, by the middle of it, begun, at least, to waver. To those who could read the signs of the times correctly, it was manifest that a rejection of the proposed Fourteenth Amendment by these communities would lead Congress forward upon that line. The President ought to have understood this, when Mr. Raymond voted for the proposed Amendment in the House. He ought to have done all in his power to influence the reconstructed communities to adopt the proposed Amendment, no matter whether the submission of it to them by the Secretary of State of the United States logically involved their recognition as "States" of the Union by the Administration at Washington, or not. They were not in a position to exact the precise conclusion of a logical process in their favor, especially as it was based on a fallacious premise, and the President did both himself and them a great wrong in not discouraging them from so doing.

A few weeks later Congress scored another victory over the President, one which did much toward wiping out the defeats of February 19th and 21st. It passed another Freedmen's Bureau Bill, and then repassed it July 16th, over the President's veto. This bill was framed with the purpose in view of avoiding those features of the bill, successfully vetoed by the President on February 19th preceding, *The Freedmen's Bureau Act of July 16th, 1866.*

which had influenced certain Republicans to sustain the President's veto. The differences between the two measures consisted in the following points. The first bill had no definite time limit; the second would expire in two years from the date of its passage. The first bill vested jurisdiction in the Freedmen's Bureau over the civil rights of freedmen and refugees in all parts of the United States. The second vested the bureau with jurisdiction over loyal refugees and freedmen without mention of place.  The first vested a most sweeping power in the Bureau to give all kinds of aid and support to the destitute refugees and freedmen. The second contained only the more moderate provision of the original law of March 3d, 1865, on that subject. Finally the first gave the Bureau jurisdiction over the civil rights of freedmen and refugees, not only when the deprivation of them was the consequence of rebellion, but when it was effected by *any local law*, ordinance, police regulation or other regulation. The second, on the contrary, limited the jurisdiction of the Bureau to those cases where the deprivation was the consequence of rebellion.

The President could not, however, see much difference between them. He claimed that his objections to the first bill were valid against the second. The second measure, he contended, was only a war measure for a definite period, in a time of peace. It was the prolongation for a definite time of military jurisdiction over civil matters, when the civil courts both "State" and Union were open and in the unhindered discharge of their business. And he held the ground that Congress had no more constitutional power to create, or perpetuate, military jurisdiction over civil matters for a definite period in time of peace than for an indefinite period. He referred to the fact that the Civil Rights measure, just passed over his veto, met all

The veto of the measure.

the points provided for in the Freedmen's Bureau bill, and affirmed that all of the provisions of that law would be executed by him through ordinary civil means, in so far as they should not be repealed by Congress or declared unconstitutional by the courts.

From the point of view of to-day it is difficult to see why the President was not right. There is no doubt that the Freedmen's Bureau with its powers, jurisdiction and charities, was a far greater source of irritation in the South than was the presence of the United States army. While its superior officers were generally men of ability and character, a large number of the subalterns were canting hypocrites and outright thieves. They kept the negroes in a state of idleness, beggary and unrest, and made them a constant danger to the life and property of the whites; and their veritable tyranny over the white population did more to destroy Union sentiment among the whites and make them regard the United States Government in a hostile light than anything which had happened during the whole course of the rebellion. It was an institution which ought to have been dispensed with the instant that the necessity which called it into existence passed away. The law of March 3d, 1865, had still about eight months to run, and Congress would be in session again four months before it would expire. There was ample opportunity for prolonging the law, and that law, it was to be presumed, was less needed in 1866 than in 1865. It took all of the party discipline of the Republicans to prevent sufficient disaffection in their ranks to sustain the President's veto. On the merits of the question alone they could not have done it. They were in error, and many of them knew it, but they were now in to fight the President and they must stand together.

Correctness of the President's views.

The veto of the bill was dated July 16th, and the two Houses repassed it over the veto on the same day. The new law was to be executed through the War Department, as the original measure had been, and the Secretary of War had begun to manifest that indecent hostility to the President which disgraced the last years of the Administration. The President was largely cut off from even the knowledge of what was taking place in the operations of the Freedmen's Bureau, and Mr. Stanton now managed it in such a manner, whether intentional or not, as to cause the greatest possible friction between the Government and the whites of the South, and thus to retard the process of Reconstruction and to destroy what had been already accomplished in that direction.

The veto overridden.

Besides Stanton, three other members of the Cabinet had showed their disaffection toward the President's policy. They were Mr. Speed, the Attorney-General, Mr. Dennison, the Postmaster-General, and Mr. Harlan, the Secretary of the Interior. During the course of the month (July) these three gentlemen resigned their offices, and were replaced by Mr. Stanbery, Mr. A. W. Randall, and Mr. O. H. Browning. Their sense of propriety would not permit them to retain high office under the President while differing with him so widely in regard to the fundamental question of Reconstruction. Mr. Stanton, however, took a different view of his duty. He seemed to feel that he was under obligations to his country to remain in the President's Cabinet, at the head of the most important branch of the Administration at that moment, and protect the country against the purposes of the President. He was sustained in this view by the Republican majority in Congress, which soon entered upon its course of depriving

Disaffection in the Cabinet.

Stanton's attitude toward the President.

CONGRESSIONAL PLAN OF RECONSTRUCTION

the President of his military control even, by transferring his functions to the Secretary of War and the General of the army. To the men of the present day, Mr. Stanton's conduct appears, at least, lacking in a proper sense of delicacy. It may be regarded in an even more serious light. It may be looked upon as a conspiracy with the Republican majority in Congress to rob the President of his constitutional prerogatives, to change the form of government from the presidential system to the parliamentary system of administration. It is difficult to find any sufficient defence for Mr. Stanton's course. It is impossible to clear him of the appearance of great egotism or of great greed of office, in not resigning along with his dissatisfied colleagues.

The President knew of this difference of feeling between himself and his War Secretary at the time of his reorganization of the Cabinet in July, and would undoubtedly have been glad to receive his resignation, but he did not ask for it. The newspapers which sustained the Administration did, however, and predicted that it would be forthcoming. The Republican leaders, on the other hand, encouraged Stanton to hold on to the office, and represented to him that the welfare of his country demanded the sacrifice of his personal feelings in the matter.

It was now generally proclaimed throughout the North that the rebel chieftains had repossessed themselves of the reconstructed "State" governments and were making use of "State" powers to re-enslave the freedmen. It was also proclaimed that the life and property of Union men, of whatever race, at the South were utterly insecure, and that at least a thousand men had been murdered in that section within a year's time, without any considerable number of the murder-

The opinion and feeling in the North concerning the condition of things in the South.

ers having been brought to justice. And it was asserted that the President of the United States had deserted the party of the Union, the party which had elevated him to the chief magistracy of the land, and was now conspiring with his old party friends, the Democrats, in both the North and the South, to drive the Republican party from power and restore the régime of the Democracy of 1860.

At this moment a horrible tragedy was enacted in New Orleans which seemed to give verification to some, if not all, of these statements. It seems that the late Confederate leaders resident in Louisiana, having received pardon from the President of the United States upon fulfilling the conditions of the President's amnesty proclamation, had got possession in 1864 of the reconstructed "State" government of Louisiana, with the exception of the governorship and some of the judicial offices. The constitution of 1864, made by sincere Union men, did not exactly suit them, and the legislature in the spring of 1866 took into consideration a bill for calling another convention together for the purpose of framing a new constitution, but the Administration at Washington frowned upon the movement and the legislature abandoned it. In like manner, the men who formed and established the constitution of 1864 were displeased with the fact that the "State" government under it had been captured at the polls by the old electorate of Louisiana, reinstated through the President's amnesty. They also wanted to change the constitution, to so change it as to create an electorate which would bring them back into power again. This meant negro suffrage. Just before the convention of 1864 adjourned, it passed a resolution vesting in the presiding officer of the convention the power, and imposing on him the duty, of reconvoking the convention in case the constitution framed by it should not be ratified at the polls, or for any other necessary reason, for the purpose of taking such measures as might be needful for forming civil government in Louisiana.

Of course, when the constitution framed by the convention was adopted by popular vote and a "State" government was set up under it, common sense and common honesty would hold that the convention had been finally dissolved, no matter how the wording of the resolution might be forced in the opposite direction. The men of "'64" saw in this wording their only chance, however, to rescue the "State" government from the hands of the amnestied electorate, and in their desperation they were determined to attempt to make use of it. A number of the members of the old convention got together informally on the 26th of June. The president of the old convention did not call them together, and he would not preside at the informal meeting. He made some trivial excuse; but there cannot be much doubt in regard to his real reason. This informal meeting then proceeded to elect a *pro tempore* president, Judge Howell, an office-holder under the constitution of 1864. It was this man who issued the proclamation of July 7th, reconvoking the old convention of 1864. The time appointed by him was the 30th of July at noon, and the place designated by him was the Mechanics' Institute Building at New Orleans. The men called together were the members of the old convention, but to provide for any vacancies that might have happened or might happen in the former membership of this old body, Judge Howell called on the Governor, Mr. Wells, to issue writs of election. The governor did so, and ordered an election of such delegates to be held September 3d. He thus manifested his approval of the movement.

Naturally the party of the amnestied viewed this scheme for depriving them of the "State" government by means of a new constitution, framed by a defunct convention, and certain to contain a provision for negro suffrage, with the most intense hostility. They were not placated either by being referred to the consideration that the constitution framed by this convention must be submitted to the suffrages of the existing electorate, and must be ratified by a majority of the same, before it could be put into operation. They had a suspicion that the whole thing was instigated by the wicked Republicans at the North, and that the voting upon such a proposed constitution would be controlled by them through the military of the United States Government.

They, therefore, resolved to nip the plan in the bud by preventing the assembly of the convention, or forcing it to disperse if it did assemble. The mayor of the city, Mr. Monroe, the same who was mayor when the Union army entered the city in 1862, applied to the General in command of the United States troops in Louisiana, General Absalom Baird, to know what attitude the military authorities would take toward the convention, and informed General Baird that he intended to disperse the convention if it should attempt to assemble without having the approval of these authorities. General Baird was acting for General Sheridan, who was absent from his post, and he replied with much more caution than he would probably have done had he been alone responsible. He told Mayor Monroe that he thought the Governor of the "State," rather than the mayor of the city, was the man to interfere with the assembly of a body professing to be a "State" convention, if there was to be any interference at all, and he gave the mayor to understand that his proposed course might be perilous. This was the

25th of July. Two days later the mayor went again to the General, this time accompanied by the Lieutenant-Governor, who was of the party of the amnestied. He now told General Baird that the police would not undertake to prevent the assembly of the convention, or disperse its members when assembled, but that its members would be indicted by the grand jury and arrested by the sheriff. The General seemed to think that the convention could lawfully assemble, but agreed with the mayor and Lieutenant-Governor that both he and they would request instructions from Washington.

The General applied to the Secretary of War, and the mayor applied to the President. The General informed the Secretary of the movement to assemble a convention; that it had the approval of the Governor; that the Lieutenant-Governor and the municipal authorities considered it unlawful and proposed to prevent it by arresting the delegates; that he had declared to them that he would not permit them to do this, unless the President should so instruct him; and he asked for orders, in the premises, by telegraph. The Lieutenant-Governor and the Attorney-General of the "State" informed the President of the movement to assemble the old convention; informed him that negroes were assembling, incendiary speeches were being made calling them to arm themselves, and the President was being denounced; that the Governor was in sympathy with the movement; that the matter was before the grand jury; and that it was contemplated to have the members of the convention arrested by criminal process; and they asked the President to inform them whether the military authorities would interfere to prevent the execution of the processes of the criminal court.

Secretary Stanton did not reply to General Baird's application at all. He did not even communicate the General's application to the President. He afterward explained that he did not consider that Baird's telegram required any reply. Baird had said in his despatch that he had informed the Lieutenant-Governor and the city authorities that he would not allow them to arrest the delegates and break up the convention unless instructed to do so by the President. The Secretary did not propose to send the General any such orders, or to allow any such to be transmitted to him from the President through the War Department, and so the Secretary thought it best to let the matter rest where the General had placed it. He did not know that the President had been applied to by the other side, and the President did not inform the Secretary of the despatch which he had received. The confidence between the two men had been already so largely destroyed as to prevent even consultation upon these grave subjects.

The President, on the other hand, answered the application made to him. He telegraphed to the Lieutenant-Governor that the military would be expected to sustain, and not to obstruct, or interfere with, the proceedings of the criminal court. He did not send any orders to General Baird, however. Whether the Lieutenant-Governor showed his telegram from the President to General Baird or not is not positively known, so far as the writer of these pages has been able to discover, but it is probable that he did.

It was certainly then the understanding on all sides, at least, that the "State" and municipal authorities would deal with the delegates to the convention, if they interfered with them at all, through the grand jury and the officers of the criminal court, and not through the police. This did not mean, of course, that the police should not be present in the neighborhood of the convention for the purpose of keeping the public peace. They were ordered to assemble at the stations on the morning of the 30th (July) and to bring their arms. According to General Sheridan's report to the President, the riot was occasioned by the marching of a procession of negroes, about one hundred strong and partly armed, through several of the streets to the locality of the convention. It occurred about an hour after the members of the convention had assembled. Naturally a number of people, mostly of the lower orders, gathered on the sidewalks of the streets through which the procession passed. Hooting and jeering followed. Then a shot was fired, probably by a negro in the procession. Then other shots followed and the crowd rushed after the procession, which soon arrived in front of the building in which the convention sat. Brickbats now flew from each side and the riot was in full progress when the police appeared on the scene. The procession rushed into the building, leaving a few of its members outside. One of these and a policeman came to blows, when another shot was fired, upon which the policemen began firing through the windows of the building. After a few moments a white flag was displayed from one of the windows, whereupon the firing ceased and the policemen rushed into the building. Once in the building they fired their revolvers upon the persons present indiscriminately and with terrible effect. The persons who succeeded in escaping from the building were also fired on by the police and by citizens, and many were killed or wounded. Nearly two hundred persons were killed or injured, mostly negroes, but some whites, and among them some members of the proposed convention. There were no United States troops in the city at the hour of the riot, their barracks being outside. General Baird had ordered four companies to take position near the place of the convention, but owing to the fact that he had got the impression that the convention would assemble at 6 P.M., he had ordered them to repair to the assigned position at 5 P.M. They, consequently, did not arrive until the riot was over and the convention was dispersed.

Each party considered the other the aggressor. The Republicans of the North viewed the massacre as a new rebellion, while the amnestied Southerners considered the riot the result of a justified resistance to an attempt to force negro suffrage and then negro rule upon them. It is very nearly certain that the first shot was fired by a negro, but this would not justify the wholesale massacre executed by the police. It could, therefore, be held by the Republicans with a great show of truth that the public authorities of the reconstructed "State" government of Louisiana not only would not extend the equal protection of the laws to all persons, but would themselves deprive persons even of life without due process of law.

The issue of the campaign of 1866 was thus made up. It was simply whether Congress should reconstruct the President's reconstructed "States," or rather should pronounce the President's Reconstruction, and the Reconstruction effected by the amnestied Southerners, null and void, and proceed to do the work *de novo*, with the purpose of creating adequate guarantee for life and property and for the equal protection of the laws to all.

The issue of Reconstruction in the campaign of 1866.

Although it was not a Presidential year, the election of the members of the House of Representatives with such a problem to deal with, and the election of "State" legislatures which would consider the question of adopting the proposed Fourteenth Amendment to the Constitution, made the canvass of 1866 a truly national

CONGRESSIONAL PLAN OF RECONSTRUCTION 99

one. Four National Conventions were held during the summer and early autumn, two of each party.

The Administration party led off with their great meeting in Philadelphia on the 14th of August. There were a few prominent Republicans among the delegates, such as Montgomery Blair, Raymond, Dix, Cowan, Doolittle and Browning, but the vast majority of them were Democrats. All of the Southern delegates were such. The larger number of the Northern Democrats were conservative men of the stamp and style of R. C. Winthrop, W. B. Lawrence, S. J. Tilden, J. P. Stockton, J. E. English and Reverdy Johnson, but there were also present men of more radical anti-national creed, like Fernando Wood, J. G. Sinclair, and James Campbell. Even Clement L. Vallandigham presented himself as a delegate. There were many, however, who objected to his presence and he withdrew. The doctrines put forward at this meeting were simply those of the President's Reconstruction policy, the doctrines that the "States" in our Federal system are indestructible and immaculate, and under submission to national authority always possessed of the rights of local self-government and of representation in the National Government. These doctrines were developed into such extreme forms of statement, and such extreme results were boldly accepted as their logical consequences, that the cause of the Administration was damaged rather than helped at the North by the work and experiences of the convention.

The National Conventions of the summer of 1866.

Inasmuch as there had been a great display of harmony between the leading men of the South and the Northern delegates in the convention of the 14th of August, making it appear that the Democrats were the party of peace and reunion, while the Republicans were in favor of a continuation of the hostile status, the Southern Republicans, or as they called themselves the loyal Union men of the South, assembled in considerable numbers in Philadelphia on the 3d of September, for the purpose of conferring with the leading Republicans of the North in regard to the condition of things in the South. Such men as John Minor Botts, William G. Brownlow, George W. Paschal, Thomas J. Durant, M. J. Safford, Thomas H. Benton, Lewis M. Kenzie, G. W. Ashburn, and many more of almost equal reputation came to counsel with the leaders of the Republican party. Many of the most important of these were there, Trumbull, Greeley, Morton, Chandler, Schenck, Schurz, Matthews, Curtin, Cameron, Gerry, Speed, the ex-Attorney-General, and Creswell. These are only a few names of the eminent men who were present.

The delegates separated into two bodies, one body comprehending the representatives from the South, and the other those from the North. This was done in order to leave the Southerners free from undue Northern influence. Mr. Speed presided over the Southern assembly, and in his opening words declared the purpose of the convention to be to determine and proclaim whether the assertion of the late Confederates that their constitutional rights were being denied them in not admitting their Representatives- and Senators-elect to seats in Congress was true, or whether, on the other hand, the claim of the emancipated that their civil and natural rights were being denied them was true. He soon left no doubt upon the minds of his hearers as to his own view and belief, and he denounced the President's reconstruction work, both in principle and results, most roundly. On account of the intimate relation in which he had stood to the President as his legal adviser, and on account of the fact that he was a citizen of one of the old slave-holding "States," his words had tremendous effect in steeling the purpose of the Republicans of the North.

Under the inspiration of Mr. Speed's speech, the Southern convention framed and fulminated an address which arraigned the President as almost a traitor to his party and the Union, and as a friend of rebels and of sympathizers with rebels, described the results of his Reconstruction policy and acts as most deplorable, and urged the speedy adoption of the proposed Fourteenth Amendment to the Constitution as the only possible cure for the evils which were afflicting the country. This address made up the issues of the campaign. The dividing line of the parties now separated those who favored the adoption of the proposed Fourteenth Amendment from those who did not. The issue was simple, and the vote upon it was decisive, as we shall see.

The Administration party now attempted to divide the late soldiers, as it had attempted to divide the Republicans, with but little better effect. They got together a convention of the veterans at Cleveland, Ohio, on the 17th of September, and had the venerable General Wool preside over it. There were many good men and true present, among them Gordon Granger, Rousseau, Custer, McClernand, and Thomas Ewing; and they accused the Republicans of attempting to stir up another civil war over the question of negro suffrage, and urged their old comrades to insist that the status of peace, and all the consequences thereof, existed and must be preserved.

This movement was met on the other side by the assembly of a Republican soldier convention at Pittsburg on the 25th and 26th of September, for the purpose of upholding Congress in its fight with the Administration over the question of Reconstruction. The convention was presided over by General J. D. Cox, and a host of the most capable officers of the armies of the Union, lately disbanded, participated in its deliberations and resolves. They denounced the President's Reconstruction policy, pronounced their adherence to Congress, and declared for the adoption of the proposed Fourteenth Amendment as the indispensable measure for the re-establishment of peace, justice and union.

During the summer and autumn the orators and politicians of both parties pursued the canvass upon the basis of the doctrines put forth by the conventions. A very large number, an unusually large number, of the leading men of the country, took part in the great debate. Even the President of the United States took part in it.

The canvass of 1866.

On the 28th of August he started from Washington to go to Chicago to be present at the laying of the corner-stone of the Douglas monument. He took with him General Grant, Admiral Farragut, three of his Cabinet officers, Seward, Randall and Wells, and a large number of lesser lights. Crowds gathered at all the principal stopping-places, and the President spoke to them in defence of his policy of Reconstruction and of his acts in the execution of it. He denounced his enemies and opponents bitterly, and descended to undignified and even vulgar altercation with individuals in the crowds. In his speech at St. Louis, on September 28th, his hot temper betrayed him into an attempt to throw upon Congress, the radical Congress, as he called it, the blame for the New Orleans riot, and he went to the imprudent extreme of almost making an excuse or a quasi-excuse for the riot. The whole performance of the President upon the journey was termed "swinging around the circle," and it both degraded the great office and its

The "swing around the circle."

incumbent, and injured the prospects of the Administration party in the campaign.

The President had on the 20th day of August, a week before setting out upon his tour, finally proclaimed the insurrection and Civil War at an end in every part of the country. He had, on the 2d day of April preceding, declared the insurrection at an end everywhere except in Texas, and the proclamation of August 20th gave official witness to its cessation in Texas. It is certainly a prerogative of the President to proclaim the cessation of opposition to his execution of the laws of the Union, and then to execute the same thereafter through civil, instead of military, officers. If the President had meant no more than this by his proclamations of the termination of the insurrection, the position would have been unassailable. But he evidently intended his proclamations as furnishing a basis for his Reconstruction work, or at any rate as furnishing a great reason for the general recognition of the validity of that work. This we can easily gather from the speeches he made as he "swung around the circle" in the campaign of 1866. He felt that he had solid ground under his feet, and did not appreciate the fact that he was resting one of his doctrines upon another, the latter being no more self-evident than the former. He felt quite sure of victory, until what were called the "October States," at that time, Pennsylvania, Ohio, Indiana and Iowa, held their elections. The two "September States," Vermont and Maine, had largely increased their Republican majorities, which the President had probably expected and allowed for, but when the four "October States" gave only twelve seats in the House of Representatives to the Democrats and nearly fifty to the Republicans, it was pretty clearly revealed

[sidenote: The President's final proclamation declaring the Civil War ended.]

[sidenote: The October elections.]

that the Administration was on the eve of a terrible defeat. It was as overwhelming as these figures indicated. The final results showed that the Republicans had elected one hundred and forty-three of their candidates to seats in the House of Representatives, while the Democrats had succeeded in securing only forty-nine seats. With the exception of Delaware, Maryland and Kentucky, all the "States" represented in Congress had given the Republican party strong majorities. The strength of the Democratic party was again in the South, where the Democratic candidates for any kind of office had almost universally succeeded. In the Senate the Republicans constituted more than a two-thirds majority of the members, and with their almost three-fourths majority in the House, there could be no question that, in a contest between the President and Congress, the former would be obliged to yield.

The Republican triumph in the elections of 1866.

Notwithstanding all this, however, the President, in his Message to Congress of December 3d, returned to the contest. He reargued his case from every point of view, and with both moderation and great force. He restated what had been done toward Reconstruction, declaring that peace had been restored everywhere, that all the laws of the United States and all the machinery of the United States Government were in unimpeded operation everywhere throughout the length and breadth of the land, and that loyal "State" governments had been restored everywhere, and lacked but one thing of completion, viz., the admission of Representatives and Senators from ten of the eleven "States" in which secession ordinances had been passed to seats in Congress. He contended that all the departments of the United States Government had proceeded upon the view that the "States" were indestructible—the Congress, in the dec-

The President's Message of December 3d, 1866.

laration, at the outset, that the war was not to be waged in any spirit of oppression, nor for any purpose of conquest or subjugation, nor purpose of overthrowing or interfering with the rights or established institutions of the "States" which were the scene of rebellion, but to defend and maintain the supremacy of the Constitution and all laws made in pursuance thereof, and to preserve the Union, with all the dignity, equality, and rights of the several States unimpaired, and in many other acts and resolutions; the Judiciary, in all proceedings affecting the reconstruction communities as "States"; and the Executive, in the entire plan of Reconstruction created by Mr. Lincoln and followed out by himself. He further contended that in recognizing these "States" as restored to their former relations, Congress was not running any risk of having disloyal men thrust into the legislative chambers of the nation, because each House of Congress could reject members-elect on account of disloyalty, and could continue to reject until the constituencies should send up such persons as the House could approve, and could expel any member whose conduct should reveal disloyalty. He therefore urged Congress to acknowledge the Reconstruction of the "States" lately in rebellion, in principle, and to apply the powers of the two Houses in regard to the elections, returns and qualifications of their respective members to the individual persons elected to seats.

The President's argument fell, however, upon deaf ears. This was, it is true, the second session of the Thirty-ninth Congress, and was not, therefore, composed of the persons just elected; but the influence of the recent elections over its members had been to cow the conservatives, strengthen the radicals, and cause the wavering to incline to the side of the extremists. They took the ver- *Ineffectiveness of the President's argument.*

dict of the people to be that Congress should ignore the President's work in Reconstruction, develop a plan of its own, put it into operation, and base it upon a newly constructed electorate in the South, in which the lately emancipated should participate. The attitude of the legislatures of the President's reconstructed "States" in regard to the proposed Fourteenth Amendment also strengthened them greatly in this view and purpose.

Rejection of the proposed Fourteenth Amendment by the legislatures of the Reconstructed "States." Before the first day of January, 1867, all of these except three had rejected it by overwhelming votes, and these three followed the same course a little later. It was said and believed in Washington that they had rejected the proposed Amendment contemptuously, and under the advice of the President of the United States. It was the angry rejection of the proposed Amendment *The effect of this on the temper of the North.* which did more than anything and everything else to convince the people of the North that Reconstruction must be now undertaken by Congress, and must proceed upon the basis of a new electorate at the South which Congress should create.

CHAPTER VII

THE CONGRESSIONAL PLAN (*Completed*)

Negro Suffrage in the District of Columbia—The First Attempts at Impeachment—Stories of Outrages at the South—The Reconstruction Bill—Passage of the Bill by the House—The Bill as Finally Agreed upon—The Condition that the Fourteenth Amendment must be Ratified by a Sufficient Number of States to make it a Part of the Constitution—The Tenure-of-Office Bill—The Supplementary Reconstruction Bill—The Assignment of the Commanding Generals to the Military Districts Created by the Reconstruction Acts—The Re-establishment of Martial Law in the South—The President's Instructions to the Generals in Interpretation of the Reconstruction Acts—The Congressional Interpretation of the Reconstruction Acts—The President's Veto of the Bill Interpreting the Reconstruction Acts—The Veto Overridden—The Suspension of Stanton from Office.

THE Congress had but just put itself in working order, when a bill was introduced and passed extending the suffrage to negroes in the District of Columbia. The Republicans reasoned that they could not with good grace force negro suffrage on the South before establishing it in the District, and that the District was the best place in the country to try the experiment first. The bill went to the President on the 26th of December, six days after the adjournment of Congress for the Christmas vacation, although it had passed the Houses on the 13th and 14th. The President held it until January 5th, 1867, and then returned it to the Senate with his veto.

Negro suffrage in the District of Columbia.

The Message was a strong paper, and to an impartial mind at this day it is a convincing paper. There is no question that Congress had the constitutional power to establish negro suffrage in the District. The President did not dispute that. He simply argued that in legislating for the District, Congress stood in a relation to the inhabitants of the District analogous to that which the legislature of a "State" bore to the inhabitants of the "State," and that as the legislature of a "State" would not act in opposition to the expressed will of a large majority of the voters in the "State," so Congress in legislating for the District of Columbia ought not to disregard the expressed will of a large majority of the voters in the District. He then referred to the vote of the District upon this very subject, taken in December of 1865, only one year before, when out of a poll of 6,556, one of the largest votes ever cast in the Capital city, only thirty-five ballots were cast for negro suffrage, and in Georgetown out of a poll of 813 only one ballot was cast for negro suffrage. He further argued that Congress ought not to make the District a place for trying political experiments of so grave a character as conferring suffrage, the highest privilege of American citizenship, upon a race of men just emerging from the ignorance and vice attendant on a condition of slavery. And he finally asked the Congress to reconsider an act which appeared to him to be the degradation and possibly the destruction of American suffrage.

The President's veto of the bill establishing negro suffrage in the District of Columbia.

There is no gainsaying that this was good reasoning, but Congress was in no frame of mind to give ear to the counsel of the President. It took the ground that in legislating for the District it was acting for the whole United States and not simply for the inhabitants of the District, and that there was no place in the entire country where political experiments could be more safely tried than in the District, since Congress had plenary legislative power in the District and could discover and correct mistakes and defects in its legislation more easily and promptly there than anywhere else.

Both Houses repassed the bill over the President's veto by the necessary two-thirds majority, the Senate on the 7th of January and the House on the 8th, and negro suffrage was established in the District of Columbia. The President's veto so angered some of the extremists that resolutions of impeachment were introduced into the House, and a resolution for the appointment of a committee to inquire whether there were reasons for impeachment was actually carried, and a committee was appointed. The committee sought everywhere and in every way for grounds upon which to arraign the President at the bar of the Senate, but for the moment it failed. *The first attempts at impeachment.*

At the same time the halls of Congress were ringing with the most extravagant tales of outrages against the negroes and loyal men of the South at the hands of the late rebels, and of the collusion of the newly established "State" governments with the same. In addition to this, the other three of the ten newly constructed "State" legislatures rejected the proposed Fourteenth Amendment, two of them by unanimous vote, and the other by every vote but one. *Stories of outrages at the South.*

While, as we have seen, the Congress did not pass the proposition to make the acceptance of the proposed Fourteenth Amendment by the newly reconstructed "States" the condition of recognizing them as "States" of the Union, and admitting the Senators- and Representatives-elect from them to seats in Congress, yet the popular mind had so conceived the matter, and the order of events in the case of Tennessee had given this conception the force of precedent. The Republicans in Congress and the North could now fairly claim that they had offered to recognize the President's reconstructed "States," although these bodies were without constitutional warrant, upon the most moderate terms which consideration for the necessary consequences of the Civil War and the victory of the Union would allow, and that their offer had been rejected in every case, except, of course, that of Tennessee—rejected by such majorities and in such a manner as to make the rejection amount to defiance. It was true that logically and constitutionally Congress had no power to make the acceptance of something not at the time a part of the Constitution a condition for the admission of the new "States," or the readmission of old "States," into the Union ; and Congress had not done this formally. It is also true, both in good logic and in sound constitutional law, that the proposed Fourteenth Amendment should not have been submitted at all to bodies that were not conventions of the people in, or legislatures of, "States" in the Union. Logically and constitutionally the whole thing was irregular. But it was as it was, and all understood that the way to cut the knot was for the legislatures of the reconstructed " States " to adopt the proposed Fourteenth Amendment, as Tennessee had done. When they refused to do so, it was natural and it was necessary that Congress should at last overturn all of the President's proceedings in Reconstruction, and all of the proceedings made under his guidance, and begin *de novo*, and upon the true constitutional principle of the exclusive power of Congress to admit new " States " into the Union, or, more scientifically expressed, to create new States or control their creation on territory

The Fourteenth Amendment as the condition of recognizing the revival of statehood.

of the Union in which loyal civil government did not exist.

There can be no question in the mind of any sound political scientist and constitutional lawyer that Congress was in the right, logically, morally, and legally, in insisting upon brushing aside the results of executive Reconstruction in the winter of 1867, and beginning the work itself from the bottom up. It ought to have done so in 1865. It ought to have created, so soon as armed resistance to the execution of the laws of the United States ceased, regular Territorial civil governments throughout the country which had been in insurrection, and then have admitted these Territories as "States" whenever the conditions warranting the same should have been attained. The phantom of the "indestructible State" had too strong an influence over the minds of all at that moment to admit of such a solution of the question. But after the experiences of 1865 and 1866, and the discussions in the last session of the Thirty-ninth Congress, the minds of the Republicans at least, both in and out of Congress, were prepared to break away from the influence of this idea and to view the process of Reconstruction as nothing but the admission of new "States" into the Union, new "States" founded on territory and including inhabitants that had indeed once formed "States," but had renounced Statehood in the Union through disloyalty to the Union, and had been brought back to the position of territories, civilly unorganized in local instance, but subject to the exclusive jurisdiction of the central Government. From such a point of view, the method of procedure was plain. While it is strange that the Congress did not follow this course in 1865, it is simply astounding that it made such a mess of it in 1867.

The correctness of the Republican view.

The Reconstruction bill was presented from the Committee of fifteen on Reconstruction to the House of Representatives on the 6th of February by Mr. Stevens. It was a thoroughly drastic measure. Instead of creating Territorial civil government in the usual manner, with an electorate designated by Congress, and with powers under the control of Congress, and sustained, if necessary, by the military of the United States, which would have been amply sufficient to meet all the real or proper exigencies of the case, the bill began by declaring that the pretended " State " governments of the so-called Confederate States did not protect adequately life or property, but countenanced and encouraged lawlessness and crime; and that it was necessary that peace and good order should be enforced in the so-called Confederate States until loyal " State " governments could be legally established therein; and then went on to enact that the said so-called Confederate States should be divided into five military divisions and made subject to the military authority of the United States, Virginia to constitute the first division, North Carolina and South Carolina the second, Georgia, Alabama, and Florida the third, Mississippi and Arkansas the fourth, and Louisiana and Texas the fifth; that the General of the army should assign an army officer of not less rank than a brigadier-general to the command of each of these divisions, and detail sufficient military forces, and place them under the command of each of said generals, to enable him to enforce his authority in the district over which he should be placed; that these commanders might use civil tribunals in the enforcement of the laws if they should see fit, but that, if these were not effective they might institute and govern through military commissions; that no sentence of these commissions should be executed until approved

CONGRESSIONAL PLAN OF RECONSTRUCTION

by the commanding officer of the district; and finally, that the United States courts and judges should issue no writs of Habeas Corpus against the proceedings and judgments of these commissions.

There was hardly a line in the entire bill which would stand the test of the Constitution. In the first place, the Congress of the United States, or any other part of the Government of the United States, can establish martial law in any part of the territory of the United States only when and where there is armed resistance to the execution of the laws of the United States, or of some "State" or Territory whose jurisdiction is being defended by the Government of the United States. Such was not the condition anywhere in the South. The Executive had proclaimed that such resistance had ceased everywhere several months before; that he had appointed civil officers throughout the South for the execution of the laws of the United States, in many cases with the advice and consent of the Senate; that these laws were in operation everywhere; and that the United States courts were open everywhere and in the unhindered discharge of their functions and duties. It was not pretended, of course, that there was armed resistance to the execution of the laws of the reconstructed "States," and that the military of the United States was to act simply in support of "State" authority. There were here and there, it is true, some of the remains of the military authority of the United States, exercised during the period of the insurrection, but they were a very poor basis upon which to found a resumption of the reign of martial law throughout the length and breadth of the South. No sane and just mind can consider for a moment such a ground as sufficient in policy, morals or constitutional law. While the people of these districts

The bill indefensible from the constitutional point of view.

which had attempted to secede from the Union had forfeited their rights to the "State" form of local government, they still had, after they had ceased from armed resistance to the Government of the United States, the rights guaranteed to the criminal by the Constitution of the United States—the right to be presented by a grand jury and tried by a petit jury in the civil tribunals of the United States, under the ordinary forms and guarantees of the common law, even though the crime charged should be treason itself.

In the second place, the bill undertook to rob the President of his constitutional prerogative of commandership-in-chief over the army, and vest the same in the General of the army. This was so evident that no one could fail to see that it was a bill directed as much against the powers of the President of the United States as against the late Confederates of the South.

<small>The bill in its attempt to rob the President of his office of Commander-in-chief.</small>

And in the third place, the bill assumed to suspend the writ of Habeas Corpus, substantially, while the Constitution forbids this to be done by any part of the Government of the United States, except in time of war or public danger. There was no war, and to say that there was public danger of the character meant by the constitutional exception was to exaggerate the condition of things entirely beyond all fact or reason.

The bill was the most brutal proposition ever introduced into the Congress of the United States by a responsible committee, and it would never have been tolerated except at such a time of partisan excitement and exaggerated suspicions. Even under such conditions Congress would not pass it as introduced, but incorporated into it many modifying provisions, most of which, however, while reflecting the honest sentiments of the lawmakers, give little

<small>The brutality of the measure.</small>

CONGRESSIONAL PLAN OF RECONSTRUCTION

evidence of good political science or sound constitutional law.

The two points in the bill which the conservative Republicans were unable to accept were, first, the establishment of martial law for an indefinite period and without any provision for a way of future escape from its rigors; and, second, the usurpation of the President's constitutional prerogative of commandership-in-chief of the army. It soon became manifest that the bill could not pass without the introduction of a clause covering the first point and without a change of the provision in regard to the second. A number of the conservative Republicans had indicated these things, when Mr. Blaine squarely asked Mr. Stevens to incorporate an amendment in the bill which should provide a way of escape from the martial rule which the bill proposed to establish. Mr. Blaine's amendment held out the promise of the admission of each of the ten communities now to be thrown into military divisions to its proper position as a "State" of the Union when it should adopt the proposed Fourteenth Amendment and conform its constitution and laws thereto, should provide by its constitution for universal male suffrage without regard to race, color or previous condition of servitude, and should adopt a constitution with such a provision in it by popular vote, and when Congress should approve of the said constitution. *The opposition of conservative Republicans to the bill.* *Mr. Blaine's proposed changes in the bill.*

There is no doubt that all this, while reflecting the good moral feeling of Mr. Blaine, was bad political science and was the very contradictory of sound constitutional law. As has been pointed out several times already, it would have been good constitutional law had the United States Congress simply delayed the admission or readmission *Criticism of Mr. Blaine's propositions.*

of these communities as "States" of the Union until after the proposed Fourteenth Amendment, and any other desirable amendment, should have been framed and adopted. Their admission then would have been into the *same* Union with all the other States. But to demand of them, as the condition of admission, their acceptance of things not yet in the Constitution of the United States, things not obligatory on the "States" already in the Union, was tantamount to the creation of a new sort of union with another kind of constitution by an Act of Congress. This question had been thoroughly talked out, fought out, and decided in 1820, and for nearly fifty years it had been the settled principle of constitutional law that Congress has no such power. It has been also pointed out that a sound political science of the federal system of government teaches the same principle.

Mr. Stevens acted correctly, from the point of view of political science and constitutional interpretation, when he declined to accept Mr. Blaine's amendment, or to allow a vote to be taken on it, and the House of Representatives also acted correctly from the same point of view when it voted down a proposition from Mr. Blaine to send his amendment along with the bill to the Judiciary Committee of the House with instruction to report it back with the bill. But it is not to be inferred from the debates that either Mr. Stevens or the House was actuated in this course of conduct by the above mentioned considerations. The expansion of the powers of government inevitably consequent upon a long period of war seemed to have made them all very nearly forget that there was anything but government in our political system. The chief thought was that one Congress could not bind another with any such promises as those held

CONGRESSIONAL PLAN OF RECONSTRUCTION 117

out in the Blaine amendment, and that each Congress must at all times be left to its own discretion in the determination of every question. The House passed the bill as it came from the Committee on Reconstruction without change or amendment, and on the 13th of February it appeared in the Senate. *Passage of the bill by the House.*

This more conservative and deliberate body regarded the bill as too radical, and after considerable debate upon a proposed amendment, offered first by Senator Williams of Oregon, and then by Senator Reverdy Johnson, which was in substance the Blaine proposition, laid it aside by general consent and allowed Senator Sherman to offer a substitute for it. *The bill in the Senate.*

This substitute contained the gist of the Blaine amendment, and also changed the provision which proposed to deprive the President of his constitutional prerogative of commandership-in-chief of the army. While the bill was thus made a less brutal measure, and in one respect a less unconstitutional measure, it still rested upon a very shaky foundation so far as constitutional law was concerned, and it was opposed by all the Democratic Senators. It was passed, however, by a large majority, every Republican who voted voting in favor of it. *The Sherman substitute.*

When it was returned to the House of Representatives for concurrence, the Radical Republicans developed a most hostile opposition to the changes which had been made by the Senate. They claimed that the Senate bill proposed to bind future Congresses by pledges which the existing Congress had no right to make and no power to execute, and that it also proposed to use the rebel element of the population of the South in the work of reconstructing loyal "State" gov- *The substitute in the House.*

ernments. After a long and acrid debate, the House rejected the Senate's substitute by a union of Democratic votes with the votes of the Radical Republicans. This result and the manner of its attainment so frightened the Republicans, however, that they quickly came to an understanding among themselves in the House, and with their party colleagues in the Senate, and passed the Senate's substitute, so amended as to prevent disloyal men, as designated in the proposed Fourteenth Amendment, from voting for delegates to a reconstruction convention, or being delegates therein, or being officers in any so-called "State" government before the admission of the Senators and Representatives from that "State" into Congress, and so amended further as to pronounce all professed civil governments existing in any of the late so-called Confederate States, except of course Tennessee, provisional only, until Senators and Representatives from the same should be admitted to seats in Congress, and subject, as provisional governments, to the paramount authority of the United States which should control them, and might supersede or abolish them at any time. The Senate also accepted these amendments, and on the 20th of February the bill was placed in the hands of the President.

The Senate substitute rejected by the House.

The bill as finally agreed upon.

It contained the following declarations and provisions. First, the preamble designated the ten communities reconstructed under the President's direction as "the rebel States of Virginia, North Carolina, South Carolina, Georgia," and so on. This was certainly an untruth. If they were "States" at all, they certainly were not rebel "States." They might with some appearance of correctness and sincerity have been termed the late rebel "States," but to be called simply rebel "States" was, to say the very least, one of the

The contents of the bill as passed.

grossest exaggerations to be found in the wording of the statutes of Congress. It was simply a play on words whereby to justify a dubious procedure. It was at the very best, a confounding of the supposed sentiments of the population of these regions with actual political status. Second, the preamble declared that no legal "State" governments or adequate protection for life or property existed in these "rebel States." As a legal proposition the first part of this declaration was true, and as a matter of fact the second part was substantially true. It would have been an unprecedented thing if anything like an adequate protection of life and property had been re-established, in the short period of two years, in communities which had been disturbed, demoralized and destroyed by four years of civil war, especially when the outcome of the conflict was total defeat and the utter destruction of the basis of the old social, political, and economic systems. It was, however, a serious question whether such a situation required drastic measures rather than mild and soothing measures.

The Republican Congress decided, after much deliberation, that the former were necessary to the maintenance of peace and good order, and, therefore, enacted that the "said rebel States" should be divided into five military districts, as previously described in the original bill; that the President should assign to the command of each of these an army officer of not lower rank than brigadier-general, and place under his command a sufficient force to enable him to perform his duties and execute his authority in his district; that these commanders should have the power to govern these districts by martial law in so far as, in their judgment, the reign of order and the preservation of the public peace might demand, under the limitations simply that "all persons put under military arrest by virtue of this act shall be tried without unnecessary delay, and no cruel or unusual punishment shall be inflicted, and no sentence of any military commission or tribunal hereby authorized affecting the life or liberty of any person, shall be executed until it is approved by the officer in command of the district—and no sentence of death under the provisions of this act shall be carried into effect without the approval of the President."

Then came the provision which offered the terms of escape from this new military régime. They were, first, the exercise of universal manhood suffrage, that is the suffrage of all male citizens, twenty-one years of age, without regard to race, color or previous condition of servitude, who were not disfranchised for participation in rebellion or for felony at common law, and who had resided for one year in the so-called "rebel State," in the election of delegates to a constitutional convention in the so-called "rebel State"; second, the framing of a "State" constitution by a convention composed of delegates so elected, and not disqualified by participation in rebellion or by the commission of felony, which constitution should conform in all respects to the Constitution of the United States and which should contain, as a permanent principle, the same law of suffrage as that prescribed by this Act for the election of the delegates to the convention; third, the ratification of this constitution by a majority of the voters, as designated by the law of suffrage for the choice of delegates to the convention, voting upon the question of ratification; fourth, the approval by Congress of this constitution; and fifth, and last, the adoption of the proposed Fourteenth Amendment to the Constitution of the United States by the legislature created by such adopted and approved "State" constitution, and by a sufficient number of the legislatures of other "States" to make it a part of the Constitution of the United States.

The measure contained, in the last place, a sort of saving clause in regard to the existing civil governments which had been established in all these communities under the direction of the President, and which were now to be displaced. It had been already provided, in section third, that the military commander of a district might use the existing civil courts, if he saw fit to do so, so long as the reign of law and order might be so preserved, and the final section provided that any civil government which might exist in these districts should be regarded as provisional, and should be in all respects subject to the paramount authority of the United States, which should control, and might abolish, modify, or supersede the same, and that the voters for the election of the officers of such provisional governments should be required to have only the qualifications prescribed in this Act for voters for the delegates to the said "State" convention, and persons elected to place and office in such provisional governments must not have the disqualifications prescribed in the proposed Fourteenth Amendment to the Constitution of the United States. It had evidently occurred to the Republican leaders that they might have to make use of some of the machinery of the existing civil governments established under the direction of the President in these regions in executing their own plan of Reconstruction.

All of the points of the measure have been commented on, except the provision in the fifth section, which makes the adoption of the proposed Fourteenth Amendment to the Constitution of the United States by a number of "States" sufficient to ratify it a condition precedent to the admission of any one of these so-called "rebel States" to representation in Congress. The adoption of the proposed amendment by the particular "rebel State" seeking representation was not sufficient.

The condition that the proposed Fourteenth Amendment be ratified by a sufficient number of "States" to make it a part of the Constitution. It must be ratified by at least three-fourths of all the "States." No matter how speedily and sincerely the legislature of Virginia might ratify the proposed Amendment, and fulfil all the other conditions required by the Act, Virginia must remain under military despotism until a very large number of the Northern "State" legislatures had pleased to ratify the proposed Amendment. This was certainly a pretty hard condition, and it was not a very fair way of forcing the legislatures of the Northern States to adopt the proposed Amendment. It was, however, an efficient weapon, and Congress had the legal power to use it. It was unconscionable, though it was one of the things about this measure which was constitutional.

Hand in hand with this bill went another measure, the purpose of which was to limit the customary power of the President, if not his constitutional power, over the civil official system, the so-called Tenure-of-Office bill. *The Tenure-of-Office bill.* On the first day of the session, December 3d, 1866, Mr. Williams of Oregon introduced this bill in the Senate, while at the same moment a bill was introduced and passed in the House repealing that section of the Confiscation Act of July 17th, 1862, which authorized the President to extend pardon and amnesty by proclamation to persons participating in the rebellion. The Senate passed the latter bill or resolution on the 8th of January, 1867, and the President, not considering that the Congress could either give or take away his power to pardon secured to him by the Constitution, simply pocketed the resolution, and it became a law on and from the 21st of January, having been presented to the President on the 9th.

The propositions contained in the Tenure-of-Office bill were, however, of a very different significance. There was no clause in the Constitution which by express literal grant vested the power to dismiss from office in the President, but the clause which made the President solely responsible for the execution of the laws was interpreted by the first Congress as doing so. Madison took the ground that the President must have this power in order to secure the necessary obedience in his subordinates, and declared that the convention which framed the Constitution so understood it and so intended it. This is certainly sound political science and correct constitutional interpretation. It had also been the practice of the Government from the beginning. The Whigs had undertaken to reverse it in their contest with Jackson, and Webster had given his opinion that good political science required that dismissal from office should be treated as an incident of appointment, and should be effected in the same manner as appointment, i.e., with the concurrence of the Senate, and that the decision of 1789 on this subject was, in his opinion, erroneous from the point of view of a proper interpretation of the Constitution as well. But the Whigs did not succeed, as we have seen, in their attempt to break down Presidential prerogative and introduce parliamentary government, and the practice of the Government on this subject remained, after, as before, the fourth decade of the century, the same.

During the experiences of the years 1865 and 1866 the Republicans feared that the President would use this great power of dismissal from office in order to make the entire official system solid with himself on the subject of Reconstruction, and toward the end of 1866 they suspected and asserted that he was dismissing officers

The reasons for the Tenure-of-Office bill.

from their positions simply on the ground of a difference of opinion with himself on this subject, and they professed to believe that he would make a clean sweep of all such as soon as Congress should adjourn. There is little doubt that excessive partisan feeling made them exaggerate greatly what the President had done and what he intended to do. The President was guided by Mr. Seward in all public matters except his imprudent speeches, and Seward's conservative and diplomatic disposition and methods were all against any such radical and reckless procedure. Besides, it was the constitutional right of the President to require obedience in their official acts from his subordinates, and to dismiss them when in his opinion their views of policy interfered with the discharge of their official duties as he required them to be discharged. The Thirty-ninth Congress, however, resolved to disregard the precedents set by all of its predecessors and to dispute the President's prerogative of control over the tenure of his subordinates.

The bill drafted for this purpose made the removal of all officers, appointed by and with the consent of the Senate, except only members of the President's Cabinet, subject to the consent of the Senate. This consent might be given in the form of a ratification of the nomination of a successor to any officer.

The contents of the bill.

It allowed the President, during a recess of the Senate, the power of suspension for misconduct in office, crime, legal disqualification or incapacity, and of making appointment of a suitable person to discharge temporarily the duties of such suspended officer, but it required of the President a report of all such suspensions to the Senate within the first twenty days of the next meeting of the Senate, with the reasons therefor, and reinstated the suspended officer in case the Senate should not concur in the suspension. If the Senate should concur, the President must remove the officer, and appoint, with the advice and consent of the Senate, another person in his place.

From the point of view of the present this would seem, in all conscience, to have been a sufficient usurpation of the President's constitutional powers to have satisfied the most radical and reckless interpretation of the organic law. *Discussion of the bill.* But the bill had hardly come under discussion when Senator Howe moved to strike out the clause excepting the Cabinet officers from its operation, and although the Senate refused to pass this amendment, the House of Representatives did so when the bill came before it. The Senate, however, refused to concur on the ground, of course, that the intimate and confidential relations which should exist between the President and the members of his Cabinet made it necessary that the President should have only the men of his own choice in these positions. The strennous insistence of the House, however, forced the Senate to a compromise upon the subject, and the bill was finally made to provide that the members of the Cabinet should " hold their offices, respectively, for and during the term of the President by whom they have been appointed, and for one month thereafter, subject to removal by and with the consent of the Senate." That is, that a Cabinet officer might hold his position against the will of the President who appointed him during the entire term of the President and for one month of the term of his successor unless the Senate should agree to such officer's removal either directly or by ratification of the nomination of a successor.

The bill as finally enacted contained, moreover, the most stringent provisions for its enforcement. It made the acceptance or exercise of any office or the attempt to exercise any office contrary to the Act a high misdemeanor, punishable by a maximum fine of ten thousand dollars or a maximum imprisonment of five years, or both in the discretion of the court ; and it made the removal, appointment, or employment of any officer contrary to the provisions of the Act, or the preparation, signing, sealing, countersigning or issuing of any commission of office or letter of authority in respect to any such appointment or employment high misdemeanors, punishable with the same extreme penalties. Lastly, it forbade the officers of the Treasury and all officers of the United States to pay any money, salary or compensation to any person claiming to hold any office or employment contrary to the provisions of this Act, and made the violation of this order a high misdemeanor, punishable with the same extreme penalties as in the other cases.

The provisions for enforcing the measure.

This monstrous measure went to the President on the same day with the Reconstruction bill, the 20th of February. It is not to be wondered at that he felt that the Republican chiefs were offering him intentional personal insult, as well as that the legislative department of the Government was attempting an unwarranted encroachment upon the constitutional prerogatives of the Executive. It is rather to be wondered at that, in his message to Congress on these subjects, he succeeded so well in ignoring the personal affronts intended by Congress, and in confining himself so closely to a discussion of the public questions and considerations involved in the measures.

The President's vetoes of these bills.

The vetoes of these bills were sent to Congress on the same day, March 2d. To the publicist and historian of this day they are masterpieces of political logic, constitutional interpretation, and official style. If not written by Mr. Seward, they must have been edited and revised by him. These documents showed most convincingly, both from constitutional provisions, opinions of contemporaries, statutes of Congress, judicial decisions, and the uniform practices of the Government, that Congress had no power to establish or reestablish martial law anywhere in the country, except when and where war or armed rebellion existed as a fact, a condition which did not then exist anywhere in the length and breadth of the land; and that Congress had no power to force the President to retain agents and subordinates in office against his judgment and will. No good political scientist and no sound constitutional lawyer will, at this day, disagree with the contention of the President upon these two points, and it is very difficult to understand how the great leaders of the Republican party could, at that day, have differed with him.

Undoubtedly, in some of the baser minds among them, the determination to create Republican party "States" in the South was a very weighty consideration, but just as undoubtedly the consideration with the majority of them was the conviction that the work of the four years of war might have to be done all over again unless a new political people, a new body of suffrage holders, should be created at the South, whose members had never been disloyal. But even from this point of view again, it is difficult to understand how they could have failed to see that the Constitution required that this should be done through the forms of Territorial civil government, instead of through the forms of martial law. Put the best light upon their conduct that is possible, there is still left the conviction that the fanaticism of extreme partisanship had an undue influence over them all.

<small>Republican motives in Reconstruction.</small>

The contest with the President had blinded their perceptions as to the morality, legality and propriety of the means they were willing to employ in securing the victory over him.

As this contest developed it dwarfed, to say the least, all other considerations. Even as late as when the Reconstruction bill was passed, the majority of the Republicans refused to vote to take the President's military prerogatives from him. In less than a fortnight from this time, however, they voted, in a section of the Army Appropriation bill, "that the head-quarters of the General of the army of the United States shall be at the city of Washington, and all orders and instructions relating to military operations issued by the President or Secretary of War shall be issued through the General of the army, and, in case of his inability, through the next in rank. The General of the army shall not be removed, suspended, or relieved from command, or assigned to duty elsewhere than at said head-quarters, except at his own request, without the previous approval of the Senate; and any orders or instructions relating to military operations issued contrary to the requirements of this section shall be null and void; and any officer who shall issue orders or instructions contrary to the provisions of this section shall be deemed guilty of a misdemeanor in office; and any officer of the army who shall transmit, convey, or obey any orders or instructions so issued contrary to the provisions of this section, knowing that such orders were so issued, shall be liable to imprisonment for not less than two nor more than twenty years, upon conviction in any court of competent jurisdiction."

Congressional encroachment on the President's military prerogatives.

To the mind of any unprejudiced constitutional lawyer, at the present day, this act must appear as a gross usurpation by Congress of the President's military powers conferred upon him by the Constitution. The Constitution makes the President the Commander-in-Chief of the army and navy, and gives Congress no power whatsoever over the methods or channels by, and through, which he may issue his military commands. Neither does the Constitution give Congress any power to assign any of the officers or troops of the army to any particular position. These are all functions of the commandership-in-chief, and, unless expressly granted by the Constitution to some other department of the Government, belong to the President.

It was not only a usurpation by Congress to pass such an act, but it was a mean thing to do it as a section of an appropriation bill; and there is no escaping the suspicion that it had a sinister purpose, namely, to entrap the President in the commission of what Congress had made a high misdemeanor, and open the way for his impeachment and expulsion from office. The President signed this bill, however, in order to save the appropriations for the support of the army, although he protested strongly against the seizure of his constitutional powers by the Congress.

On the same day that the vetoes of the Reconstruction bill and the Tenure-of-Office bill were sent to Congress, this body passed a bill supplementary to the first measure. It was in the nature of an administrative measure for the purpose of carrying out the new plan of Reconstruction. *The supplementary Reconstruction bill.* It ordered the commanding generals of the respective districts to cause a registration to be made before September 1st next following of all male citizens of the United States, twenty-one years of age and over, resident in each county or parish in the "State" or "States" included in their respective districts, who were qualified as prescribed by the Reconstruction Act to vote for delegates to a constitutional convention, and who had taken an oath asserting citizenship and residence, and freedom from disfranchisement on account of participation in rebellion or the commission of felony, and had sworn that they had never engaged in insurrection or rebellion against the United States, or given aid and comfort to the enemies of the United States after having been members of Congress or of a "State" legislature, or officers of the United States or of a "State" of the Union, and that they would henceforth faithfully support the Constitution and obey the laws of the United States and encourage others to do so.

It next made it the duty of the commanding generals to order elections, at such times after the completion of the registrations and at such places as they might choose, for delegates to constitutional conventions in the "States" comprised in their respective districts. It required them to give thirty days' notice of the elections, and it fixed the number of delegates to each convention at the number of members in the lower House of the legislature of the "State" concerned in the year 1860, except in the case of Virginia, where, on account of the separation of West Virginia from the old Commonwealth, the number of deputies to the Virginia convention was made to correspond with the number of members in the lower House of the legislature of 1860, representing the territory not included in West Virginia. The bill further directed the commanding generals to distribute the representation in the conventions among the districts, counties and parishes of the "States" in accordance with the number of registered voters in each.

The bill then provided that at the elections for delegates, the voters should vote on the question as to

CONGRESSIONAL PLAN OF RECONSTRUCTION 131

whether there should be a constitutional convention or not, and that such convention should be held only when a majority of the inscribed electors voted upon this question, and a majority of those voting voted in the affirmative. It then ordered the commanding generals, in case the voters did so decide for conventions and elect delegates thereto, to call such within sixty days from the date of the elections, and to notify the delegates to assemble at a given time and place, and frame constitutions according to the provisions of the bill and of the former Act to which it was supplementary, and, when framed, to submit the same to the registered voters for ratification with a notice of thirty days.

The bill then further provided, that if, at such elections, a majority of the registered voters voted upon the question of ratification, and a majority of those voting voted in favor of ratification, the presidents of the respective conventions should transmit copies of the respective constitutions to the President of the United States, who should transmit them to Congress, and that Congress should declare the respective "States," whose conventions had framed these constitutions and whose voters had adopted them, entitled to representation in Congress, provided Congress was satisfied that there had been perfectly free elections, and that no force, fraud or intimidation had been perpetrated at them, and that the constitutions presented met the approval of a majority of the qualified electors and were in conformity with the requirements of the Reconstruction Act.

Finally, the bill put into the hands of the commanding generals the appointment of the officers of the elections, and the control of the machinery of the elections, only requiring them to hold the elections by ballot, and to proclaim the results of the elections in accordance with the returns made to them by their boards of registration.

Congress had passed a resolution ordering the assembly of the Fortieth Congress so soon as the Thirty-ninth Congress expired, and in accordance therewith the newly elected Congress opened its session on the 4th of March, 1867, instead of on the first Monday of the following December. The Congress was, therefore, in position to deal at once with a veto of the supplemental bill to the Reconstruction Act, in case one should be sent in.

<small>Congress in permanence.</small>

On the 23d of March the veto appeared. The President argued that the oath required by the bill from every person before his name could be admitted to registration, viz., "that he had not been disfranchised for participation in any rebellion or civil war against the United States," was so entirely uncertain in its meaning that it would prove a most terrible means of oppression in the hands of the military officers and their appointed agents, and declared he could never approve of an election law whose plain and manifest purpose was to disfranchise the great body of respectable white people, and create a new electorate on the basis of universal negro suffrage. He contended that the existing constitutions of the ten "States" to be re-reconstructed conformed to the long-established standards of loyalty and Republicanism, and that the new test of these qualities now set up by Congress, viz., universal negro suffrage, was a gross exaggeration, and would make many of the Northern "States" themselves unrepublican. The President did not expressly say that this bill was unconstitutional, but he quite distinctly implied it. In this, however, he was wrong, unless his doctrine that the rebellious com-

<small>The veto of the supplemental Reconstruction bill.</small>

CONGRESSIONAL PLAN OF RECONSTRUCTION

munities remained "States" of the Union throughout the rebellion, or had been reconstructed by his plan, was true, that is, unless these communities were "States" of the Union at the time Congress passed this bill.

On the other hand, from the point of view of the correct legal principle in regard to this subject, the principle which holds that the result of general rebellion within a "State" against the Constitution and laws of the United States is the loss of the "State" form of local government, and brings the territory and population of the former "State" under the exclusive jurisdiction of the central Government, Congress certainly had, and has, the power to create the electorate in such territory at its own discretion, Congress was referred, and is referred, in such a case, only to its own sense of right and policy.

<small>Criticism of the veto.</small>

But there is no question, now, that Congress did a monstrous thing, and committed a great political error, if not a sin, in the creation of this new electorate. It was a great wrong to civilization to put the white race of the South under the domination of the negro race. The claim that there is nothing in the color of the skin from the point of view of political ethics is a great sophism. A black skin means membership in a race of men which has never of itself succeeded in subjecting passion to reason, has never, therefore, created any civilization of any kind. To put such a race of men in possession of a "State" government in a system of federal government is to trust them with the development of political and legal civilization upon the most important subjects of human life, and to do this in communities with a large white population is simply to establish barbarism in power over civilization. The supposed disloyalty, or even the actual disloyalty, of

<small>Criticism of the Reconstruction Acts.</small>

the white population will not justify this. It will justify the indefinite withholding of the "State" form of local government. It will justify the throwing of a "State" of the Union back under the form of a Territory of the Union. It will even justify the establishment of martial law. But it is not to be cured, nor is the welfare of the whole land, or any part of it, to be promoted, by the subjection of the white race to the black race in politics and government. It was a great wrong to the negroes themselves. It made the white men among whom they must live their most bitter enemies, when they most needed them for friends, and it made the negroes trifling and corrupt politicians, when they should have been devoting themselves exclusively to the acquirement of property and education. It was argued, as will be well remembered, that they could not acquire property and education without the ballot. But this is another sophism. The mainstay of property is the courts; and under a Territorial form of local government Congress could have established a system of free schools. It was not at all necessary to have recourse to negro suffrage and negro "State" governments in order to secure the negroes in their personal liberty, and the possession of property, and to aid them in the acquirement of education.

There was another alternative, and a better one. In fact, there were two other conceivable ways of doing these things, either of which would have been better than the one chosen. The one was, as has been already suggested, to establish Territorial civil governments in the late rebellious region and maintain them there until the civil relations between the two races became settled and fixed. The other was to so amend the Constitution of the United States, before the readmission of the "States" which had renounced the "State" form of local government under the Union, as to give Congress and the national judiciary the power to define and defend the fundamental principles of civil liberty. Neither of these methods would have demanded martial law or universal negro suffrage. It is entirely surprising, from the point of view of to-day, that one or the other of these methods or a combination of both was not resorted to, instead of the monstrous plan that was carried out. There is no way to explain this sufficiently, except upon the reflection that the passions of the men of that day had become so inflamed and so completely dominating that they obscured reason, drowned the voice of prudence, and even dulled the sense of decency. There were a few who favored universal negro suffrage from an exalted and exaggerated humanitarianism, but the mass of the Republicans sustained it as a punishment to the late rebellious whites, and as a means of establishing Republican party "State" governments in the South. Many claimed, indeed, that it was the only alternative to long-continued martial law rule, but they were either very ignorant or very insincere.

In prompt obedience to the requirements of the two Reconstruction Acts, the President issued his general order through the Adjutant-General's office, on March 11th, assigning General Schofield to the command of the first military district, as created by these Acts, with his head-quarters at Richmond, Virginia; General Sickles to that of the second, with his head-quarters at Columbia, South Carolina; General Thomas to that of the third, with his head-quarters at Montgomery, Alabama; General Ord to that of the fourth, with his head-quarters at Vicksburg, Mississippi; and General Sheridan to that of the fifth, with his head-quarters at New Or-

The assignment of the commanding generals to the military districts created by the Reconstruction Acts.

leans, Louisiana. On the 15th this order was so modified as to change the assignment of General Thomas from the command of the third district to that of the Department of the Cumberland, and to substitute General Pope for him in the command of the third district.

These officers betook themselves at once, with the forces attached to their several commands, to their respective stations, and assumed the government of their respective districts by martial law. No opposition whatever was made to any of them by the populations thus made subject to their despotic rule.

The re-establishment of martial law in the South.

Very soon, however, the generals found great difficulty in interpreting the Reconstruction Acts, especially in respect to the oath required for enfranchisement, both as to the persons who might take it and as to its consequences, and in respect to the powers of the boards appointed to superintend the elections. They applied to the President for information upon these points. The President submitted their application to his Attorney-General and to his Cabinet, and with the full concurrence of all the members thereof, except only Mr. Stanton, issued through the Adjutant-General's office in the War Department, on the 20th of June, the following instructions:

The President's instructions to the generals in interpretation of the Reconstruction Acts.

First: That the oath prescribed in the second Act defined all the qualifications required for suffrage, and that any person who could take that oath should have his name entered on the list of voters; that the boards of registration provided in that Act could not require any other, or any additional, oath from the person applying for registration, nor " administer an oath to any other person touching the qualification of the applicant or the falsity of the oath taken by him," but that the person taking the oath must be registered as a voter, and if it could be afterward proved that he had sworn falsely, he could be punished for perjury.

Second: That an unnaturalized alien could not take the oath, but a naturalized alien could, and that no other proof of naturalization could be required of him.

Third: That "actual participation in rebellion or the actual commission of a felony" did not amount to disfranchisement, but there must be a law made by competent authority declaring disfranchisement, or a judicial sentence inflicting it, and that no law of the United States had declared the penalty of disfranchisement for participating in rebellion alone.

Fourth: That a person who had engaged in rebellion, but had not theretofore held an office under a "State" or the United States, or not been a member of a "State" legislature or of Congress, and not taken, as such, an oath to support the Constitution of the United States, was not disfranchised or disqualified from voting.

Fifth: That persons who were militia officers in any " State " prior to the rebellion were not disfranchised by participating in the rebellion.

Sixth: That "an act to fix upon the person the offence of engaging in rebellion under this law must be an overt and voluntary act, done with the intent of aiding or furthering the common unlawful purpose," and that "a person forced into the rebel service by conscription or under a paramount authority which he could not safely disobey, and who would not have entered such service if left to the free exercise of his own will," was not disfranchised or disqualified from voting.

And lastly: That disloyal sentiments, opinions or sympathies, or anything said or written which fell short of an incitement to others to engage in rebellion, did not disfranchise or disqualify from voting.

Some other instructions were given which were concurred in by the entire Cabinet, Mr. Stanton included, but the recital of them is not essential to this narrative. It must be added, however, that the President's view of the relation of the military commanders to the "State" governments created under his direction and with his aid was one which gave these governments a more independent and permanent character than the language of the Reconstruction Acts seemed to warrant.

The Congressional interpretation of the Reconstruction Acts. When, then, the instructions of June 20th to the generals became known, another bill was introduced into Congress and passed which put the Congressional interpretation upon the Reconstruction Acts.

It declared that the true intent and meaning of these Acts was that the civil governments then existing in the "rebel States" of Virginia, North Carolina, etc., were not legal "State governments," and that, if thereafter they should be allowed to continue to exist at all, they must be subject in all respects to the will of the military commanders of the respective districts, and to the paramount authority of Congress; and it provided that the generals in command of the respective districts might suspend or remove any person from any office under these illegal and pretended governments, and detail or appoint some other person to discharge the duties and exercise the powers said to pertain to such office. The acts of the district commanders in regard to these things were made subject to the disapproval of the General of the army, but not to that of the President, and stood until so disapproved. The same powers in regard to these matters were vested, by this bill, in the General of the army as in the district commanders, but were not accorded by it to the President; and it was made the duty of the General of the army and the district commanders to remove from such pretended offices "all persons who were disloyal to the United States, or who used their official influence in any manner to hinder, delay, prevent, or obstruct the due and proper administration of the Reconstruction Acts."

The bill, furthermore, provided that the boards of registration should have the power, and that it should be their duty, to ascertain the fact as to whether a person applying for registration as a voter was entitled to registration under the Reconstruction Acts, and to refuse registration, if in their judgment he was not, and that the fact that he was willing to take the oath prescribed in the Reconstruction Acts, or had taken it, was not conclusive upon the registration boards in making their inquiries and forming their decisions. And it, finally, declared that the true intent and meaning of the oath prescribed in the Reconstruction Acts for persons who had held office under a "State" government or membership in a "State" legislature, before the rebellion, was that whether such persons were holding such positions at the time of the commencement of the rebellion or at some time prior to the same, and whether they had taken an oath to support the Constitution of the United States or not, they were disqualified from registration and were disfranchised, if, after holding such positions, they had "engaged in insurrection or rebellion against the United States, or given aid or comfort to the enemies thereof"; and it gave to the commanders of the districts the power to extend, in their discretion, the time for completing the original registration of the voters, as provided for in the Reconstruction Acts, to October 1st following, and to the boards of registration the power, and imposed upon them the duty, to revise, during the first five of the last fourteen days before any election under the Reconstruction Acts, the registration lists and to strike off any name from said lists which, in their judgment, ought not to be there, and to add any name, which, in their judgment, ought to be there, and required them to disregard any Executive pardon or amnesty as relieving the disability of any person for registration, if such person had committed any act which without such pardon or amnesty would disqualify him.

This bill, it will be readily seen, was a wholesale repudiation of all the instructions given by the President to the generals in command of the districts from which, in the Cabinet council, Mr. Stanton had dissented. The President immediately realized this, of course, and it increased his distrust of Stanton immensely. From that moment forward he regarded him as the spy of Congress upon all his official acts, and he was resolved to remove him upon the first opportunity, that is, so soon as Congress should adjourn.

The bill passed the Houses on the 13th of July, was presented to the President for his signature on the 14th, and on the 19th he returned it with a veto message to the House of Representatives. The President contended in his argument that this new measure was not simply an interpretation of the existing Reconstruction Acts, but was in many respects a large advance upon them. The existing Acts, he contended, made the reconstructed "State" governments at the South subject to absolute military authority in many important respects, but not in all respects, while the new measure proposed to extend the despotism of the military commanders over everything. Against such a measure, in time of peace, he protested as being in violation of every guaranty of

The President's veto of the bill interpreting the Reconstruction Acts.

individual liberty contained in the Constitution. He dwelt upon the unfitness of military officers to discharge the duties and exercise the powers pertaining naturally to civil office, and he pointed out the inconsistency, as he thought, of the declaration of Congress that the ten "State" governments at the South were illegal with the attempt of Congress to carry on these *illegal* "State" governments by "Federal agency," when Congress had no power to carry on a *legal* "State" government through "Federal agency"; and he stopped, as he thought, the way of escape from this argument by pointing out that the entire legislation of Congress down to the passage of the Reconstruction Acts distinctly involved the recognition of the ten communities now to be put under absolute military rule in all respects as "States" of the Union.

But the most vigorous and unanswerable part of the message was the protest against the robbery of the constitutional powers of the Executive by the attempt of Congress, in this measure, to confer some of those powers upon other persons. The President expressed himself so warmly upon this point, that the Republicans began to whisper around their suspicions of sinister purposes on his part, just as if such a declaration to Congress itself was not proof to the contrary. He said : "Whilst I hold the chief executive authority of the United States, whilst the obligation rests upon me to see that all the laws are faithfully executed, I can never willingly surrender that trust or the powers given for its execution. I can never give my assent to be made responsible for the faithful execution of laws, and at the same time surrender that trust and the powers which accompany it to any other executive officer, high or low, or to any number of executive officers. If this executive trust, vested by the Constitution in the President, is to be taken from him and vested in a subordinate officer, the responsibility will be with Congress in clothing the subordinate with unconstitutional power and with the officer who assumes its exercise."

The radical Republicans interpreted this language, at once, as meaning that the President proposed to so interfere with the execution of the Reconstruction Acts as to avoid their intent and destroy their effect. And the talk about impeachment was again revived. The President, however, meant nothing of the kind, and but for exaggerated suspicion and party hatred the language of the message would have been held to mean only an appeal to Congress to desist from its unlawful attempt to rob the Executive of his constitutional powers, and to the people to elect men to Congress who would obey the principles of the Constitution in their legislative acts.

Ideas and suspicions about the meaning of the message.

The Houses passed the bill over the President's veto immediately, by an overwhelming majority, and almost in a spirit of derision. The next day, July 20th, Congress adjourned to the 21st of the following November.

The veto overridden.

The unfortunate relations of Mr. Stanton with the President, and with the other members of the Cabinet were the thing which was destined to produce the catastrophe. He had become unbearable to the President, and to the most of his colleagues. He ought in all decency to have resigned his portfolio as Speed and Harlan and Dennison had done the year before. The President asked him to resign in a note of the 5th of August. Stanton, feeling sure of the support of the large majority in Congress, contemptuously refused. The President could now in the recess of Congress suspend him without violating the provisions of the Tenure-of-Office Act, or raising the

The suspension of Stanton from office.

CONGRESSIONAL PLAN OF RECONSTRUCTION

question of its constitutionality. The President at last resolved to take the matter into his own hands and rid himself of Stanton's presence in his confidential counsels. On the 12th of August he sent an executive order to Stanton suspending him from the office of Secretary of War, and another to General Grant authorizing and empowering him to act as Secretary of War *ad interim*. Stanton yielded to this order under protest. He wrote the President that he could not legally suspend him from office and declared that he submitted only to superior physical force. Grant accepted the appointment, although he had, four days before, advised the President against disturbing Stanton. Grant entered upon the duties of the office at once, and Stanton went off to New England to recuperate health, spirits and courage for his battle with the President which was bound to come unless the President should yield and take him back again, so soon as Congress should assemble.

By a series of orders issued during the same month (August) General Hancock was substituted for General Sheridan in the command of the fifth military district and General Canby for General Sickles in the command of the second district. Both of the generals thus relieved were great favorites at the North, especially Sheridan. The President felt that they were too much imbued with the military spirit to make good administrators of civil affairs. But the people of the North saw in these changes only the purpose of the President to place his political friends among the army officers in command of the military districts, and through them to modify the intent of the Reconstruction Acts in the course of their execution.

<small>Changes among the commanders of the military districts.</small>

CHAPTER VIII

THE EXECUTION OF THE RECONSTRUCTION ACTS

The Attempt to Prevent the Execution of the Reconstruction Acts in Mississippi and Georgia—The Case of Mississippi vs. Johnson—The Case of Georgia vs. Stanton—The Operations of the Commanders—The Registration—The Number Registered—The Change in the Electorate in the South—The Elections—Efforts of the Commanders to Get the Vote Out—The Result of the Elections—The Character of the Convention Delegates Chosen—The Work of the Conventions—The Vote upon Ratification—Fraudulent Voting and Unlawful Voting—The Recall of Pope and the Appointment of Meade in His Stead—Rejection of the Constitution in Alabama—The Statute of Congress Changing the Proportion of Votes to Registration in the Ratification of a Constitution—Criticism of the Statute—Ratification in Arkansas—Ratification in North Carolina, South Carolina, Georgia, Florida and Louisiana—Second Attempt in Georgia to Obstruct Reconstruction—Rejection of the Constitution in Mississippi.

ALTHOUGH the Supreme Court of the United States had said, in the case of Kendall vs. the United States, in 1838, that so far as the President's power is derived from the Constitution he is beyond the reach of any other department, except in the mode prescribed by the Constitution, through the impeaching power, and had also indicated, in the cases of the Cherokee Nation vs. the State of Georgia, in 1831, and Luther vs. Borden, in 1849, that it had no jurisdiction over political questions, there still prevailed in many minds the idea that the Court was the ultimate in-

The attempt to prevent the execution of the Reconstruction Acts in Mississippi and Georgia.

EXECUTION OF THE RECONSTRUCTION ACTS 145

terpreter of the Constitution in all cases of whatever nature, and that no person was exempted from its jurisdiction on account of official station. Under the influence of this idea, W. L. Sharkey, the ex-provisional Governor of Mississippi, appointed by President Johnson in 1865, undertook to obtain from the Supreme Court of the United States an injunction restraining the President of the United States from carrying the Reconstruction Acts of March, 1867, into effect. He was aided in this attempt by the Hon. Robert J. Walker, and their client in the case, as set up by them, was the "State of Mississippi." In a powerful argument, noted for both clearness and frankness, Mr. Johnson's Attorney-General, Mr. Stanbery, demonstrated that the President of the United States cannot be made subject to the jurisdiction of any court, while in office, except only the Senate of the United States, as the constitutional court of impeachment. The plea of Mr. Stanbery is also notable for another thing, viz.: the frank way in which he notified the Southerners that the President's opposition to these laws ceased with their successful passage over his vetoes, and that the President intended to execute them in spirit and letter, as it was his sworn duty to do. The Court decided, in 1866, in the case of Mississippi vs. Johnson, that "a bill praying an injunction against the execution of an act of Congress by the incumbent of the presidential office cannot be received, whether it describes him as President or as a citizen of a State." *The case of Mississippi vs. Johnson.*

Under the delusion that this decision was based entirely upon the official exemption from jurisdiction of the person sought to be made defendant, Hon. Charles J. Jenkins, Governor of Georgia, under the reconstructed constitution of 1865, undertook, as representing the "State of Georgia," to obtain an injunction against Stanton as Secretary of War, Grant as General of the army and Pope as commander of the third military district, restraining them from putting the Reconstruction Acts of March, 1867, into operation. Mr. Stanbery again came forward, in the case of the State of Georgia vs. Stanton, with a most able argument against the jurisdiction of the Court over the question involved, it being, as he contended, a political question pure and simple, and the Court again sustained him, deciding that it possessed no jurisdiction over the subject-matter presented in the bill for relief.

The case of Georgia vs. Stanton.

The generals now had free hand to go ahead according, pretty much, to their own discretion. The law gave them, first until September, and then until October, to complete the registration, and they themselves appointed and extended the times of registration at will. They constituted the boards of registry chiefly of army officers, Freedmen's Bureau officers, discharged Union soldiers, and negroes. Where white residents could be found who could take the iron-clad oath, the oath prescribed by Congress July 2d, 1862, they were also used in constituting these boards. The registration was quite successful in bringing out most of those qualified to register. The reason for this was not ready acquiescence on the part of the whites in the Reconstruction Acts, but it was the calculation that by registering and not voting on the question of holding a convention, or on the question of constitutional ratification, one or both of these propositions might be defeated, since the act of March 23d provided, as we have seen, that a majority of the registered voters must vote in order to carry them in the affirmative.

The operations of the commanders.

The registration.

In Alabama the registration reached the number of 165,813, of whom 104,518 were negroes or colored. In

EXECUTION OF THE RECONSTRUCTION ACTS 147

Arkansas it reached the number of 66,831, of whom less than half were known to be colored, although no exact account of the proportion was reported. In Florida it reached the number of 28,003, of whom 16,089 were colored. In Georgia it reached the number of 191,501, of whom 95,168 were colored. In Louisiana it reached the number of 129,654, of whom 84,436 were colored. In Mississippi it reached the number of 139,690, of whom, it was well known, a large majority were colored, although no exact figures giving the proportions were reported. In North Carolina it reached the number of 179,653, of whom 72,932 were colored. In South Carolina it reached the number of 127,432, of whom 80,550 were colored. In Texas it reached the number of 109,130, of whom 49,497 were colored. In Virginia it reached the number of 225,933, of whom 105,832 were colored.

The numbers registered.

It will thus be seen that of the ten "States" to be reconstructed five were to be recreated through an electorate in which the majority would be negroes and mulattoes, about all of whom had been, three years before, slaves; while in the other five the majority of the constructing electorate would be whites by a comparatively small number. This was a tremendous *bouleversement* of the political society of these sections. A large majority of the old leaders were disfranchised completely and a goodly number of the old Unionists were deterred by social considerations from taking any part in the work, while negroes, "poor white trash," "carpet-baggers" and a few self-denying respectables formed the new electorate for recreating "State" governments.

The change in the electorate in the South.

There is no doubt that Congress had the constitutional power to do this thing, on the theory, of course, that these communities were not "States" of the Union;

but it was a reckless thing, and a monstrous thing. Anybody of common sense and common honesty could, at the time, have foreseen some of the horrible results which were sure to follow.

So soon as the registration was completed, the commanders ordered elections to be held and the vote to be taken, first, upon the question of convention or no convention, and, at the same time, for the choice of delegates to the conventions. The commanders did their best to get out the vote. They met every device for keeping the negroes away from the polls and foiled it by means of their arbitrary powers, and they kept the polls open for two and three days, and in the case of Georgia, for five days. There is no doubt that there was repeating, although the military authorities exerted themselves most sincerely to prevent it. Their purpose was not, in any case, to permit fraud, but to give every opportunity to the freedmen to vote. Their efforts were aided by the fact that the elections in the Northern "States" during the autumn showed, in most quarters, large Democratic gains, and by the fact that in one of the great Northern "States," Ohio, the proposition to enfranchise negroes by an amendment to the "State" constitution was rejected by a large popular majority. The effect of these facts was to encourage the whites in the South, who had registered with the intention of defeating the proposed reconstruction by abstention from voting, to vote with the hope of securing a majority of the delegates to the proposed conventions.

The result was that in all the communities to be reconstructed as "States" a majority of the registered voters voted on the question of convention or no convention, and a large majority of those voting voted in

EXECUTION OF THE RECONSTRUCTION ACTS

every case for the holding of the convention. The figures were as follows: In Alabama, of the 165,813 registered voters, 96,866 voted on the question of convention or no convention, and 90,283 voted for holding the convention. In Arkansas, of the 66,831 registered voters, 41,134 voted on the question, and 27,576 of these voted in favor of holding the convention. In Florida, of the 28,003 registered voters, 14,503 voted on the question, and of these 14,300 voted in favor of holding the convention. In Georgia, of the 191,501 registered voters, 106,410 voted on the question, and of these 102,283 voted in favor of holding the convention. In Louisiana, of the 129,654 registered voters, 79,089 voted on the question, and of these 75,083 voted in favor of holding the convention. In Mississippi, of the 139,690 registered voters, 76,016 voted on the question, and of these 69,739 voted in favor of holding the convention. In North Carolina, of the 179,653 registered voters, 125,967 voted on the question of convention or no convention, and of these 93,006 voted for holding the convention. In South Carolina, of the 127,432 registered voters, 71,046 voted on the question, and of these 68,768 voted for holding the convention. In Texas, of the 109,130 registered voters, 56,129 voted on the question, and of these 44,689 voted for holding the convention. And in Virginia, of the 225,933 registered voters, 169,229 voted on the question, and of these 107,342 voted for holding the convention.

The great mass of those who registered and refrained from voting were the whites who were opposed to the Congressional Acts for Reconstruction, and hence the persons voting were chiefly the newly enfranchised. This was likewise true in the voting for the delegates to the conventions, with the result that radical men were, for the most part, chosen. They were new men to the political society of the South. There were a few of the old Whigs among them, who had remained true to the Union in their sentiments during the rebellion, but the most of them were "carpet-baggers," that is adventurers or new settlers from the North, "poor white trash" and negroes. In the South Carolina convention there were 63 negro delegates to 34 white. No such hideous bodies of men had ever been assembled before upon the soil of the United States for the purpose of participation in the creation of a "State" of the Union, and but for the control exercised over them by the military commanders, and the co-operation between the commanders and the small conservative white element in these bodies, the result of their work would have been the most ghastly travesty of justice, common-sense, and common honesty which the republic had ever been called upon to witness.

<small>The work of the conventions.</small>
During the winter and spring of 1867-68 the work of these conventions went on under the greatest extravagance and incompetence of every kind. The constitutions which came from them provided for complete equality in civil rights and, in some cases, in advantages of a social character, such as equal privileges in public conveyances, etc. They also not only established negro suffrage, as in fact was required by the Reconstruction Acts, but they, in most cases, disfranchised those whites whom the proposed Fourteenth Amendment would disqualify from holding office. In Alabama, Arkansas and Louisiana they went even further than this and disfranchised also, in the case of the first two, all who "had violated the rules of civilized warfare," and in the case of the last, all who had voted for secession, or had advocated treason against the United States in the press or the pulpit. It is true

EXECUTION OF THE RECONSTRUCTION ACTS

that in most cases ways were provided for removing these disabilities, but they were generally connected with such self-stultifying requirements as to make them worthless.

The restrictions upon eligibility to hold office or mandate were in general the same as those imposed on the exercise of the suffrage, and in some cases they went even further, as in the cases of the Mississippi and Virginia instruments, by both of which anybody who had voluntarily participated in the rebellion, or had voluntarily given aid or comfort to those who had, was disqualified.

The next step in the procedure was the submission of these constitutions to the voters. The registration was effected in the same manner as for the vote on the question of holding the conventions, and the election of the delegates; and the elections were held, as before, under the direction and control of the military commanders. The voting upon the question of ratification came off first in Alabama. General Pope had issued orders that the votes of persons registered in one precinct might be received in another, and that "State" officers and legislative members should be elected at the same election with the vote on ratification, and by the same voters. There is no doubt that the General only desired to secure the freedmen, who were then moving about restlessly, in their right of suffrage under the Reconstruction Acts, and to expedite the process of reconstruction so far as possible. But he undoubtedly opened the door to fraudulent voting by offering unrivalled opportunities for repeating, and he also violated the law and practice under the Constitution of the United States in regard to the qualified electors of "State" officers and legislators. Such officers and legislators could have been constitutionally elected only by the electors desig-

[margin: The vote upon ratification. Fraudulent voting and unlawful voting.]

nated in the constitution submitted for adoption. The qualifications of the electors who vote upon the question of the adoption of the first "State" constitution are necessarily fixed by Congress, but Congress has no constitutional power to fix the qualifications of the electors of "State" officers and legislators. Neither has the constitutional convention, which frames the first "State" constitution any such power, for the constitution which it frames is only a proposition, and ratification by the electors designated by Congress is necessary to its validity. Furthermore, any resolution which it might pass ordering the election of "State" officers or legislators by the electors designated by the Congressional statute is only a proposition to those electors, which must be accepted by them by a preliminary vote before they can proceed to the election of such officers and legislators. The General certainly did not understand these niceties of constitutional law and practice, and his desire to hurry up the re-establishment of civil government was rather laudable than otherwise. The President, however, who had in his Attorney-General one of the ablest lawyers of the country, understood well the constitutional limitations upon the General's powers and duties. He recalled the reckless commander and sent the more conservative Meade to take his place, December 28th, 1867.

The recall of Pope and the appointment of Meade in his stead.

Before the election came off, however, a bill was introduced into Congress, and passed the House of Representatives, and was making its way, a little more slowly, but surely, through the Senate, which authorized the election of "State" officers and legislators in the communities suffering reconstruction at the same time that the vote should be taken upon the ratification of the new constitutions and by the same electors. Congress had not a whit more power to

Rejection of the constitution in Alabama.

EXECUTION OF THE RECONSTRUCTION ACTS 153

do this than the commanders, and the President knew this well enough, but he gave no instructions to Meade, and so the commander permitted the voting for "State" officers and legislators at the same election that the vote was taken upon the question of the ratification of the constitution and by the same electors. But the registered voters refrained from voting upon the question of ratification in sufficient numbers to reduce the vote to several thousand less than half the registration. The proposed constitution was thus rejected under the provision of the Reconstruction Acts which required a vote exceeding the half of the registration, as well as a majority of that vote, for ratification. The "State" government chosen at this same election was thus in the air.

The Senate now passed the House bill providing that the approval of a majority of those voting, no matter what the proportion of the vote to the registration might be, should be regarded as a sufficient ratification of the proposed "State" constitutions for the communities suffering reconstruction; and although this Act was passed more than a month after the vote on the constitution was taken in Alabama, and although, furthermore, General Meade reported that a majority of the registered voters had not voted on the question of ratification, and that he interpreted this to mean that a majority of the registered voters did not want the constitution, yet Congress, as we shall see later, applied this new law of March 11th to the Alabama election which had taken place in the first days of the preceding February.

The statute of Congress changing the proportion of votes to registration in the ratification of a constitution.

In the original requirement that the vote to be effective must exceed half of the registration, Congress was still upon the ground of correct principle. When it left this ground it virtually accepted the principle that republican "State" governments may be legitimately created by a minority of the lawful voters against the will of a majority of the lawful voters, and that, too,

Criticism of this statute. not by allowing that minority to demonstrate its political superiority to the majority by greater intelligence, or shrewder management, or even by brute force, *but by the aid of power coming from without.* Now this is not, in correct political science, "State" government in a federal system, autonomous local government, at all. It is provincial government in local affairs, more or less complete as the necessity for the outside aid is more or less continuous. The Republicans had denounced the Johnson "State" governments upon the ground, among other grounds, that they were minority governments, minority governments in the vague and uncertain sense that not a majority of the adult males had been enfranchised, and not in the clear and distinct and unmistakable sense that a minority of the enfranchised, supported by the military power of the United States, might impose its will upon a majority of the enfranchised. There was nothing disloyal in the registered voters of Alabama giving Congress to understand that a majority of them preferred the continuance of the military régime, or the creation of a Territorial government for them by Congress, to the "State" constitution offered them. But it was utter self-stultification for Congress to take the ground that the Johnson "State" governments were unrepublican because they did not enfranchise all adult males of whatever race, color, or condition of mind or estate and overthrow them on that ground, and then proceed to create new "State" governments in their places upon the basis of a minority of the already duly qualified and registered voters. No impartial student, at this day, can view this terrible inconsistency in any other light than that of a high political crime.

EXECUTION OF THE RECONSTRUCTION ACTS

While the Senate was proceeding with the bill, another of the Southern communities was rapidly approaching the date fixed for voting upon the proposed "State" constitution, viz., Arkansas. The bill was passed by Congress the day before the voting began in Arkansas, but it was not known in Arkansas that it had been passed until near the close of the second day of the election. It could, however, be claimed that it was applicable to the case, and it certainly made all figures unnecessary except in regard to the actual voting. The "State" officers and legislators under the constitution to be adopted were chosen at the same time, by the Congressional electorate in Arkansas, and not by the "State" electorate, created by the new constitution. *Ratification in Arkansas.*

In the course of the next two months, April and May, voting upon the question of ratifying the new "State" constitutions took place in North and South Carolina, Georgia, Florida and Louisiana. As the Congressional Act of March 11th was in full force at this time, the result was affirmative in all cases. *Ratification in North Carolina, South Carolina, Georgia, Florida and Louisiana.*

During the Reconstruction proceedings in Georgia Governor Jenkins had refused to issue an order to the "State" Treasurer to pay a sum of forty thousand dollars, on the ground that the "State" legislature (Johnson government) had not made any such appropriation. For this refusal Meade removed him and the "State" Treasurer and Controller General, and appointed military men in their places. These new officers seized the "State" buildings, but Jenkins succeeded in getting away with the money in the treasury. He went to Washington and undertook to institute a proceeding in the Supreme Court of the United States against Generals Grant and *Second attempt in Georgia to obstruct Reconstruction.*

Meade to restrain the officers appointed by Meade from levying taxes upon the people of Georgia, and from collecting the same and the other income of the "State," as well as from exercising other functions. The Court gave its permission to the filing of the bill, but put off the hearing of the argument until the next term, and before this arrived, the new constitution had been ratified, and new "State" officers elected along with the ratification. In the other communities mentioned no opposition to the reconstruction process was offered.

On the other hand, the opponents of the proposed "State" constitution in Mississippi went into a most ear-

Rejection of the Constitution in Mississippi. nest and energetic campaign against its ratification and succeeded, at the election on June 22d, in rejecting the same by between seven and eight thousand majority. Many of the better class of negroes voted with their old masters, that is with such of these as were allowed by the Congressional acts to register and vote, against ratification. Those in favor of ratification claimed that fraud was practised by their opponents, in the face of the fact that they had the elections in their own hands, and they petitioned the military authorities to put the proposed constitution, notwithstanding its rejection at the polls, into operation. This these authorities refused to do.

CHAPTER IX

THE ATTEMPT TO IMPEACH THE PRESIDENT

Grant in the War Office—The President's Message of December 3d, 1867—The President's Special Message Concerning the Suspension of Stanton—The Senate Resolution in Regard to the Suspension of Stanton—Grant's Disobedience toward the President—The Unbearable Situation in which the President now Found Himself—The Dismissal of Stanton from Office—General Thomas Appointed Secretary of War *ad interim*—Stanton's Resistance—Thomas and the President—The Attitude of the Senate toward the Dismissal of Stanton—The Movements in the House of Representatives—The Arrest of General Thomas—Thomas's Second Attempt to Take Possession of the War Office—The House Resolution to Impeach the President—The Withdrawal of Stanton's Complaint against Thomas—The Fear of the Republicans to Test the Tenure-of-Office Act before the Courts—The Managers of Impeachment—The Charges against the President—The President's Answer to the Complaint—The Withdrawal of Mr. Black from the President's Counsel—The Contents of the President's Answer—The Replication of the House to the President's Answer—The Trial—Conduct of the Managers—The Evidence in the Case—The Argument—The Law in the Case—Mr. Stanton's Violations of Law—The Nomination of General Schofield to be Secretary of War—The Vote upon Impeachment—The Truth of the Matter—The Abdication of Stanton—Schofield's Confirmation as Secretary of War, and His Acceptance of the Office.

DURING this same period, another act in the drama of Reconstruction was being played, a fit companion piece to what was occurring in the unhappy communities of the South. It was the attempt to dispose of the President, and the presidency, by the impeachment of the President.

The history of the President's relations to Mr. Stanton, his Secretary of War, has already been given down to the suspension of Mr. Stanton in August of 1867, and the designation of General Grant to succeed him *ad interim*. Grant immediately assumed the duties of the office, and Mr. Stanton then regarded General Grant as a friend of the President in the controversy between himself and the President.

Grant in the War Office.

In his annual Message to Congress, the Fortieth Congress, of December 3d, 1867, the President said nothing directly in regard to his suspension of Mr. Stanton from office. He put forward a strong argument, couched in moderate and respectful language, against the policy and constitutionality of the Reconstruction Acts, as measures establishing martial law in times of peace, and as doing it for the purpose of establishing negro rule over the Southern communities, and he urged the repeal of these Acts, and the immediate admission of the Representatives and Senators from these communities, or "States" as he considered them, to their seats in Congress. What he said upon these subjects is, for the most part, entirely convincing to the impartial mind, at this day, and all of it was apparently animated with true patriotism and earnest desire to promote the common weal. At the close of the argument, however, the President introduced into his Message some ambiguous expressions which were unfortunate, to say the least, and which roused to a high degree the suspicions and the hatred already entertained against him by the radical Republicans.

The President's Message of December 3d, 1867.

He wrote as follows: "How far the duty of the President 'to preserve, protect, and defend the Constitution' requires him to go in opposing an unconstitutional act of Congress is a very serious and important

THE ATTEMPT TO IMPEACH THE PRESIDENT 159

question, on which I have deliberated much and felt extremely anxious to reach a proper conclusion. Where an act has been passed according to the forms of the Constitution by the supreme legislative authority, and is regularly enrolled among the public statutes of the country, Executive resistance to it, especially in times of high party excitement, would be likely to produce violent collision between the respective adherents of the two branches of the Government. This would be simply civil war, and civil war must be resorted to only as the last remedy for the worst of evils. Whatever might tend to provoke it should be most carefully avoided. A faithful and conscientious magistrate will concede very much to honest error, and something even to perverse malice, before he will endanger the public peace; and he will not adopt forcible measures, or such as might lead to force, as long as those which are peaceable remain open to him or to his constituents. It is true that cases may occur in which the Executive would be compelled to stand on its rights, and maintain them regardless of all consequences. If Congress should pass an act which is not only in palpable conflict with the Constitution, but will certainly, if carried out, produce immediate and irreparable injury to the organic structure of the Government, and if there be neither judicial remedy for the wrongs it inflicts nor power in the people to protect themselves without the official aid of their elected defender—if, for instance, the legislative department should pass an act even through all the forms of law to abolish a co-ordinate department of the Government—in such a case the President must take the high responsibilities of his office and save the life of the nation at all hazards. The so-called Reconstruction Acts, though as plainly unconstitutional as any that can be imagined, were not believed to be within the class last mentioned.

The people were not wholly disarmed of the power of self-defence. In all the Northern 'States' they still held in their hands the sacred right of the ballot, and it was safe to believe that in due time they would come to the rescue of their own institutions. It gives me pleasure to add that the appeal to our common constituents was not taken in vain, and that my confidence in their wisdom and virtue seems not to have been misplaced." These last words referred undoubtedly to the recent rejection, by popular vote, in a number of the most important Northern "States," of proposed amendments to "State" constitutions conferring suffrage upon negroes.

Most of the Republicans in Congress interpreted this whole paragraph in the Message as a threat to violate the Reconstruction Acts, although this was disavowed, rather indistinctly it is true, and to violate also the Tenure-of-Office Act. It is very difficult to say what the President was aiming at in giving such a warning to a body already excited against him to a high degree. It was certainly a *faux pas* of the worst kind, to say the least about it.

<small>The interpretation placed by the Republicans on the President's Message.</small>

Just nine days later the President sent his special Message to the Senate in regard to his suspension of Mr. Stanton. The gist of it was that mutual confidence between himself and Mr. Stanton no longer existed, and that when he asked Mr. Stanton to resign Mr. Stanton had declined to do so and had strongly intimated that his reason for declining was his own lack of confidence in the President's patriotism and integrity. The President claimed that such an attitude, on the part of a subordinate toward his superior, was unendurable, was in fact official misconduct of a grave order, and he also referred to Stanton's withholding Baird's telegram from

<small>The President's special Message concerning the suspension of Stanton.</small>

him just before the New Orleans riot. The President furthermore discussed Mr. Stanton's letter in reply to his order to him suspending him from office and commanding him to turn over the records and property of the office to General Grant. This letter contained a declaration by Mr. Stanton denying the right of the President, under the Constitution and laws, to suspend him from office, without the advice and consent of the Senate, and without legal cause, and affirming that he yielded, under protest, to the superior force wielded by the General of the Army who had been designated to succeed him.

This contention of Mr. Stanton that the President could not suspend him under the Constitution and laws of the United States gave the President the opportunity of saying that Mr. Stanton must be claiming the protection of the Tenure-of-Office Act of March 2d, 1867, and of revealing to the Senate Mr. Stanton's most decided condemnation of that Act when it was a bill before the President. The President asserted that Mr. Stanton, as every other member of his Cabinet, advised him that the bill was unconstitutional, in that it was a dangerous encroachment upon the President's constitutional prerogatives, and urged him to veto it. He also said that all the members of his Cabinet who had been appointed by Mr. Lincoln—and Stanton was one of these—appeared to be of the opinion that their tenures were not fixed or affected by the provisions of the bill. The conclusion arrived at by the President evidently was that the Tenure-of-Office Act did not cover Mr. Stanton's case, but left it under the law and practice existing before the passage of that measure, and that if it did cover it, the Act was unconstitutional, and was so considered by Mr. Stanton himself, and every other member of the Cabinet.

It is hardly credible that the President intended to recognize the validity of the Act by sending this Message to the Senate. It is true that the second section of the Act provided that the President might suspend an officer during a recess of the Senate, and designate an *ad interim* successor, and must, within the first twenty days of the next meeting of the Senate, report the suspension to the Senate, and it does appear, from a casual view, that the President was acting under the authority of this provision, or rather under the duty imposed by it, in suspending instead of removing Mr. Stanton and in making this report of Mr. Stanton's suspension to the Senate. But the President could claim that he was proceeding under his general constitutional power and duty of suspending from office, as a power included in the power of removal, and of sending such communications as he saw fit to Congress or to either House thereof. And the fact that he disputed the constitutionality of the Act in the Message itself is good internal evidence that he did not consider that he was in any way acting under the authority granted to him by it, or in any way estopping himself, so to speak, from making future declarations against the constitutionality of the Act, or even from disobeying its requirements.

The Senate, however, conceived at once that the President was acting under the Tenure-of-Office Act, and after considerable discussion, passed a resolution, on the 13th day of January, 1868, which provided that, "having considered the evidence and reasons given by the President in his report of December 12th, 1867, for the suspension of Edwin M. Stanton from the office of Secretary of War, the Senate does not concur in such suspension." The body then instructed its secretary to send copies of this resolution to the President, General

The Senate resolution in regard to the suspension of Stanton.

THE ATTEMPT TO IMPEACH THE PRESIDENT 163

Grant and Mr. Stanton. It is also evident that General Grant supposed the President was acting under the Tenure-of-Office Act both in suspending Stanton, in appointing himself *ad interim,* and in making report of these proceedings to the Senate; for upon receiving his copy of the Senate's resolution from the secretary of the Senate, he immediately left the room of the Secretary of War, locking the door after him and giving the key to the Adjutant-General, and repaired to the official head-quarters of the General of the army. Stanton manifestly regarded the matter in the same way, for upon receiving his copy of the notice of the Senate's action, he went to the room of the Secretary of War, and resumed the duties of Secretary of War without further ceremony. He did not even go to see Grant, but sent word over to the head-quarters of the General of the army summoning Grant to wait upon him in the Secretary's room.

There is no question now in any calm and impartial mind that the Senate acted most inconsiderately, not to say wrongfully, in passing that resolution. The situation was a perfectly plain one. The President and Stanton could not work together, since they had lost all confidence in each other. Common-sense and common decency required in such a case the retirement of the subordinate. The Senate itself had committed itself to this view in the discussion and votes upon the Tenure-of-Office bill, in its original form and in its final form. General Grant, the man who stood first in the confidence of the whole people, was in possession of the War Office. He had held it already nearly six months, and had in that short time improved the administration of it very greatly. At the end of the six months, at farthest, the President was held by the law of 1795, a law whose constitutionality

Criticism of the Senate resolution.

he did not dispute, to make a nomination to the Senate of a permanent incumbent. The Senate would then be able to prevent the appointment of any person to the office who did not have the confidence of the Senate and the country. No possible harm could thus have come to the country from acquiescing in Stanton's suspension, and it is hard to see that anything but harm did come to it in not doing so. No perfectly fair and unprejudiced mind could have failed to see that then; but the radical Republicans—and most of the Republicans in Congress at that moment were radical, or at least intensely partisan—were bent upon attacking and destroying the President in any way they could. They were ready to lay traps for him, and then to so excite him by encroachments upon the prerogatives and the dignity of his office as to make him fall into them. They were determined to sustain Stanton against the President, the subordinate against his lawful superior, simply because they despised the President. They claimed that the welfare of the country demanded it, and most of them probably thought so, but everybody can see the fallacy of that now, and anybody fit to be a Senator of the United States ought to have been able to see it then.

It is also a question whether General Grant did not act hastily, and inconsiderately, not to say wrongfully, in yielding the post without dispute to Mr. Stanton. The President certainly understood General Grant to promise him to hold on to the office in case the Senate should not approve of Stanton's suspension, and thereby compel Stanton to have recourse to the courts to regain possession, and thus secure a judicial determination of the constitutionality of the Tenure-of-Office Act, or to give the office back to the President before the Senate reached its determina-

<small>Criticism of General Grant's act.</small>

tion, so that he might have opportunity to put it into the hands of a man who would be willing to incur this responsibility; and the President was able to back this understanding by the testimony of five members of his Cabinet. On the other hand, General Grant was just as sincere in his view that his remarks to the President on the subject did not amount to a promise, and if they did, he had fulfilled it when on the 11th of January, two days before the Senate acted, he indicated to the President his unwillingness to involve himself in a lawsuit to test the constitutionality of the Tenure-of-Office Act. It is true that when he spoke with the President, on the 11th, he did not offer to resign the office, and that it was understood that he would see the President again on the subject, and that he did not see the President, nor attempt to see him, before the Senate acted. But he explained this apparent failure to keep faith by saying that he was extremely busy during the two days between the 11th and the 13th, and that the Senate had acted much more hastily than he expected it would.

There is little doubt that General Grant thought the Senate would acquiesce in Stanton's suspension, and was taken by surprise when it did not do so, and that until the action of the Senate on the 13th, he had never seriously considered that any opportunity or necessity for a judicial proceeding would arise. When, then, the alternative was suddenly presented to him of obeying the Tenure-of-Office Act, or disputing its constitutionality by forcibly holding possession of the War Office, he decided that it would be wrong for the General of the army to assume the attitude of defiance to Congress, whatever a civilian might consider his duty to be. He thought that such an act on his part would look like a contest between the civil and military powers of the Government, and he was unwilling to provoke it.

The President blundered very seriously when he did not accept the explanation from General Grant and drop the matter. The General was friendly in his feelings toward the President, and when Stanton repossessed himself of the War Office in his cavalier way, without seeking any understanding with Grant, and sent the General a rude summons to wait upon him, the General was very naturally and properly indignant with Stanton. The way was here open for the President to make a close friend of General Grant, by simply appreciating Grant's point of view in surrendering the War Office, and saying nothing more about it. But the President was not a prudent man when crossed in his purposes. He generally thought that the motives of all men who differed with him were bad. He showed in this trait his common origin and his vulgar breeding. He thought that Grant had deceived him and made a scapegoat of him, and he resolved to have it out with him. He did not seem to understand at all that in an issue of veracity between General Grant and himself, the country would believe Grant, no matter who told the truth, and who the lie. The utter impossibility of coming out winner in a contest with a national hero, no matter what the merits of the case might be, does not seem to have occurred to him at all. And so he plunged into that unfortunate controversy with General Grant in the public prints, which made Grant his enemy for life, at a time when he needed most his friendship, and might have had it by the exercise of a little common prudence.

The outcome of this whole course of crimination and recrimination was that the country came to the belief that the President first tried to force the responsibility of a violation of the Tenure-of-Office Act upon the popular General of the army, and then, when the Gen-

THE ATTEMPT TO IMPEACH THE PRESIDENT

eral foiled him in his purpose, undertook to impugn his honor and his integrity, and destroy his character before the public. An impartial study of the facts and the correspondence will not sustain any such view now, but in the state of feeling then prevailing, no such impartial study was possible. The President ought to have known this, and to have controlled his indignation until a more propitious time. *The result of the controversy between the President and General Grant.*

General Grant's letter closing the controversy is dated February 11th. In the interval between his quitting the War Office and this latter date, the President instructed the General not to obey any orders from Stanton until he knew they came from the President. *Grant's disobedience toward the President.* This instruction was given, first, verbally on January 19th. Grant demanded, on January 24th, a written order from the President on the subject, and repeated this request on the 28th. The President replied on the 29th that "General Grant is instructed, in writing, not to obey any order from the War Department, assumed to be issued by the direction of the President, unless such order is known by the General commanding the armies of the United States to have been authorized by the Executive." Grant responded, on January 30th, that he had been informed by the Secretary of War that he (the Secretary) had not received from the Executive any order or instructions limiting or impairing his authority to issue orders to the army as had theretofore been his practice under the law and the customs of the Department, and that while this authority to the War Department was not countermanded it would be satisfactory evidence to him (the General) that any orders issued from the War Department by the formal direction of the President were authorized by the Executive. This was coming very nearly up to the line between obedience and disobedience on the part of the General of the army toward the constitutional Commander-in-chief of the army and navy of the United States. The General must have himself felt that he was on rather shaky ground, for in the closing paragraph of his letter of February 11th he disclaimed any intention of disobeying "any legal order of the President distinctly communicated." But this was still an ambiguous situation. Who was to determine whether an order of the President to the General was legal or not? If the President, then there was no need of qualifying the word "order" by the word "legal." The language used, therefore, indicates that the General considered it within *his* power to decide this question. But if the subordinate can determine upon the legality of the orders of his superior, and disobey them in case he considers them illegal, then farewell to all discipline in civil or military service. It is very clear from these expressions of the General that Stanton's successful insubordination was already exercising its demoralizing influence, and was confusing the minds of those high in command in regard to the interpretation of their duties and responsibilities.

The situation was utterly unbearable for the President. Here was the constitutional Executive of the United States, the Commander-in-chief of the army and the navy, virtually excluded by one of his own subordinates from any relation to the business of one of the most important departments of the Government for which he alone was responsible, and his subordinate sustained in this attitude by the legislative branch of the Government.

The unbearable situation in which the President now found himself.

Matters were now rapidly approaching a crisis which could be avoided only by the resignation of the President or by the retreat of the Senate from its indefensible position. If both stood firm the clash must follow, and that too very quickly. On the 21st (February) it came. The President addressed an order of that date to Mr. Stanton dismissing him from the office of Secretary of War, and another order of the same date to General Lorenzo Thomas, Adjutant-General of the army, commanding him to take possession of the War Office and administer its affairs *ad interim*. He, on the same date, informed the Senate of his action, and transmitted to that body a copy of the orders to Stanton and Thomas. *The dismissal of Stanton from office.*

Upon receiving the order, General Thomas repaired immediately to the Secretary's room in the War Office, and handed to Mr. Stanton both of the documents, they having been put into his hands by the President's private secretary. Upon reading the one addressed to himself, Mr. Stanton immediately asked General Thomas whether he wished him to vacate at once or would give him time to remove his private property. Thomas replied, "act as you please." Stanton then read the order addressed to Thomas designating him Secretary *ad interim*, and asked Thomas for a copy of it. *General Thomas appointed Secretary of War ad interim.*

Thomas then left the Secretary's room and went into his old room, the Adjutant-General's room, to have a copy of the order made. He returned at once with it, and when he handed it to Mr. Stanton, the latter said: "I do not know whether I will obey your instructions, or whether I will resist them." General Thomas had certified the correctness of the copy, and had signed himself Secretary of War *ad interim*. The two then went into General Schriver's room just across the hallway, and there Stanton declared outright that Thomas should not issue orders as Secre- *Stanton's resistance.*

tary of War, and that if he did he (Stanton) would countermand them, and he then and there directed General Schriver and General Townsend, both of whom were present, to disobey any orders coming from General Thomas as Secretary of War. Mr. Stanton then caused General Townsend to prepare a written order to Thomas, signed by Mr. Stanton as Secretary of War, which was as follows: "Sir: I am informed that you presume to issue orders as Secretary of War *ad interim.* Such conduct and orders are illegal, and you are hereby commanded to abstain from issuing any orders other than in your capacity as Adjutant-General of the army."

General Thomas then went over to the White House to see the President about the matter. He told the President of his conversation with Mr. Stanton, and repeated to him Stanton's replies verbatim. The President simply said to him: "Very well; go and take charge of the office and perform the duties." Thomas did not, however, return to the Secretary's room in the War Office that day, and did not see Mr. Stanton again on that day.

<small>Thomas and the President.</small>

While these things were occurring in the executive offices matters were seething at the other end of the avenue. The Senate was deliberating, if we may call such a stormy procedure as took place a deliberation, upon the President's communication. It very quickly passed the following resolution: "Whereas, the Senate have received and considered the communication of the President stating that he had removed Edwin M. Stanton, Secretary of War, and had designated the Adjutant-General of the army to act as Secretary of War *ad interim:* Therefore, Resolved by the Senate of the United States, That under the Constitution and laws of the United States the President has no power to remove

<small>The attitude of the Senate toward the dismissal of Stanton.</small>

THE ATTEMPT TO IMPEACH THE PRESIDENT 171

the Secretary of War and designate any other officer to perform the duties of that office *ad interim.*" A copy of this resolution was sent to the President, another copy to Mr. Stanton, and another to General Thomas.

The excitement in the other House was still more intense and irrational. The Senate resolution had hardly passed when the radical Mr. Covode presented a motion to the effect that "Andrew Johnson, President of the United States, be impeached of high crimes and misdemeanors." This resolution was referred to the Committee of the House on Reconstruction, which was, as we have seen, composed of members nearly all of whom were radical Republicans. *The movements in the House of Representatives.*

Encouraged and strengthened by these movements in the legislature, and hearing that Thomas had threatened to force his way into the office, Mr. Stanton resolved to forestall all possible movements of General Thomas for gaining possession of the office of Secretary of War. He procured a warrant of arrest for the General, and on the next morning, the morning of the 22d, the warrant was served on General Thomas just after he had risen from his bed, and before he had taken his morning meal. The officers who arrested him, the Marshal of the District, and his assistant, and a constable, took the General at once before Judge Cartter, the Chief Justice of the District of Columbia. On the way from the General's residence to the court-room, the General asked the officers to allow him to see the President, and inform the latter of his arrest. The Marshal went with the General to the White House, and was present at the interview between the General and the President. It lasted but a moment. The General told the President that he was under arrest. The President replied that he was satisfied to have the case go into the courts, that he wanted it judicially determined. He then directed the General to go to the Attorney-General, Mr. Stanbery. The Marshal permitted him to call at Mr. Stanbery's apartment in his hotel, and inform the Attorney-General of his arrest. He then took him before Judge Cartter. Nobody was with the General before the Judge, except the officers who had arrested him. The Judge held him to bail in the sum of five thousand dollars to appear on the following Wednesday morning, the 26th. After about an hour friends of the General came in and signed his bail bond, and the General was released, the Judge informing him that he was not suspended from any of his official functions. The General then went back to the White House and informed the President of his release under bail, and the President again replied that he wanted the case in the courts.

Finally, the General went over to the rooms of the Secretary of War. There he found some six or eight members of Congress with Mr. Stanton, evidently awaiting the *dénouement*. He demanded the office. Stanton ordered him to his room as Adjutant-General. He refused to obey. He demanded the office of the Secretary of War a second and a third time, and a second and a third time Stanton refused to yield it to him and ordered him to his room as Adjutant-General. The General then left the room of the Secretary of War, and went across the hall into General Schriver's room. Stanton followed him and asked him if he insisted on acting as Secretary of War. The General replied that he did, and would demand the mails of the War Office. The two then fell into a friendly chat, General Thomas saying that he had had nothing to eat or drink that day and requesting Mr. Stanton the next time he might have him arrested not to do it before

[marginal note: Thomas's second attempt to take possession of the War Office.]

THE ATTEMPT TO IMPEACH THE PRESIDENT 173

breakfast, and Stanton appealing to Schriver to bring out his whiskey, which Schriver did, and the two men, Thomas and Stanton, drank a little together on Stanton's invitation. With this Thomas's attempt to get possession of the War Office seems to have ended. On the same day the President sent to the Senate for confirmation as Secretary of War the name of Thomas Ewing, Sr. Mr. Ewing was a man of undoubted ability and of the purest loyalty. He had been one of Lincoln's best friends and supporters and was the father-in-law of General Sherman; but the Senate denied that the President had any power to send in a nomination, that is, denied that there was a vacancy.

On the same day, also, the 22d, the Reconstruction Committee of the House, to whom the resolution for impeaching the President had been referred, reported it back with the recommendation that it be passed, and the chairman, Mr. Thaddeus Stevens, urged that it might pass without debate. *The House resolution to impeach the President.* But the members began at once to debate it hotly, and continued to do so through the day and deep into the night. The following day was Sunday, the 23d. The House had, therefore, one day of recess in which to cool down. But on Monday the angry determination of the Republican leaders was even more manifest than on the preceding Saturday. All day long the war of words went on. The reproach and the odium heaped upon the President were simply immeasurable. Read from the point of view of to-day, and at this distance from the event, most of it appears highly extravagant, and some of it ridiculous and even puerile. Late in the afternoon the vote was reached, by application of the previous question rule. The House resolved to impeach the President before the Senate by a vote of 126 to 47. All those voting in the affirmative were

Republicans, and all those voting in the negative were Democrats.

By another strict party vote the House authorized the Speaker to appoint a committee to acquaint the Senate with its resolution to impeach the President before that body, and another committee to draw up the articles of impeachment. The Speaker, Mr. Colfax, appointed Mr. Stevens and Mr Bingham to constitute the first committee, and Mr. Boutwell, Mr. Stevens, Mr. Bingham, Mr. Wilson, Mr. Logan, Mr. Julian and Mr. Ward to constitute the second. This committee immediately set about its work, and on the 29th was ready to report.

The committee of the House on Impeachment.

Meanwhile the day for General Thomas to appear in court, February 26th, arrived. By this time the General had taken legal advice, and the plan of his counsel was to refuse to give further bail, allow him thus to be committed to jail, then sue out a writ of Habeas Corpus from a United States judge, and bring in this way the question of the constitutionality of the Tenure-of-Office Act to judicial determination. But Judge Cartter foiled this plan, according to the word of Judge Luke P. Poland of Vermont, who drew the complaint against Thomas, by declining to make any further order requiring bail, and on the same day Mr. Stanton withdrew the complaint, and the case was thus prevented from reaching the United States courts at all.

The withdrawal of Stanton's complaint against Thomas.

There is little doubt that the Republicans were afraid to have the Tenure-of-Office Act tested judicially They preferred recourse to the Court of Impeachment to settle the matter so far as President Johnson was concerned. It is true that Stanton alleged that he brought the case against Thomas in order to test judicially the right of

The fear of the Republicans to test the Tenure-of-Office Act before the courts.

THE ATTEMPT TO IMPEACH THE PRESIDENT 175

Thomas to the office of Secretary of War, and that he withdrew the complaint as superfluous after the House of Representatives had resolved to impeach the President, but that may have been a mere legal form of excuse.

Three days after this, as we have seen, the committee charged with preparing the articles of impeachment reported to the House. They were debated until March 3d, when they were adopted by a strict party vote, and the managers to conduct the prosecution were elected. They were Messrs. Bingham, Boutwell, Wilson, Butler, Williams, Logan and Stevens. *The managers of impeachment.*

Disregarding the legal order and form of the eleven articles of impeachment, we may say briefly that the charges against the President were :

First, that he violated the Tenure-of-Office Act in issuing an order deposing Stanton from the office of Secretary of War, and another order appointing Thomas to the office of Secretary of War *ad interim*. *The charges against the President.*

Second, that he violated the Anti-conspiracy Act of July 31, 1861, in conspiring with Thomas to expel Stanton by force from the War Office, and to seize upon the property and papers of the United States in the War Office, and to unlawfully disburse the money appropriated for the military service and the Department of War.

Third, that he violated the Act of March 2, 1867, which, among other things, directed that the military orders and instructions of the President and Secretary of War should be issued through the General of the army, by attempting to induce General Emory, the commander of the troops around Washington, to disregard this law and take his orders immediately from the President.

And fourthly, that he committed high misdemeanors

in his speeches denouncing the Thirty-ninth Congress, and declaring it to be a Congress of only a part of the "States."

These charges were presented by the managers of the impeachment to the Senate on March 5th, the day upon which the Senate organized itself as a Court of Impeachment, by assembling under the presidency of the Chief Justice of the United States, who administered the oath to the Senators as members of the court. The court directed its sergeant-at-arms to serve its summons upon the President to appear before its bar and answer to the charges preferred against him, and then adjourned to the 13th of the month. On the 13th the court reassembled. The chief clerk read the return of the sergeant-at-arms to the writ of summons, to the effect that he had served the writ upon the President at seven o'clock P.M. of Saturday, the 7th day of the month; and the President entered his appearance by his counsel, Henry Stanbery, Benjamin R. Curtis, Jeremiah S. Black, William M. Evarts and Thomas A. R. Nelson, and asked for forty days for the preparation of his answer to the charges. The first four of these men were the most noted constitutional lawyers of the country, and the fifth was one of Mr. Johnson's loyal Tennessee friends and his chief ally in the Union cause in Tennessee during the years of sorest trial. Mr. Stanbery had resigned the office of Attorney-General of the United States in order to take the leading part in the defence of the President.

The charges presented to the Senate.

The President's appearance entered by his counsel.

The managers on the part of the House very ungenerously objected to giving the President any time at all for the preparation of his answer further than what he had had since the service of the summons upon him, but the Senate re-

The President's answer to the complaint.

THE ATTEMPT TO IMPEACH THE PRESIDENT 177

solved to give him ten days, that is until March 23d. Upon the latter day the Senate resumed its sitting as a Court of Impeachment, and the President's counsel appeared with his answer to the charges made against him.

An incident occurred at this point in the history of the procedure, which should be related, although it interrupts somewhat the thread of the narrative. It was the disappearance of Mr. Black from among the counsel for the President, and the appearance of Mr. Groesbeck in his place. It was the gossip among the enemies of the President, and this gossip was sedulously spread abroad throughout the whole country by them, that Black on examining the case had become convinced of the President's guilt and had retired from the case for this reason, and for the further reason that he had become disgusted with the President's conduct. It did not become known until later that during this time Judge Black was counsel for a firm composed of one Patterson and one Marguiendo, which firm claimed a guano island in the West Indies, called Alta Vela, and that one of Judge Black's colleagues in the prosecution of the Patterson-Marguiendo claim, one J. W. Shaffer, procured a letter of the date of the 9th of March, 1868, that is one week after the House of Representatives had resolved to impeach the President, signed by General Benjamin F. Butler and approved by John A. Logan, J. A. Garfield, W. H. Koontz, J. K. Moorhead, Thaddeus Stevens, J. G. Blaine and John A. Bingham, some of them the most bitter among the President's enemies, which contained the statement that these gentlemen were clearly of the opinion that the citizens of the United States had the exclusive right to the guano beds of Alta Vela island, and an expression of their surprise that the President had not upheld this right by force against the claims of the Dominican Government to the island, and caused this letter to be placed in the hands of the President on the 16th day of March, and that on the 17th or 18th of March Judge Black had an interview with the President and urged him to send an armed vessel of the United States to Alta Vela to take possession of the island, and that the President, viewing this approach to him at this time as an attempt to take advantage of his situation, refused, and that on the next day, the 19th of March, Judge Black declined to appear further as the President's counsel in the impeachment trial.

It must have taken a good deal of self-control on the part of the President, in possession of all these facts, to keep them quietly to himself for more than a month from the time of Judge Black's retirement from his case, while his enemies were pointing the finger of a supposed triumphant scorn at him as being unworthy to have so honest a man as Judge Black among his counsel, and then to allow them to be given out only under provocation from the managers of the impeachment, taunting him with his treatment of Judge Black, and with Judge Black's withdrawal from his case.

But to return to the President's answer to the charges against him. Disregarding again legal verbiage and order, the President answered substantially that Stanton's case was not affected by the Tenure-of-Office Act, and that he held his office, according to the Constitution and laws of the United States, and the wording of his commission, at the pleasure of the President; that even if Stanton's case were covered by the Act, the President was within his right and was not thereby committing any crime or misdemeanor at all, to so act as to make up an issue before the Supreme Court of the United States, whereby the constitutionality of the Act might be tested ; that the authority given to General Thomas to act as Secretary of War *ad interim* was not an appointment nor an attempt to make an appointment, but was only a designation of a person to act temporarily until an appointment could be made by and with the consent of the Senate, a thing which the President was empowered to do by the Act of February 13th, 1795, still in force ; that he had not entered into any conspiracy with Thomas or anybody else to force Stanton out of the War Office, or to seize the property and papers of the United States in the War Office, that he could not in fact do so, since Stanton was not lawfully in the War Office, and since the President of the United States was the ultimate lawful custodian of the property and papers of the United States in the War Office, but that his communications with Thomas were orders from the President to a subordinate officer, to whom the President gave no authority to use force for their execution, and who did not use any force in his attempts to execute them, the intention of the President only being, if his authority should be resisted by Mr. Stanton, to create an issue before the Supreme Court of the United States, and secure thereby a judicial determination of the rights and powers of the parties concerned, and not to do anything unlawful ; that he had never undertaken to induce General Emory to take his orders immediately from himself in violation of the Act of March 2d, 1867, which provided that all of the military orders and instructions issuing from the President and the Secretary of War should pass through the hands of the General of the Army, but that he had only expressed to General Emory, as he had to Congress, his conviction that the Act was in violation of the Constitution, which latter conferred upon the President the Commandership-in-chief of the army and the navy ; and finally, that his speeches were simply the expression of his opinions as a free citizen of the Republic, which right was guaranteed to him and to every other citizen by the Constitution of the country, and could not be made out in any way to have any of the qualities of a crime or a misdemeanor, and that his declaration that the Thirty-ninth Congress was a Congress of only a part of the "States" was intended by him in no other sense than that of an assertion that ten "States" of the Union were not represented in it, all of which ought to be so represented when they should send loyal men to take seats therein, and that he had never intended by this declaration to deny the validity of the acts of the Congress or its power to originate and adopt an amendment to the Constitution of the United States.

After the filing of this answer, the counsel of the President asked the Court of Impeachment for thirty days' time after the replication of the House of Representatives to this answer should be filed for the preparation of the President's case. But the managers on the part of the House again very ungenerously opposed giving them any time at all for this purpose. The debate over this point lasted until after the replication of the House was filed on the following day, that is on the 24th of March. The Court of Impeachment then decided to give them until March 30th, and ordered the trial to proceed on that day.

The replication filed by the House of Representatives, on the 26th, was an exception to the answer of the President as insufficient, a denial of all the averments of the answer, a declaration of the guilt of the President of the high crimes and misdemeanors charged, and an offer to prove the same.

The replication of the House to the President's answer.

On the 30th, the trial opened with the fierce, not to say brutal, attack of Mr. Butler on the President. During the entire course of the trial, from the 30th of March until the 16th of May, the managers followed a line of conduct which no impartial student of this day can fail to condemn, and which, even in that time of hostile passion against the President, lost to them a large measure of popular favor. They tried to prevail upon the Court of Impeachment to regard itself as a political body instead of a court, to renounce all limitations upon its powers, and to accept common rumors against the President as good evidence of his guilt. On the other hand, they objected to the introduction of evidence by the President to prove the purpose of his acts, and to show the advice upon which he had proceeded in their commission. They succeeded in inducing the Court of Impeachment to refuse to hear the President's evidence upon these points, although the Chief Justice had ruled in favor of its reception. There is no doubt that their cause was greatly weakened in the public esteem by this manifestation of partisanship on the part of the court.

The evidence in the case showed no conspiracy with Thomas to do anything, and no orders to him to use any force in what he was authorized to do, and no attempt to induce General Emory to violate any law or any orders received from or through the General of the Army or any other legal authority. The case, thus, rested chiefly upon the question as to whether the President had violated the Tenure-of-Office Act; and the transactions of the President in regard to this subject were matters of record.

When one, at this lapse of time from the events, peruses the calm, dignified, convincing and masterful arguments of the President's counsel, and compares them with the passionate, partisan harangues of the managers, it is very difficult to understand how the lat-

The argument. ter could have made any serious impression at all. There was only a single point upon the law seemingly involved in the case in regard to which they held the better reason. That was the claim on their part that the President had no right to violate an act of Congress for the purpose of testing its validity before the United States courts, or for any other purpose. They argued with much force that to allow the President the power to violate an act of Congress, or to omit to execute an act of Congress, in order to make up an issue before the courts upon the question of its constitutionality, would be virtually to attribute to the President the once hated royal power of suspending the law at the pleasure of the Executive. They contended that the veto power was placed in the hands of the President for the purpose of allowing him to be heard at the proper time, and to act at the proper time, in regard to the passage of any law, and that no other power was given him in relation to the subject; that after he had exhausted this power, he was bound to execute the legislation of Congress, and could not suspend it or violate it for any purpose whatsoever; and that the constitutionality of any of the acts of Congress could be raised before the courts only by persons not charged with the execution of the law and having such interests affected by the act in question as would warrant a judicial procedure.

Judge Curtis was so influenced by the consideration that to claim such a power for the President would give him a double veto upon all of the acts of Congress, a veto when acting as a part of the legislature in the enactment of law, and then a purely executive veto which could be overcome only by an adverse judicial decision, that he expressed his contention on the subject in very cautious language. He declared that the President claimed no such general power as that, but he said "when a question arises whether a particular law has cut off a power confided to him by the people through the Constitution, and he alone can raise that question, and he alone can cause a judicial decision to come between the two branches of the Government to say which of them is right, and after due deliberation, with the advice of those who are his proper advisers, he settles down firmly upon the opinion that such is the character of the law, it remains to be decided by you, Senators, whether there is any violation of his duty when he takes the needful steps to raise that question and have it peacefully decided."

The great lawyer refused thus to commit himself upon this fundamental question of constitutional law. And well he might, for to recognize any such power in the President would be to enable him to rule with such arbitrariness as to upset the principles and practices of all free government. The President can constitutionally defend his prerogatives with the veto power, a power which nothing short of a two-thirds majority of both Houses of Congress can overcome, and he has no other power of defence confided to him by the Constitution. He must execute the laws passed over his veto upon matters which in his opinion touch his executive prerogatives, just the same as upon all other matters, and if persons not connected with the administration of the laws do not call such measures in question before the courts, the remedies provided by the Constitution for the people of the United States are either the election of members of Congress who will repeal the enactments, or else the amendment of the Constitution so as to repeal them. It was, however, a question whether, in showing the sole purpose of making an issue before the courts, the President would not clear himself of any criminal intent. Happily his case did not require this, as was demonstrated by his counsel and by Senators Trumbull and Fessenden in their opinions.

The law governing the President's case was perfectly clear to anyone who could divest himself of political prejudice and of personal hostility. It was briefly this. By an Act of the First Congress, of the date of August 7th, 1789, Congress interpreted the Constitution as giving the President the power to remove any officer of the United States, except judges of the United States courts, at his discretion, as an incident of his sole executive responsibility, and in an especial sense recognized this constitutional power as belonging to the President in the case of the heads of the governmental departments, the members of the Cabinet, as they afterwards came to be called, since these persons stood, and must stand, in a peculiarly confidential relation to the President, as his official advisers. This interpretation of the Constitution as to the President's power of removal and the practice built upon it remained untouched by the Congress until the 2d of March, 1867, when, as we have seen, Congress enacted, "that every person holding any civil office to which he has been appointed by and with the advice and consent of the Senate, and every person who shall be hereafter appointed to any such office, and shall become duly qualified to act therein, is and shall be entitled to hold such office until a successor shall have been in like manner appointed and duly qualified, except as herein otherwise provided: Provided, That the Secretaries of State, of the Treasury, of War, of the Navy, and of the Interior, the Postmaster-General, and the Attorney-General, shall hold their offices respectively for and during the term of the President by whom they may have been appointed, and one month thereafter, subject to removal by and with the advice and consent of the Senate."

It will be remembered that in the Tenure-of-Office bill as it originated in the Senate the members of the Cabinet were entirely excepted from its operation; that the House in passing the bill included them; that the Senate would not agree to their inclusion; that the bill was then sent to a conference committee; that this committee invented the compromise contained in the proviso; that this proviso was understood to give to each President the power to choose his own Cabinet officers once during his term, and therefore to remove any Cabinet officer not originally appointed by him, but holding under a commission from a former President, and remaining in office only by the sufferance of the existing President; that this was especially the true meaning of the proviso in regard to those Cabinet officers then in office, but who had been appointed and commissioned by Mr. Lincoln during his first term to hold during the pleasure of the President; and that it was upon this explanation of the meaning of the proviso that the Senate voted the resolution of the conference committee.

From all this it is entirely clear that the President had the legal power to remove Mr. Stanton, no matter whether the Tenure-of-Office Act was constitutional or not, simply because his case was excepted by the proviso in the first article in the Act from the operation of the Act, and was left to the operation of the laws in existence at the time the Act was passed. There is little question now that that Act was not in accordance with a fair interpretation of the Constitution, but it was not at all necessary to hold that view in order to clear the President of the accusation of having violated the Constitution and the laws of the land.

The law in reference to the *ad interim* appointment, or designation, of General Thomas was equally plain to the impartial eye. The Constitution provides only for vacancies that may happen during the recess of the Senate, and empowers the President to fill all such by granting commissions which shall expire at the end of its next session. By an act of May 8th, 1792, Congress empowered the President, in case of the death, sickness, or absence from the seat of government, of the Secretary of State, the Secretary of the Treasury, or the Secretary of War, whether these events should occur during a session, or a recess, of the Senate, " to authorize any person or persons, at his discretion, to perform the duties of the said respective offices until a successor be appointed, or until such absence or inability by sickness should cease."

Another act of Congress of February 13th, 1795, empowered the President, in case of vacancy from any cause in the offices of Secretary of State, Secretary of the Treasury, or Secretary of War, happening either during a recess or a session of the Senate, " to authorize any person or persons, at his discretion, to perform the duties of the said respective offices until a successor be appointed or such vacancy be filled," provided, however, that no one vacancy should be supplied in that manner for a longer time than six months.

It will be seen that neither of these statutes provided for the temporary filling of vacancies in any of the Departments, except those of State, the Treasury, and War. In practice, however, the Presidents have followed the analogies of the law of 1795, when it became necessary, in their opinion, to make a temporary designation in the other Departments. On the 22d of September, 1862, President Lincoln appointed J. B. L. Skinner Postmaster-General *ad interim.* It was Mr. Lincoln himself who called the attention of Congress to the fact that he had no literal legal authority for this, and who on January 2d, 1863, asked Congress to extend the Act of May 8th, 1792, so as to cover the cases of the other Departments, and empower the President to make *ad interim* appointments to fill vacancies in these Departments happening on account of death, sickness, or absence from the seat of government. Why the President did not ask for the extension of the Act of February 13th, 1795, which covered all vacancies happening from whatever cause, instead of the Act of 1792, which covered those only which might happen from death, sickness, or absence from the seat of government, we do not know. We only know that in January, 1863, both the President and Congress were greatly pressed by the exigencies of the war, and did things generally in haste and without much consideration. In answer to the President's suggestion, Congress passed the Act of February 20th, 1863, extending the Act of 1792 so as to cover all the executive Departments in the cases of vacancy provided for in that Act, viz., by cause of death, sickness, or absence from the seat of Government—adding resignation—and limiting the President, however, in these appointments to persons already officers in one or the other of the Departments, and providing that no one vacancy should be so supplied for a longer period than six months. The vacancies which might happen from expiration of term or by removal were not at all provided for by the Act of 1863; and as the Act of 1863 did not expressly repeal the Act of 1795, but only declared that "all acts and parts of acts inconsistent with this act are hereby repealed," the Act of 1795 remained in force as to all vacancies caused by expiration of term or by removal, whether happening during a recess or a session of the Senate.

Neither did the Tenure-of-Office Act of 1867 repeal the Act of 1795 in regard to first vacancies happening among the Secretaries of Departments by other causes than those provided for in the Act of 1863, either expressly or by implication, since these first vacancies were expressly excepted from the operation of the Act of 1867, by the proviso attached to the first article. And even if it should be held that the Act of 1867 did repeal that of 1795 entirely, yet, in that it did not forbid the President to make *ad interim* appointments in the cases where a Secretary's term expired, or a Secretary was lawfully removed by him, the President's designation of Thomas could not be considered as a violation of law but only as an act without warrant of law, the very kind of an act committed by Mr. Lincoln in his appointment of Skinner as Postmaster-General *ad interim* in 1862, and committed by other Presidents in other cases.

The managers made much of the argument that the President had recognized the validity of the Tenure-of-Office Act in suspending Stanton the preceding August, and reporting his suspension to the Senate, and in notifying the Secretary of the Treasury of the suspension, as provided in the Act, and asserted that he was therefore estopped from denying its constitutionality. But while it can be easily shown that these acts of the President did not at all militate against his claim that other parts of the statute were unconstitutional, still this was not at all necessary to the President's defence, under the view here advanced of the relations between the Acts of 1867, 1863, and 1795. It made no difference, under this view, whether the Act of 1867 was, or was not, constitutional and valid. In either case the President had violated no law, either constitutional or statutory.

The fact is that Mr. Stanton and those who abetted him were the violators of law. Every official act which he committed after receiving the notification from the President of his removal, on the 21st of February, was a usurpation of governmental powers by a private citizen, and the gathering of armed men about him with the purpose of sustaining him in holding on to the War Office after his dismissal by the President was treason. It is a question whether his official acts after the 13th of January and down to February 21st were not also usurpations. That depends upon whether the Tenure-of-Office Act was, or was not, constitutional, and whether, if it were, the right of a member of the Cabinet, suspended from office, to resume the functions of the office, after disapproval of the suspension by the Senate, was made, by the Act, to apply to such members of the Cabinet as were excepted from the operation of the first article of the Act by the proviso to that article. The best Republican lawyers in the Senate, Trumbull, Fessenden, Grimes and Doolittle, took the view of the law in the President's case as here explained. They, with one other Republican, Van Winkle of West Virginia, filed, after the vote on impeachment, opinions in the case expressing substantially this view. *Mr. Stanton's violations of law.*

It is now known that during the trial some of these men expressed to one of the President's counsel the belief that Mr. Johnson could not be convicted upon the law and evidence in the case, and that should the Senate vote to remove him, "it would be done wholly from supposed party necessity," and from fear of what the President might do in case he were acquitted, and that they suggested to this member of the President's counsel the wisdom of the President's sending to the Senate, at that *The nomination of General Schofield to be Secretary of War.*

juncture, a nomination for the Secretaryship of War, which would allay all reasonable apprehension that the President would, if acquitted, use the War Department for the accomplishment of any arbitrary purposes, and that they mentioned General Schofield as a man who would be satisfactory. These communications were made about the 20th of April. The President was immediately informed of them, as was General Schofield, and, on April 24th, the President nominated General Schofield to the Senate to be Secretary of War. Whether this move on the part of the President influenced any Senator to vote for acquittal is unknown. It certainly served to allay popular apprehension, if the testimony of the newspapers of the day may be taken on that point.

Fifty-four Senators from the twenty-seven "States" represented constituted the membership of the Court of Impeachment under the presidency of the Chief Justice. The President must, therefore, have nineteen votes in order to escape conviction. Of these fifty-four, only eight were Democrats. It was practically certain that all of these would vote for acquittal. He needed, therefore, at least eleven Republican votes in his favor. The closing of the case by the prosecution occurred on the 6th of May, and, on the 7th, the court passed the resolution to take the vote of its members upon the articles of impeachment on the 12th. On that day Mr. Chandler of Michigan informed the court that his colleague, Mr. Howard, was too ill to appear, and asked the court to adjourn to the 16th, in order to give Mr. Howard the opportunity to be present. The court agreed to this request. On the 16th, with all the members present, the voting began. The last article, the eleventh, was, by an order of the court, taken first, and the Chief Justice

The vote upon Impeachment.

put the question to each Senator : "Mr. Senator—how say you? Is the respondent Andrew Johnson, President of the United States, guilty or not guilty of a high misdemeanor, as charged in this article?" Thirty-five votes were cast in the affirmative, and nineteen in the negative. So soon as it was known that the President had been acquitted upon this article, a motion was made by Mr. Williams of Oregon to adjourn the court to the 26th. After the announcement of the vote by the Chief Justice, this motion was carried and the court adjourned to the 26th. On that day it reassembled and proceeded to vote upon the second article and then on the third, with the same result as upon the eleventh. Whereupon Mr. Williams moved that the Senate sitting as a Court of Impeachment adjourn *sine die*, and the motion was carried by a vote of 34 to 16, 4 not voting. The Republicans who voted "not guilty" were Messrs. Dixon of Connecticut, Doolittle of Wisconsin, Fessenden of Maine, Fowler of Tennessee, Grimes of Iowa, Henderson of Missouri, Norton of Minnesota, Patterson of Tennessee, Ross of Kansas, Trumbull of Illinois, and Van Winkle of West Virginia. The country and the Republican party itself were placed under the deepest obligation to these men for their courage and independent action. They saved the country from the direst results of the great political scandal of the age, and they saved the Republican party from the commission of a deed which would have destroyed its hold upon the people.

The truth of the whole matter is that, while Mr. Johnson was an unfit person to be President of the United States—which may be also affirmed of some others who have occupied the high place—he was utterly and entirely guiltless of the commission of any crime or misdemeanor. He was

The truth of the matter.

low-born and low-bred, violent in temper, obstinate, coarse, vindictive, and lacking in the sense of propriety, but he was not behind any of his accusers in patriotism and loyalty to the country, and in his willingness to sacrifice every personal advantage for the maintenance of the Union and the preservation of the Government. In fact, most of them were pygmies in these qualities beside him. It is true that he differed with them somewhat in his conception of what measures were for the welfare of the country and what not, but the sequel has shown that he was nearer right than they in this respect.

So soon as the Court of Impeachment pronounced its acquittal of the President, Mr. Stanton addressed to the President a letter announcing his relinquishment of the War Department, and his delivery of the papers and properties thereof to General Townsend, subject to the President's directions.

<small>The abdication of Stanton.</small>

The Senate now confirmed the nomination of General Schofield to be Secretary of War. The General at once accepted the appointment and entered upon the duties of his office, and administered these duties to the end of his term, according to his own testimony, in perfect harmony with the President.

<small>Schofield's confirmation as Secretary of War and his acceptance of the office.</small>

Some of Stanton's friends have tried to make out that but for Stanton's resistance and the impeachment, and its nearness to success, Johnson would have appointed a tool of his own to the War Office and have rode rough-shod over the laws of the land, and that he was frightened out of this purpose, and frightened into an implied agreement with certain Senators and General Schofield that the Reconstruction laws should be executed as Stanton understood them, and not as the President understood them. There is little ground for any such assumptions. There is certainly none in the character of the men whom the President asked to take the War Office, Grant, Sherman and Ewing; and it must be remembered that through Mr. Stanbery, in the case of Mississippi vs. Johnson, he had long before announced to the Southerners that his opposition to the Reconstruction Acts ceased with his unsuccessful veto of them, and that he should execute them both in letter and in spirit. It was Republican Senators who suggested to the President's counsel the nomination of General Schofield, a man entirely friendly with the President and acceptable to him. Neither the President nor the President's counsel approached any Senator with the proposition. It was the Republican Senators who were frightened, rather than the President or his counsel. These Senators knew that the law and the evidence were with the President, and that the Republican party was on trial, as much so as the President; and they knew that, if the Republican Senate should, upon the showing made by the President's counsel of the law and the evidence in the case, convict the President and remove him from office, the party would stand arraigned before the people for having destroyed the constitutional balance between the executive and the legislature in order to gain a partisan end. They recognized the dilemma into which the hot-headed leaders of the party in the House of Representatives had, by their hasty impeachment procedure, brought the party, and they were very much relieved to secure any understanding with the President's counsel whereby the chance of averting the catastrophe to the party, as well as to the country, might be increased. The suspicion that Mr. Stanton was playing his part for the purpose of securing the Republican nomination for the presidency in 1868, rather than from any motives of disinterested patriotism, has about as little foundation as has the theory of salutary terror, produced by the impeachment, controlling the President's subsequent actions against his own preconceived plans and purposes. Both of these speculations are no valid parts of the history of this great transaction. What we have as certain facts are that the judgment was an acquittal, that it was rendered in accordance with law and evidence, and that it preserved the constitutional balance between the executive and the legislature in the governmental system of the country; and that for this the judgment of history coincides with the judgment of the court.

CHAPTER X

RECONSTRUCTION RESUMED

The McCardle Case—The Congressional Acts Admitting the Senators and Representatives elect from the Reconstructed "States" to Seats in Congress—The Veto of these Bills by the President—The Vetoes Overridden—Ratification of the Fourteenth Amendment and the President's Proclamations Declaring Reconstruction Completed — Seward's Proclamation Declaring the Ratification of the Fourteenth Amendment by the Required Number of "States"—The Questions Suggested by Mr. Seward's First Proclamation—The Concurrent Resolution of Congress upon these Questions—The Correct Procedure—The National Conventions of 1868—Platform and Nominees of the Republican Party—Democratic Platform and Nominees—The Election and the Electoral Vote—The Conduct of the President during the Campaign—Congress and the President—The President's Last Annual Message—The President's Amnesty Proclamation of December 25th, 1868—The President's Veto of the Bill in Regard to the Colored Schools in the District of Columbia—The Fifteenth Amendment—Criticism of the Republican View—Johnson's Retirement from the Presidency—The President and the Republican Party.

DURING the period of the impeachment trial, a case was in progress before the Supreme Court of the United States, which in its final settlement was destined to deprive the President of any hope that a judicial decision in regard to the constitutionality of the Reconstruction Acts could ever be attained. We have seen that in the cases of Mississippi vs. Johnson and of Georgia vs. Stanton the President had resisted the jurisdiction of the Court when

The McCardle case.

aimed directly at the Executive and his immediate agents. This was his duty, and he performed it sincerely and successfully. But it is not to be inferred from this that he would not have welcomed a judicial decision from the Supreme Court of the United States pronouncing these Acts null and void, if it could have been reached through the forms of a proper case, one not involving the executive authority at all.

Such a case had appeared in this Court in the winter term of 1867-68, and the argument as to the jurisdiction of the Court, and the decision of this point in the affirmative, had both been made before the impeachment trial began. One William H. McCardle, arrested and held by the military authorities in Mississippi for trial before a military commission on charge of having published in a newspaper, of which he was editor, libellous and incendiary articles, petitioned the Circuit Court of the United States for a writ of Habeas Corpus. The writ was issued, and return was made by the military commander, General A. C. Gillem, admitting the arrest and detention of McCardle, but contending that these acts were lawful. The Circuit Court, on the 25th of November, 1867, remanded McCardle, who had been held in custody between the time of the return to the writ and this date by the United States marshal, to the custody of General Gillem. McCardle then appealed from this judgment of the Circuit Court to the Supreme Court of the United States. Upon a motion to dismiss the appeal, made by the counsel of the military authorities, this Court decided that under the statute of February 5th, 1867, the Supreme Court of the United States could hear the appeal, and denied the motion to dismiss it.

The question was now before the Supreme Court upon its merits, and it involved the constitutionality of the Reconstruction Acts. It was argued very ably, and the part of the Reconstruction Acts putting the districts of the South under martial law two years after the Civil War had ended, and when the civil authority of the United States was everywhere recognized and enforced, was pretty clearly shown to have been a very serious stretching of its powers by Congress, if not a distinct usurpation. The Republicans in Congress were greatly frightened, and while the case was under advisement in the Court, they hastened to repeal the Act of February 5th, 1867, and to make the repeal apply to appeals already taken under that Act, as well as to such as might be attempted in the future. The repealing bill was vetoed by the President on the 25th of March, but it was immediately repassed by the majority necessary to override the veto, repassed without the slightest regard to the President's very sound and convincing objections. This Act of the 27th of March was intended to prevent any decision upon the constitutionality of the Reconstruction Acts, and did do so most effectively, but it was an abominable subterfuge on the part of Congress and a shameful abuse of its powers.

As will be remembered, seven of the ten Southern communities, viz., North Carolina, South Carolina, Georgia, Alabama, Florida, Louisiana, and Arkansas, had already before the close of the impeachment trial ratified the "State" constitutions framed for them by the "carpet-bag, scalawag, negro conventions" held in each for them, had elected "State" officers and legislators, and the legislature of one of them, Arkansas, had ratified the proposed Fourteenth Amendment to the Constitution of the United States, as the legislature of each of them was required to do before it could be admitted to representation in Congress.

Congress now looked upon the work of its hands and pronounced it good, and proceeded to pass the acts, necessary in its conceit, to admit these communities to representation in the legislative houses of the Nation. First came the Act in reference to Arkansas, of the 22d of June, 1868, since, as has been just said, the new legislature of Arkansas had already ratified the proposed Fourteenth Amendment. It provided " that the State of Arkansas is entitled and admitted to representation in Congress, as one of the States of the Union, on the following fundamental condition : That the constitution of Arkansas shall never be so amended or changed as to deprive any citizen, or class of citizens, of the United States of the right to vote who are entitled to vote by the constitution herein recognized, except as a punishment for such crimes as are now felonies at common law, whereof they shall have been duly convicted under laws equally applicable to all the inhabitants of said State : Provided that any alteration of said constitution prospective in its effect may be made in regard to the time and place of residence of voters."

The Congressional Acts admitting the Senators and Representatives elect from the reconstructed "States" to seats in Congress.

Three days later, that is on the 25th, Congress provided in a single act for the admission of the Senators and Representatives from the other six reconstructed "States" to the national legislature in the following language : " *Be it enacted*, &c., That each of the States of North Carolina, South Carolina, Louisiana, Georgia, Alabama, and Florida, shall be entitled and admitted to representation in Congress as a State of the Union when the legislature of such State shall have duly ratified the Amendment to the Constitution of the United States proposed by the Thirty-ninth Congress, and known as Article XIV., upon the following fundamental conditions: That the constitution of neither of said States shall ever be so amended or changed as to deprive any citizen, or class of citizens, of the United States of the right to vote in said State who are entitled to vote by the constitution thereof, herein recognized, except as a punishment for such crimes as are now felonies at common law, whereof they shall have been duly convicted under laws equally applicable to all the inhabitants of said State : *Provided*, that any alteration of said constitutions may be made with regard to the time and place of residence of voters." It was also further provided that the legislature of Georgia should, by solemn public act, declare its assent to the fundamental condition that the article of the new constitution of Georgia prohibiting the courts within the "State" from entertaining any suit against any resident of the "State" for any debt existing prior to June 1st, 1865, and prohibiting the judicial and ministerial officers of the "State" from executing any process in reference to such debts, should be considered and treated as null and void.

The President had placed his veto on both of these bills. The veto of the Arkansas bill bears the date of June 20th, and that of the other bill bears the date of June 25th. There are parts of the President's argument which are entirely convincing to any candid mind at the present day. He pointed out that the fundamental condition imposed by Congress, in all these cases, upon the admission of Senators and Representatives to Congress, viz., that no change should ever be made in the suffrage qualifications provided in these "State" constitutions whereby any citizen or class of citizens of the United States having the right to vote under these constitutions should be deprived of such right, was an assumption of power by Congress to regulate a subject, within the "States," which by the

<small>The veto of these bills by the President.</small>

existing Constitution of the United States belonged exclusively to the "States," to each "State" for itself.

There can be no question that the President was entirely correct in this contention. The Fifteenth Amendment was as yet no part of the Constitution. It had not even been proposed by Congress to the "States." It is very questionable whether a majority in Congress could have been found, at that time, in favor of making such a proposition, much less the required extraordinary majority of two-thirds. And until the Fifteenth Amendment had been ratified as a part of the Constitution of the United States, Congress had no power to exact such a concession, or anything like it, from any "State" as the price of the admission of representatives from it to the Houses of the National Legislature. And even since the Fifteenth Amendment has become a part of the Constitution, the Government of the United States cannot prohibit such changes in a "State" constitution, unless the deprivation of suffrage is made on account of race, color, or previous condition of servitude.

The President also called attention to the fact that no way was provided in the bills whereby the "States" should signify their acceptance of this "fundamental condition" of admission to representation in Congress, and that no penalty was prescribed for a violation of the condition. Did Congress mean that, in case of any violation of its "fundamental condition," it would throw the "State" back under martial law, and proceed to reconstruct anew? That was a question which might well be asked in view of what Congress had already done; and it was a question which was not calculated to allay uneasiness in the minds of the people in the Southern communities.

Finally, in the veto of the Arkansas bill, the President expressed his very serious doubts whether the new "State" constitution had been ratified by the electorate created by the Acts of Congress for that purpose, since a section in that constitution prescribed that no person would be allowed to vote upon the ratification of the constitution who had not previously taken an oath to the effect "that he accepted the doctrine of the civil and political equality of all men, and agreed not to attempt to deprive any person or persons, on account of race, color, or previous condition, of any political or civil right, privilege or immunity enjoyed by any other class of men," thus adding a new qualification for registration and voting to those prescribed in the Reconstruction Acts of Congress. There is no question that the President was right about this, too. And there is no question that this new qualification was entirely null and void, in so far as it applied to voting upon, and registering to vote upon, the ratification of the constitution itself, unless we ascribe constituent power to the convention which framed the constitution, instead of the power of initiation only. We know that no constitutional convention has, or then had, any such powers in our system. It was nothing more or less than a palpable usurpation of constituent power when the convention in Arkansas presumed to add this qualification to those prescribed by Congress for voting upon the ratification of the constitution itself. Of course it would have been lawful and regular for the "State" constitution to make this additional requirement for voting in all future elections, after the constitution prescribing it should have been adopted by the electorate created by the Congressional Acts, although the requirement itself would have been unreasonable and oppressive. But for the convention, a mere proposing body, to ordain this new qualification for voting on the question of the adoption of the constitution itself was a political outrage of the first order.

Congress was not, however, in a state of mind to listen to any suggestions from the President, no matter how correct and important they might be. Both Houses promptly, almost mockingly, passed the two bills over the President's vetoes.

The vetoes overridden.

Such of the legislatures created under the new "State" constitutions as were not already in session were quickly summoned to assemble, and by July 21st all of them had ratified the proposed Fourteenth Amendment to the Constitution of the United States, and the legislature of Georgia had also pledged by solemn act that the repudiation article of the new constitution should never be enforced. By July 27th the President had issued his several proclamations, as required by the Act of June 25th, announcing the ratification of the proposed Fourteenth Amendment by these legislatures, and consequently the admission of these "States" to representation in Congress; and so far as the seven "States" of Arkansas, North Carolina, South Carolina, Georgia, Alabama, Florida and Louisiana were concerned the work of reconstruction was now completed. Virginia, Mississippi and Texas still remained under martial law.

Ratification of the Fourteenth Amendment and the President's proclamations declaring Reconstruction completed.

On the 28th day of July, Mr. Seward, the Secretary of State, issued his proclamation, declaring the ratification of the proposed Fourteenth Amendment to the Constitution of the United States by the legislatures of thirty States of the Union, and its consequent validity as a part of the Constitution of the United States.

Seward's proclamation declaring the ratification of the Fourteenth Amendment by the required number of "States."

Eight days before this proclamation, that is on the 20th, Mr. Seward had issued a proclamation declaring that the legislatures of twenty-three States, viz., of Connecticut, New Hampshire, Tennessee, New Jersey, Oregon, Vermont, New York, Ohio, Illinois, West Virginia, Kansas, Maine, Nevada, Missouri, Indiana, Minnesota, Rhode Island, Wisconsin, Pennsylvania, Michigan, Massachusetts, Nebraska and Iowa, had ratified the proposed Fourteenth Amendment, and that six "newly-constituted and newly-established bodies avowing themselves to be, and acting as, the legislatures, respectively, of the States of Arkansas, Florida, North Carolina, Louisiana, South Carolina, and Alabama" had also ratified it; that the legislatures of Ohio and New Jersey had subsequently passed resolutions withdrawing their ratification of the Amendment; and that, if these latter resolutions of the legislatures of Ohio and New Jersey should be disregarded, the proposed Fourteenth Amendment had been adopted by the legislatures of twenty-nine of the thirty-seven "States" of the Union and had thus become a valid part of the Constitution of the United States. *The questions suggested by Mr. Seward's first proclamation.*

Besides the question expressed in this Proclamation, Mr. Seward indicates by his language a further question, viz., whether the six "newly-constituted and newly-established bodies, avowing themselves to be, and acting as, the legislatures, respectively, of the States of Arkansas, Florida, North Carolina, Louisiana, South Carolina, and Alabama" were genuine "State" legislatures. They were the legislatures established under the Reconstruction Acts of Congress, but as Congress had refused to recognize the "States" for whom these bodies acted as entitled to representation in Congress, that is as "States" having the rights of "States" of the Union, until after these bodies had ratified the proposed Fourteenth Amendment to the Constitution of the United States, it was no wonder that so good a constitutional lawyer and so logical a thinker as Mr. Seward had his doubts as to whether these bodies were genuine "State" legislatures.

In order to quiet these doubts, if possible, the two Houses of Congress passed on the following day, July 21st, the following concurrent resolution:

<small>The concurrent resolution of Congress upon these questions.</small>

"Whereas the legislatures of the States of Connecticut, Tennessee, *New Jersey*, Oregon, Vermont, West Virginia, Kansas, Missouri, Indiana, *Ohio*, Illinois, Minnesota, New York, Wisconsin, Pennsylvania, Rhode Island, Michigan, Nevada, New Hampshire, Massachusetts, Nebraska, Maine, Iowa, *Arkansas, Florida, North Carolina, Alabama, South Carolina* and *Louisiana*, being three-fourths and more of the several States of the Union, have ratified the Fourteenth Article of Amendment to the Constitution of the United States, duly proposed by two-thirds of each House of the Thirty-ninth Congress; therefore, Resolved by the Senate (the House of Representatives concurring), That said Fourteenth Article is hereby declared to be a part of the Constitution of the United States, and it shall be duly promulgated as such by the Secretary of State." Upon the basis of this resolution, which decided, in so far as Congress can decide, that the consent of the legislature of a "State" to a proposed amendment to the Constitution of the United States cannot be withdrawn when once given, and that the "newly-constituted and newly-established bodies, avowing themselves to be, and acting as, the legislatures, respectively, of the States of Arkansas, Florida, North Carolina, Louisiana, South Carolina, and Alabama" were genuine "State" legislatures qualified to vote upon the ratification of a proposed amendment to the Constitution of the United States, Mr. Seward issued his proclamation of the 28th of July, above recited. As the Georgia Legislature ratified the proposed amendment on the 21st inst. and also gave its pledge not to allow the repudiation article in its constitution to be enforced, Mr. Seward included Georgia in this last proclamation.

It will be seen that both Mr. Seward and Congress counted all of the Southern communities which had ever been "States" as being "States," making the whole number of "States" thirty-seven, and the number necessary for ratification of the amendment twenty-eight. Upon this basis of calculation two more than the necessary number had ratified at the date of Mr. Seward's final proclamation. It will also be seen that both Mr. Seward and Congress, that is that both the legislative and executive departments of the Government, ignored the attempt of Ohio and New Jersey to withdraw their consent to the amendment, and fixed the precedent in the constitutional practice of the United States that a "State" legislature cannot reconsider its ratification of an amendment to the Constitution of the United States at any time. This means, when scientifically appreciated, that the ratification of an amendment to the Constitution of the United States is not an agreement between the "States," and therefore becomes valid as to each only after three-fourths of the "States," the constitutional number necessary to make the proposed amendment a valid part of the Constitution, shall have ratified it, but that ratification by a "State" legislature, and *a fortiori* by a convention of the people within a "State," is only an indirect vote of a part of the people of the United States upon a question submitted to the suffrages of the whole people of the United States. When, therefore, this affirmative vote has been once officially announced by the proper authorities within the "State" to the proper authorities of the United States there is no further control over it by the authorities within the "State."

If, however, the votes of Ohio and New Jersey had not been counted in the affirmative, there was still a three-fourths majority of thirty-seven "States" in favor of ratification. And if the ten Southern communities had been left out of the computation altogether, which would have made the Union to consist, so far as that part of it erected into "States" was concerned, of twenty-seven "States," there would still have been more than a three-fourths majority in favor of ratification, with or without Ohio and New Jersey. The correct procedure, from a scientific point of view, would undoubtedly have been to have computed the necessary majority upon the basis of twenty-seven "States," to have included Ohio and New Jersey among the "States" whose legislatures voted for ratification, and then to have admitted the ten Southern communities as "States" under the Constitution of the United States, *with the Fourteenth Amendment as an already established part of it*, concerning which they had no more to say than they had in regard to any other part of the Constitution. But, however that may be, no objection can be made to the validity of the Fourteenth Amendment on the ground of the majority by which it was ratified. In whatever way we may compute the whole number of "States" and the majority voting in the affirmative, the Amendment was lawfully ratified.

During these movements in execution of the Reconstruction Acts, the national party conventions for the nomination of candidates for the presidency and for the formation of platforms were held. That of the

Republican party assembled first, on the twenty-first day of May in Chicago, at the moment when its radical elements were filled with rage and chagrin at the failure of the impeachment of the President.

The national conventions of 1868.

It made General Joseph R. Hawley, of Connecticut, its presiding officer; adopted a platform, a large part of which was devoted to denunciation of the President, to the promise of bountiful pensions, and to a twist of the British lion's tail on the subject of expatriation; the main principles of which, however, were good faith in the payment of the public debt with sound money, and equal suffrage by Congressional law in the Southern communities; and nominated Grant and Colfax for the presidency and the vice-presidency.

Platform and nominees of the Republican party.

In pronouncing for the guaranty of negro suffrage at the South by Congressional law, the platform attempted to steer clear of the prejudices against negro suffrage at the North by a sort of proviso, which read, "While the question of suffrage in all the loyal States properly belongs to the people of those States." This was certainly inconsistent, not to say hypocritical. Negro suffrage at the North would have been a comparatively harmless thing on account of the fewness of the negroes as compared with the whites in that section, and on account of the superior average intelligence of the negroes of the North when compared with that of those of the South. There was no sound principle in this article of the platform. It was a mean, shuffling bit of partisan politics. The party itself felt it to be so in the course of the campaign, and came out finally for the settlement of the whole question of negro suffrage upon the same basis for the whole country and by means of a constitutional amendment.

The nominees immediately accepted their nominations in characteristic letters, that of General Grant being short, crisp, modest and ending with the now famous sentence: "Let us have peace," and that of Colfax being more lengthy and wordy and containing a rhetorical defence of some of the more questionable parts of the platform.

The Democratic convention assembled in New York on the 4th day of July. It was confronted at the start with the Greenback heresy, and the candidacy of the Greenback champion for the presidency, Mr. George H. Pendleton of Ohio.

Democratic platform and nominees.

This heresy was in a sentence the doctrine that all the public debt of the United States not made expressly payable in coin should be paid in United States paper, which Congress might order to be stamped, issued, and made legal tender, to any amount it might please. The shibboleth was, "the same currency for the bond-holder and the plough-holder." It had taken firm hold in Ohio, and was rapidly spreading through the valley of the Mississippi. The Eastern Democrats, however, looked upon it with disfavor, and were determined to defeat the nomination of Mr. Pendleton. They were obliged, however, to accept the platform, in so far as it related to this subject, as dictated by their Western compatriots. The third plank in the platform read, ". . . and where the obligations of the Government do not expressly state upon their face, or the law under which they were issued does not provide, that they shall be paid in coin, they ought in right and in justice to be paid in the lawful money of the United States." The fifth plank also read, "one currency for the Government and the people, the laborer and the officeholder, the pensioner and the soldier, the producer and the bondholder." It is true that the platform did not expressly pronounce in favor of an unlimited issue of paper money with which to pay the bonds, but it was generally understood that this was what was meant. The questions then of sound money and of the faithful discharge of the public obligations were thus put in issue. The Democrats also met squarely the Republican doctrine of Reconstruction. They demanded the "immediate restoration of all the States to their rights in the Union under the Constitution, and of civil government to the American people," with "amnesty for all past political offences, and the regulation of the election franchise in the States by their citizens." And they denounced the Radical party, as they termed the Republicans, "for its disregard of right, and the unparalleled oppression and tyranny which have marked its career," declared the Reconstruction Acts to be unconstitutional, revolutionary and void, and lauded President Johnson for his unflinching resistance to "the aggressions of Congress upon the constitutional rights of the States and the people."

There is no question that the platform of the Democrats, with its paper money doctrine, and its hostility to Reconstruction and universal suffrage, was a shaky foundation for any party to attempt to stand upon at that juncture. *Weakness of the platform.* Not much conscience and not much sentiment could be aroused with such tenets. Conscience and sentiment were much more amenable to the appeals of the Republican platform upon these points. Moreover, the tremendous popularity of the Republican candidates had to be reckoned with. Where could the Democrats find a candidate who would both match Grant in the popular affection and overbalance also the weakness of the platform? The New Yorkers in the convention, led by Seymour, Tilden, Schell and Kernan, had their man for this emergency, but they dared not reveal at the outset their plan. They were resolved to nominate Chief Justice Chase. They thought that Chase's well-known devotion to the principles of universal suffrage and his career as Secretary of the Treasury would satisfy the Eastern men in regard to the platform, and that his attachment to the principles of civil government versus militarism would, in some degree at least, neutralize the popularity of the military hero. The delegates from Ohio, Mr. Chase's own "State," suspected the purpose of the New Yorkers, and were determined to foil it. If they could not get Pendleton, they were determined not to have Chase. After the first six ballots without result, Pendleton, however, leading, the New Yorkers brought forward Hendricks of Indiana, in order to break down Pendleton's vote. Having succeeded in this after some six more ballots, the name of Chase was brought before the convention by a half vote from California. The purpose was probably to feel of the convention. It was highly successful. The announcement of the half vote was received with enthusiastic applause. Masking themselves behind Hancock, who was at that juncture in the lead, and Hendricks, the New Yorkers now prepared to present Chase; but the Ohioans were too quick for them. They succeeded in withdrawing Pendleton and presenting Seymour himself as their candidate, before the New Yorkers knew what they were about. Seymour, who was occupying the presidency of the convention, declared from his seat that he could not accept, but the Ohioans stuck to their nomination, and the New Yorkers had to assent. They were fairly caught in their own net.

Seymour finally yielded, and the convention addressed itself to the nomination of its candidate for the vice-presidency. The ex-Confederate General William Preston of

Kentucky presented the name of the noted Union General Francis P. Blair of Missouri for the place. The nomination was seconded by the ex-Confederate General Wade Hampton of South Carolina, and was made by acclamation. *The nominees.* While General Blair was a noted Union soldier of high ability and undoubted loyalty, he was a fierce enemy of the Reconstruction Acts of Congress, and was for this reason very popular with the ex-Confederates. In an open letter to Colonel J. O. Brodhead of St. Louis, written five days before the assembly of the Democratic convention, he not only denounced the Reconstruction Acts as unconstitutional, but advanced a method for getting rid of them and their effects in case a Democratic President should be elected. He proposed that the new President should " declare these Acts null and void, compel the army to undo its usurpations at the South, disperse the carpet bag State governments, allow the white people to reorganize their own governments, and elect Senators and Representatives." He said, further, that the House of Representatives would contain a majority of Democrats from the North, who would admit the members elected to that body from the South to seats, and that the House with the President would exert such a pressure on the Senate as to cause the doors of that body to be opened to the members from the Southern " States." When General Blair wrote this letter he was being spoken of as a candidate for the presidency, and this letter was taken as the declaration of what he would do if elected to the position of Chief Magistrate of the nation. After his nomination for the vice-presidency, in his speech and letter of acceptance, he announced the chief issue in the contest to be the relief of the South from martial law and negro domination. The ex-Confederates represented it the same way at the South, and threw themselves into the campaign with great enthusiasm for Seymour and Blair.

On the other hand, the bland, politic and persuasive Seymour pursued a much more moderate and conciliatory course, and when it became evident that General Blair's violent expressions and revolutionary purposes were ruining the Democratic prospects at the North, he went into the campaign personally, and by his diplomatic manners and fine oratory succeeded in stemming the tide which, running against the Democrats from the moment when their platform was proclaimed, had been driven on to a flood by General Blair's indiscretions, to put it very mildly, in speech and conduct. But while some lost ground was regained, it was evident that the hopes of the Democrats had been blasted.

The electoral votes of thirty-four "States" were counted, Virginia, Mississippi and Texas being still regarded by Congress as unreconstructed. Of these thirty-four, eight cast their votes for Seymour and Blair. These were New York, New Jersey, Delaware, Maryland, Kentucky, Oregon, Georgia and Louisiana. The rest went for Grant and Colfax. The electoral vote stood eighty for Seymour and Blair and two hundred and fourteen for Grant and Colfax. The popular vote stood two millions seven hundred and three thousand two hundred and forty-nine for Seymour and Blair, and three millions and twelve thousand eight hundred and thirty-three for Grant and Colfax. The exclusion of Virginia, Mississippi and Texas from the vote and the inclusion of the suffrages of the "carpet-baggers" and the negroes, under the protection of the military, in the reconstructed "States," had saved the day for Grant and Colfax. If the electorate of the South had been as in 1860, or probably as it was in the years of the Johnson governments, Seymour and Blair would have triumphed. As it was, but for the Greenback plank in the Democratic platform and the indiscretions of General Blair, they might have triumphed. [That is to say, if the Reconstruction policy of Congress had been the sole issue, it is quite possible that the Republicans would have lost the election, even with the most popular man in the North as their standard bearer.]

Meanwhile the President had continued to ply the Congress with his vetoes and messages and to address the country with his proclamations. He had thought that he ought to be vindicated by being nominated by the Democrats for the presidency, and had actually received sixty-five votes on the first ballot. His failure before the convention ought to have taught him that he was no longer a factor to be reckoned with in the domain of politics, and that his proper course was to execute quietly the functions of his office to the end of his term, and then retire to private life. But he seemed to think that his political opinions were still of great value, and in a very few days after the adjournment of the Democratic convention he addressed a message to Congress advising a most radical change in the structure of the government by means of constitutional amendment. He therein recommended that Congress should propose to the "States" so to amend the Constitution as to provide for the election of the President and Vice-President by a direct vote of the people, for the ineligibility of these officers for a second term, for the designation of the members of the Cabinet in a certain order, beginning with the Secretary of State, as the persons to discharge the duties of the President in case of a vacancy in the presidential office by the death, resignation or removal of both the President and the Vice-President, for the election of the Senators by the direct vote of the people,

The conduct of the President during the campaign.

and for the limitation of the terms of the United States judges to a period of years. There was sound reason for the third of these suggestions, the designation by the Constitution of the Cabinet officers in a certain order as the successors to the powers and duties of the President, when the country might be without both a President and a Vice-President, and it has since then been made law under the form of a statute of Congress.

But the Congress was not then in a mood to hear anything from Mr. Johnson. Two days later, July 20th, the President vetoed the joint resolution passed by the two Houses, excluding from the electoral college in the coming presidential election the votes of "States" lately in rebellion which should not have been reorganized under the Reconstruction Acts of Congress. In this veto he went over his whole argument once more against the constitutionality of these Acts and in favor of his own method of Reconstruction. But the Congress treated the message with contempt and promptly repassed the resolution.

Congress and the President.

On the 9th of December President Johnson sent his last annual Message to Congress. It was a grave, dignified and statesmanlike document both in form and content. In it he told Congress plainly and respectfully that its Reconstruction policy had arrayed the races against each other at the South, had impaired, if not destroyed, the kindly relations that had previously existed between them, and had given mortal offence to the civilized race by placing the uncivilized race in domination over it; and he urged that legislation which had produced such baleful consequences ought to be abrogated. He also told Congress that it had seriously impaired the power of the President to exact the necessary accountability of the public officers by its Tenure-of-Office Act, and had embarrassed

The President's last annual Message.

the Executive in the exercise of his constitutional military functions by the Act of March 2d, 1867; and he urged the repeal of both of these measures. He also gave a most serious and startling account of the condition of the public finances, and of the consumption of the wealth of the Nation by the bondholders, officials and pensioners. He pointed out that the public debt, which in 1860 was 64,000,000 dollars, had become 2,527,129,552 dollars; that the annual expenditure, which was, in 1860, 63,000,000 dollars, had become 336,000,000 dollars and more, and that the expenditure per capita, which was two dollars in 1860, had become nearly ten dollars. And he suggested the ways in which this threatening condition might be relieved, viz., by a refunding of the bonds at a lower interest, by a speedy resumption of specie payment, by a reduction of the army and of the horde of Reconstruction officials in the South, and by a strict accountability of the revenue officials to their superiors and of these latter to the President. From the point of view of sound political science, good public policy and true patriotism all of these suggestions were at least worth consideration, but Congress took no more notice of them than it did of the distant murmurs of the waters of the Potomac.

Only once again did the Congress break over its apparent resolve to ignore the President, and that was upon the occasion of his issue of his universal and unconditional pardon and amnesty to all persons who had participated, either directly or indirectly, in the rebellion, with the restoration of all their rights, privileges and immunities under the Constitution and the laws made in pursuance thereof. The date of this document was December 25th, 1868. On the 5th of January, 1869, the Senate called him to account for this by a res-

<small>The President's amnesty proclamation of December 25th, 1868.</small>

olution calling upon him "to transmit to the Senate a copy of any proclamation of amnesty made by him since the last adjournment of Congress, and also to communicate to the Senate by what authority of law the same was made." The President replied on the 18th, sending a copy of his proclamation of December 25th, 1868, and declaring that he issued it by authority of the second section of Article second of the Constitution, which vested in the President the power to grant reprieves and pardons for offences against the United States, except in cases of impeachment, and in accordance with precedents established by his predecessors in office, Washington, Adams, Madison and Lincoln. The Senate did not say that he had no right to claim any constitutional prerogative, and that he was not worthy to act under precedents set by Washington, Adams, Madison, and Lincoln, but most of the Senators evidently so thought. The proclamation had no effect upon the qualifications for suffrage in the face of the Reconstruction Acts and the "State" constitutions framed and established in accordance with them. It was little more than the bull against the comet.

As a sort of final stroke the President vetoed the bill concerning the transfer of the control of the colored schools in the District of Columbia, and the bill for raising the duties on imported copper and copper ores. He gave excellent reasons for both of these vetoes, but Congress had long ceased to be guided by reason in matters which related to the President.

<small>The President's veto of the Bill in regard to the colored schools in the District of Columbia.</small>

On its side it was busy with a project which, though not intended as a blow at him particularly, was not in accordance with his view that the regulation of the suffrage within the "States" was, and should be, left to the "States" respectively, and exclusively, viz., the proposed Fifteenth Amendment to the Constitution. Reference has already been made to the inconsistent doctrine, we might almost say the timorous subterfuge, of the Republican platform on the matter of negro suffrage, and to the growing conviction on the part of the Republicans during the campaign that this question must be settled for the entire county alike, and by a constitutional amendment. At the opening of Congress in December, and during the first days of the session, the proposition was presented which finally took on the form given it by the conference committee of the two Houses in the words: "The right of citizens of the United States to vote shall not be denied or abridged by the United States or by any State on account of race, color, or previous condition of servitude. The Congress shall have power to enforce this article by appropriate legislation." It was passed by both Houses with the requisite two-thirds majority on the 26th of February and sent to the legislatures of the "States" for ratification. The Republicans had at last come to the view that the emancipation of the freedmen involved their civil equality with the whites, and that such equality could not be maintained unless they possessed the elective franchise, and that it was cowardly for the "States" of the North to force negro suffrage on the South without accepting it for themselves.

The Fifteenth Amendment.

It is certainly true that full freedom implies civil liberty and civil equality, but there was another way, and a better way, to have secured these than by the immediate and universal suffrage of the newly emancipated in all their ignorance, immorality and poverty, and that was by the nationalization of civil liberty, and its protection and enforcement by the United States courts. Most of the Repub-

Criticism of the Republican view.

licans believed, at that moment, that that had been secured by the Fourteenth Amendment; and there can be little question that a very important consideration with such was the fear that after Reconstruction should be accomplished, the Southern "States" might amend negro suffrage out of their "State" constitutions, and thus destroy the Republican party in these "States," unless the Constitution of the United States should be so amended as to prevent it. The most radical among them were no doubt moved chiefly by the extravagant humanitarianism of the period, which had developed in their minds to the point of justifying not only the political equality of the races, but the political superiority, at least in loyalty to the Union, the Constitution and republican government, of the uncivilized negroes over the whites of the South; but that this conviction was not very strong among the masses of them can be readily concluded from the fact that that party is to-day the party which is following the European idea of the duty of civilized races to impose their political sovereignty upon uncivilized, or half civilized, or not fully civilized, races anywhere and everywhere in the world. No party can, in so short a time, so completely change its fundamental principle of political ethics when it is really and conscientiously believed in by the masses of the party.

This proposed Fifteenth Amendment was not sent to the President for his approval, but went, according to the custom, to the Secretary of State, to be submitted to the "State" legislatures. The President was now within a very few days of the end of his term. His sun had fairly set, and the disrespect felt for him by the members of the dominant party in Congress and out of Congress was expressed in the rude and quite unprecedented refusal of General Grant to sit in the same carriage with him in the pro-

Johnson's retirement from the presidency.

cession from the White House to the Capitol, on the 4th of March, for the ceremonies of the inauguration of the new President. Discredited, despised, and scoffed at, as a traitor to his party, to his political creed, and to his country, Mr. Johnson stepped down from the high office which he had occupied during one of the two most critical periods in American history since the establishment of the present Constitution.

[And yet it is certainly true that the Republican party had left him rather than that he had left the party. This party began simply as a Union party and an anti-slavery extension party. Mr. Johnson, an original Democrat, joined with the Republicans upon this basis, and he never left it.] On the other hand, when the necessities of the war for the Union made it evident that the slaves within the Southern communities which had declared secession, and were engaged in rebellion, must be proclaimed free, Mr. Johnson still went with the Republicans in the justification of this measure. And when, finally, the war was ended and the Union was preserved, and the Republicans decided that the legitimate outcome of the victory was the prohibition of slavery everywhere within the United States by an amendment to the Constitution, Mr. Johnson still marched with them, at the head of the column. [It was only when they became more and more radical in their policy, and insisted upon transforming rather than restoring the "States" of the South, by placing civil rights under national protection instead of "State" protection, disfranchising the whites of the South, and enfranchising the negroes, and upon overcoming the Executive's objections to these movements not simply by overriding the veto, but by generally subordinating the Executive to Congress — it was only then that he

The President and the Republican party.

separated from them and fell back naturally on such support as he could get, which was chiefly from the Democratic party.

No fair mind can claim that the Republicans in their quarrel with the President had not departed from their solemn declaration made in Congress assembled in those dark July days of 1861, just after the first great defeat of the Union arms, "That this war is not waged upon our part in any spirit of oppression, nor for any purpose of conquest or subjugation, nor purpose of overthrowing or interfering with the rights or established institutions of the Southern States, but to defend and maintain the supremacy of the Constitution, and to preserve the Union, with all the dignity, equality, and rights of the several States unimpaired." And it was upon the basis of this understanding that the Democrats in Congress, Mr. Johnson among them, stood with the Republicans in the prosecution of the war. It is indeed a serious question of political casuistry as to how far declarations of policy are binding upon a political party. They are certainly not like agreements entered into between sovereign states, and the law of development rather than the law of contract must be the constructive force in party creed. But this, at least, must be held, viz., that a man originally not of a given political party, but acting with it upon the basis of a given creed, cannot be accused of being an apostate from that party if he does not continue with it when it adopts a new creed in many respects the very opposite of that given creed, except in the most groveling sense of machine politics; and that when he and it do part company, more by its own departures from the given creed than by his, he is certainly not on that account to be necessarily considered as a traitor to his country. The truth is, that while all men who occupy high station are peculiarly subject to wanton, as well as ignorant, assaults upon their purposes and their conduct, [few men that have occupied so high a station have ever been so unreasonably slandered and vilified as Andrew Johnson. His own unfortunate and irritating manners and methods will account for a good deal of the misunderstanding of his character, but the violence of the times was the occasion of a great deal more of it. The true Union men of Tennessee will, however, never forget the hope, and encouragement, and support which he gave to them, when they were left in the lurch by their own natural leader, John Bell; and the Nation should for this, if nothing else, write his name in the book of its heroes.]

CHAPTER XI

PRESIDENT GRANT AND RECONSTRUCTION

The Situation at the Moment of Grant's Accession to Power—The Georgia Question—The Attitude of the New President toward Reconstruction—The Virginia Case—Grant's Message to Congress of April 7th, 1868, and His Proclamation of May 14th—Ratification of the Virginia Constitution and Election of "State" Officers under it—The Restoration of Virginia to Her Federal Relations—Ratification of the Mississippi Constitution and Election of " State " Officers and Legislative Members under it—The Restoration of Mississippi to Her Federal Relations—Ratification of the Texas Constitution and Election of " State " Officers and Legislative Members under it—Restoration of Texas to Her Federal Relations—Grant and the Tenure-of-Office Act — Congress and the Tenure-of-Office Act after Grant's Accession to the Presidency—The Modification of the Tenure-of-Office Act—The President's Dissatisfaction with the Measure — The Facts in the Georgia Case — New Conditions Imposed on Georgia—The Final Restoration of Georgia to Her Federal Relations—Negro Rule in the South from the Point of View of Political Science and Ethnical Principle.

AT the moment of Grant's accession to power, four of the Southern communities were still denied recognition as "States" upon the floor of Congress. Three of the four had not yet adopted "State" constitutions, viz.: Virginia, Mississippi and Texas; and the fourth, Georgia, the representatives from which to the lower House of Congress had been admitted in December of 1868, was still unrepresented in the Senate, for the reason that the legislature of Georgia, after electing United States Senators,

The situation at the moment of Grant's accession to power.

had rejected the negro members-elect of that body on the ground that negroes were not eligible to legislative seats in Georgia.

When the news of this procedure reached Washington, the Senate held back from admitting the Senators-elect from Georgia to seats and did not admit them during the last session of the Fortieth Congress; and at the opening of the Forty-first Congress, on March 4th, 1869, the day of Grant's inauguration, one of the first acts of the respective Houses was to refuse admittance to the representatives from Georgia to *either House*, and to refer their credentials to the Committee of each House on Elections. *The Georgia question.*

In his inaugural Address the new President made no reference to these questions, but he had hardly been one month in the presidential office before he recognized the difficulties with which his predecessor had been beset, and asked and almost demanded of Congress relief from them. On the 7th day of April he addressed a message to Congress requesting that body to provide for submitting to the voters of Virginia the "State" constitution drafted and adopted by a constitutional convention at Richmond nearly a year before, and recommending that "a separate vote be taken upon such parts as might be thought expedient," and that the constitution, "*or such parts thereof as shall have been adopted by the people,*" should be submitted to Congress on the first Monday of the following December, and that the officers provided for under the said constitution should be chosen at the same election. *The attitude of the new President toward Reconstruction.*

The President also suggested that the constitution framed by the convention in Mississippi and rejected by the voters might be resubmitted in the same way. The events in Mississippi culminating in the rejection of the proposed State constitution by the voters in June of 1868 have been already related.

The case of Virginia, on the other hand, which differed in several material respects from that of any of the others, has not been as yet sufficiently stated for a clear understanding of the President's meaning in his recommendations to Congress of April 7th. It will be remembered that a loyal government of Virginia, with its seat first at Wheeling and then at Alexandria, existed during the entire period of the Civil War, and that from 1861 to 1864 Virginia, under this government, had been represented in Congress, and that it was this government which consented to the partition of Virginia recognized by Congress. On the 23d day of May, 1865, this government transferred itself from Alexandria to Richmond, having been recognized by President Johnson on May 9th as the true government of Virginia. The legislative department of it met in session on the 20th of June following. The Governor, Mr. Pierpont, recommended, in his message to that body, that a constitutional amendment should be drafted, and proposed by it to the voters for ratification, which would enfranchise, and qualify for office, a much larger proportion of the people than was the case under the revised constitution of Virginia of 1864, adopted by the loyal convention at Alexandria. The legislature followed the Governor's advice and proposed an amendment to the voters which granted suffrage and eligibility substantially to the old ante-bellum electorate and eligibles on the condition of future loyalty to the United States. This proposition was voted on at the elections held on the 12th of October for the choice of members of the legislature and of the lower House of Congress, and was ratified by a large majority. The election was held in every county and the result was fairly representative of the people. There was lacking but one thing more for the complete restoration of the "State" to its federal relations, viz., the admission of the Senators and Representatives from it to seats in Congress. They presented themselves at the opening of the Congressional session on the first Monday of December following, and were excluded, along with the Senators and Representatives from the other "Johnson States," by the Stevens resolution.

For more than a year, however, this government continued to act as the "State" government of Virginia, under the limitations placed upon it by the presence of the military of the United States, and the interference of the commanding general in behalf of the freedmen. On January 15th, 1866, the legislature chosen at the October elections of the preceding year passed the vagrant act, which defined as vagrants "all persons who, not having wherewith to maintain themselves and their families, live idly and without employment, and refuse to work for the usual and common wages given to the laborers in the like work in the place where they are," and which authorized the condemned vagrant to be hired out, and his wages applied to his own use or the use of his family, and, in case of his running away from the hirer, to be apprehended on the warrant of a justice and returned to the hirer, who should have one month of service extra, and without wages, for the interruption of the service contracted for, and other trouble and expense, and should also have the right, by permission of the justice, to work the returned vagrant with ball and chain, in order to prevent a repetition of his flight. On the 24th, just nine days after the passage of the act, General Terry, the military commander at Richmond, issued an order setting aside this measure as to the freedmen. He based his order on the *The Vagrant Act.*

tendency of the statute to influence employers to combine for the purpose of lowering the wages of the freedmen to a point that would pauperize them and drive them into vagrancy; and create thus the very situation which, under the operation of the measure, would lead to a species of servitude worse than the old domestic slavery. He had no reliable facts of experience upon which to base his theory. It was a bit of political and economic prophecy on his part. It was sufficient, however, to call down maledictions from the Congress at Washington and the people of the North upon the legislature at Richmond and the people of Virginia and of the South generally.

<small>General Terry's order setting aside the Vagrant Act.</small>

Congress, however, gave this legislature one more opportunity to redeem itself. The proposed Fourteenth Amendment to the Constitution of the United States was submitted to it for ratification in June of 1866. After long deliberation upon it, the legislature rejected it on the 9th of January, 1867. This act sealed the fate of that legislature. Virginia was brought, with the other Southern communities which had rejected or not adopted the proposed Amendment, under the Reconstruction Acts of March, 1867, and became the first military district under those Acts, with General Schofield as commander. Schofield ordered the election for delegates to a constitutional convention, by the voters designated in the Reconstruction Acts, to be held in November of 1867, and ordered the delegates so elected to assemble in Richmond on the 3d of the following December. These orders were successfully executed under the supervision and control of the military. Schofield himself appeared in the convention, and urged the delegates to be moderate in the propositions for the disfranchisement and disqualification of those who had participated in rebellion. But the delegates

<small>Virginia made a Military District.</small>

PRESIDENT GRANT AND RECONSTRUCTION 227

elected under the Reconstruction Acts, and by the electorate created through them, were not only radical, but bent upon retaliation. They would not listen to the wise counsel of Schofield, but drafted and adopted such provisions in regard to suffrage qualifications and eligibility to office and mandate as would have put the "State" government, based on such a constitution, in the hands of negroes, "scalawags" and "carpet-bag" adventurers. The opposition to these provisions on the part of the commander and the Administration at Washington was, however, sufficiently effective to delay indefinitely the submission of the constitution to the voters. Near the end of the year 1868, a conference of prominent Virginians assembled at Richmond and appointed a committee, and sent its members to Washington to petition Congress to allow the disfranchising and disqualifying clauses, and the clauses in reference to county organization, to be voted on separately from the other parts of the proposed constitution. This committee proceeded to Washington in January of 1869, and argued their case before committees of both of the Houses of Congress, and also presented the same to the new President-elect, General Grant.

It was in consequence of such representations and prayers, that President Grant sent his message of April 7th to Congress, requesting authority to accede to the petition of the Virginians, and that Congress immediately conferred the authority upon him. Armed with this authority, the President issued a proclamation on the 14th day of May, 1869, commanding the "State" constitution framed for Virginia by the convention which assembled on December 3d, 1867, at Richmond, to be submitted to the voters, on July 6th, 1869, for ratification or rejection, and also commanding that those pro-

Grant's message to Congress of April 7th, 1868, and his proclamation of May 14th.

visions disqualifying persons from voting and holding office who had in any way aided the rebellion against the United States should be separately submitted.

At the election ordered by the President, the constitution without these clauses was ratified, and the conservative Republican candidates for office and legislative membership were elected.

Ratification of the Virginia Constitution.

At the next session of Congress, in December of 1869, the Senators and Representatives presented themselves for admission. Their claims were sustained by the President, who reported to Congress that Virginia had fulfilled all of the conditions required of her for readmission to her full privileges as a member of the Union, having among other things ratified by legislative acts both the Fourteenth and Fifteenth Amendments to the Constitution of the United States, and urged the admission of the Senators and Representatives from the "State" to Congress. After a good deal of discussion and some wrangling, the bill for the accomplishment of this object was passed, and, in the last days of January of 1870, Virginia was restored to her proper federal relations, on the conditions that the constitution of the "State" should never be so amended as to deprive any person enfranchised therein of the suffrage, or any citizen or class of citizens of the United States of the educational rights and privileges provided therein, or any citizen of the United States of the equal right to hold office, on account of race, color or previous condition of servitude, or of the school rights provided in the constitution of the "State." The Congressional Act also undertook to purge the new "State" legislature by requiring that every member must take an oath that he was not disqualified by the Fourteenth Amendment to the Constitution of the United States, or that, if he had been, he had also been

The restoration of Virginia to her Federal relations.

relieved by the Congressional Act authorized for the case in the Amendment.

The Act of Congress of April 10th empowered the President to deal with the question of Reconstruction in Mississippi in the same manner as in Virginia. By virtue of this power, the President issued a proclamation, on the 13th of July, 1869, commanding the resubmission to the voters of the constitution adopted by the Mississippi convention, on the 15th of May, 1868, and rejected by the voters as stated on a previous page, and designating the 30th day of November, 1869, as the date of the election. As in the case of Virginia, the President ordered a separate vote to be taken upon the disfranchising and disqualifying clauses of the constitution which prohibited any person from voting or holding office who had given any aid or comfort to persons in rebellion. *Ratification of the Mississippi constitution.*

The result of the vote on the constitution was the same as in Virginia. The constitution was ratified without these clauses; and on the 23d of February, 1870, the bill for the restoration of Mississippi and the admission of the Senators and Representatives from the "State" to Congress, on the same conditions as those exacted of Virginia, became law. *The restoration of Mississippi to her Federal relations.*

The Act of April 10th, 1869, also invested the President with the power of ordering the submission of the constitution framed and adopted by the convention at Austin, Texas, in June of 1868, to the voters for ratification. By virtue of this authority, the President ordered a vote to be taken upon this instrument on the 30th day of November, 1869. This proposed constitution did not contain any such disfranchising and disqualifying clauses as those which rendered the Virginia and Mississippi instruments ob- *Ratification of the Texas Constitution.*

noxious to the intelligence of these communities, and the vote was, therefore, ordered to be taken upon the entire constitution at once. The result was ratification; and on the 30th of March, 1870, the Congressional measure for the complete restoration of Texas to her proper federal relations, upon the same fundamental conditions as those required of Virginia and Mississippi, became law.

<small>Restoration of Texas to her Federal relations.</small>

Thus while the new President did not, as his predecessor had done, dispute the power of Congress to direct and control the reconstruction of the disrupted Southern communities as "States" of the Union, he appealed to Congress for the authority to relieve some of them still suffering under military rule from the hard alternative of negro domination, and when Congress gave him the power requested, he used it for the amelioration of the situation. This was true statesmanship. If President Johnson had done this instead of insisting upon his constitutional power to reconstruct, independently of Congress, these communities, and repeating continually his unsound, though specious, arguments in support of his view, it is quite possible that he might have maintained his influence, in some degree at least, with the Republican majority, and at the same time, and in consequence thereof, might have accomplished something in the interest of a true conservatism in Reconstruction. This is not, however, certain. Johnson had none of Grant's vast popularity with the people of the North whereby to overawe Congress, and there is no doubt, deny it as we may to conscious reflection, that down below consciousness there was a sort of distrust of a Southern Union man on the part of a large portion of the people of the North. Mr. Johnson had to suffer under the influence of this feeling, like all others of his class, and whenever he suggested any moderate course in the treatment of former rebels, he fell under the suspicion of masking sympathy with their sentiments under a pretence of Unionism. He was, thus, rather an object of Congressional distrust from the first, and could probably never have done so much as Grant succeeded in doing for conservatism in Virginia and Mississippi, even though he had recognized the power of Congress in the work of reconstruction, and had preferred respectful requests, instead of asserting presidential prerogatives.

Likewise the new President found, as soon as he began the work of administration, that the Tenure-of-Office Act was an unendurable hindrance to the efficient discharge of his duties. None of Mr. Johnson's Secretaries, it is true, gave him any trouble by attempting to hold on to office for the one month allowed them after the expiration of Mr. Johnson's term. The men nominated by President Grant for his Cabinet of chiefs and advisers were immediately confirmed, and, with one exception, inducted into office. These men were E. B. Washburne, of Illinois, as Secretary of State; A. T. Stewart, of New York, as Secretary of the Treasury; A. E. Borie, of Pennsylvania, as Secretary of the Navy; J. D. Cox, of Ohio, as Secretary of the Interior; E. R. Hoar, of Massachusetts, as Attorney-General; and J. A. J. Creswell, of Maryland, as Postmaster-General. No immediate nomination was made for the Secretaryship of War, and General Schofield remained for a few days at the head of the Department. The President soon found that Mr. Stewart, being a large importer of foreign goods, was disqualified by statute from holding the office of Secretary of the Treasury. He first suggested to the Senate the removal of the disability by a joint resolution of Congress, and, on objection being made to the introduction of a

Grant and the Tenure-of-Office Act.

bill repealing the disqualifying statute, he withdrew the suggestion. Mr. Stewart then relieved the situation by sending in his declination, and the President nominated Mr. G. S. Boutwell of Massachusetts for the office, which nomination was immediately confirmed, and Mr. Boutwell took immediate charge of the Department. Mr. Washburne, the Secretary of State, resigned the office within a few days, and Mr. Hamilton Fish, of New York, was nominated and appointed to succeed him. General Schofield next resigned the War Office, and was succeeded by General John A. Rawlins of Illinois. Finally, Mr. Borie resigned in June the Secretaryship of the Navy, and was succeeded by Mr. G. M. Robeson of New Jersey. The Senate put nothing in the way of these changes. But President Grant made up his mind in a very few days after his inauguration not to have his hands tied in regard to any of the officers for whose acts he was responsible. He gave the Republican leaders in Congress to understand that he would allow the existing incumbents of the offices to remain in office, unless they should commit some such offence as would call for their suspension, so long as the Tenure-of-Office Act should remain on the statute book. The Republicans were hungry for a new distribution of the spoils. They called it a righteous desire for the "cleaning of the Augean stables." Whatever it was, they were thrown into a great state of trepidation by this covert threat of the President not to clear the way for their friends.

On the 9th day of March, less than a week after the accession of the new President to power, a bill was introduced into the House of Representatives providing for the immediate repeal of the Tenure-of-Office Act, and was passed, immediately and without debate, by a vote of 138 to 16. These 16 were naturally Republicans.

The Democrats voted for the repeal on principle. When the bill reached the Senate it was sent to the Judiciary Committee. This Committee quickly reported to the Senate a substitute for the bill of the House. This substitute provided that the Tenure-of-Office Act should be suspended from operation until the next session of Congress. *Congress and the Tenure-of-Office Act after Grant's accession to the presidency.* No more shameless piece of partisanship was ever advanced on the floor of the Senate than this. It simply meant, suspend the Act when the Republicans wanted to get the offices, and keep it in force when they might be in danger of being put out. The Senate itself could not be brought to vote this proposition of its Judiciary Committee. It was withdrawn by the committee, and Mr. Trumbull proposed to supersede the existing law with a measure which would allow the President to suspend from office without assigning any cause for the same to the Senate, or even reporting the suspension to the Senate, and to nominate to the Senate a person to fill the vacancy, and in case of rejection by the Senate to nominate another person; and only when the session of the Senate should come to a close without a ratification should the suspended officer be restored.

It was pretty clear that the President would not find any trouble with such a measure as this, but it seemed to the House that the Senate was trying to cling to a certain control over the Executive, and the House refused concurrence in the bill. The matter was finally referred to a conference committee, and this committee speedily matured and reported a measure, which allowed the President, during a recess of the Senate, to suspend any civil officer appointed by and with the consent of the Senate, except judges of the United States courts, until the end of the next session of the Senate, and to designate some other person *The modification of the Tenure-of-Office Act.*

to discharge the duties of the vacant office in the meantime, and made it the duty of the President simply to nominate to the Senate, within thirty days from the beginning of its next session, some one to succeed to the office permanently, and in case the Senate should refuse to ratify the nomination, to nominate another person. Both Houses accepted the recommendation of the Committee and the bill agreed upon by its members became law April 5, 1869.

Still the President was not satisfied with it. He thought that any control whatever of the Senate over dismissal from office was not warranted by the Constitution, and he regarded the attempt of the Senate to cling to any shadow of such a power as a personal affront to himself.

The President's dissatisfaction with the measure.

In his first annual Message, that of December 6th, 1869, he earnestly recommended the total repeal of the Tenure-of-Office Acts, and declared them both unconstitutional, and inconsistent with "a faithful and efficient administration of the Government." His recommendation was probably an effective warning to Congress against any attempt to hamper him by claiming any power under them to control his dismissals and suspensions, but they still remained on the statute book for nearly two decades longer. The glaring inconsistency of a bare and bald repeal of the Acts was too great even for the partisan Congress. It was willing to make them practically null and void, but it wanted a shadow with which to cover its nakedness. At any rate, the position taken by President Grant toward them was a complete vindication of President Johnson's views concerning them, and, in no small degree, of his deeds also.

At the date of this Message all of the Southern communities had completed the acts required by Congress for their restoration as "States" of the Union, but the result of the elections held in Mississippi were not known in Washington. The President simply expressed the hope that the constitutions submitted in these communities to the voters would be ratified, and "thus close the work of Reconstruction." As we have seen, the elections resulted as the President hoped, and these communities were restored, on the basis of the "State" constitutions adopted, to their proper federal relations.

The case of Georgia still remained, however, unsettled, and the President suggested that Congress should enact a law authorizing the Governor of Georgia, Mr. Bullock, "to convene the members originally elected to the legislature, requiring each member to take the oath prescribed by the Reconstruction Acts, and none to be admitted who were ineligible under the third clause of the Fourteenth Amendment." The situation was briefly as follows: The Senators and Representatives from Georgia had been refused admission to seats in Congress at the first session of the Forty-first Congress which convened the 4th of March, 1869, because the legislature of Georgia had expelled the colored men elected to that body as ineligible, and had rejected the proposed Fifteenth Amendment to the Constitution of the United States. It is true that the Senators from Georgia had been elected by the legislature before the colored members were expelled, and that the Representatives had been admitted to seats in the House during the last session of the Fortieth Congress, and that the ostensible reason for not admitting the members to the lower House of the Forty-first Congress was that they had not been elected to the Forty-first Congress. However, Georgia had no representation in either House of Congress at the date of President Grant's first annual Message in December of 1869.

The facts in the Georgia case.

Her "State" government seems, therefore, to have been considered by Congress as being still only provisional, despite the fact that by the Act of June 25th, 1868, she had been declared entitled to admission to representation in Congress upon conditions which she had subsequently fulfilled.

A bill had been introduced into Congress soon after the opening of the session beginning March 4th, 1869, dealing with the subject. It was claimed in the preamble of this bill that the Georgia legislature had not purged itself of disloyal members as required by the Fourteenth Amendment to the Constitution of the United States, that it had violated the constitution of Georgia and the Constitution of the United States and the fundamental principles of the Reconstruction Acts by expelling the negro members for ineligibility, and that the civil authorities in the "State" could not, or did not, protect the loyal citizens in the enjoyment of their rights and liberties or even in their persons. The bill proposed to meet these difficulties by providing that the Governor of Georgia should reconvene the originally elected members of the legislature, reseat the expelled negro members, and expel such members as could not swear that they were not disqualified by the Fourteenth Amendment to the Constitution of the United States. It may be remarked here in passing that the Fourteenth Amendment does not disqualify anybody, in express language, from being a member of a "State" legislature. It disqualifies all persons who have engaged in rebellion after having taken an oath, as a member of Congress or of a "State" legislature, or as a United States or a "State" officer, to support the Constitution of the United States, from holding a seat in Congress or from being an officer of the United States or of a "State," *but not from holding a seat in a "State" legislature.* The word officer in the public jurisprudence of this country does not include membership in a legislative body. But to return to the bill. It provided finally for making United States troops in Georgia subject to the Governor's call for assistance. This bill was so seriously opposed by the Democrats and the conservative Republicans that it did not pass, and during this session Congress did nothing further for the restoration of Georgia.

On the other hand, the conservatives in Georgia undertook to do something for themselves. They got up a test case in the Supreme Court of the "State" to determine the rights of negroes to hold office. The case was that of White and Clements, and the office involved was a county court clerkship. Of course the decision was not binding upon the legislative houses in judging of the eligibility of their members, but it was thought that it would have an influence upon their views. The court decided that under the new constitution of Georgia and the code of Georgia negroes could hold office, since the constitution of 1868 declared that all persons born or naturalized in the United States and residents in Georgia were citizens of Georgia, and the code declared that among the rights of citizens was the right to hold office. Of course the legislature could abolish or amend the code. After the rendering of this decision the conservative members of the legislature requested the Governor, Mr. Bullock, who was a radical Republican, and a New Yorker by birth, to reconvene the legislature for the purpose of reseating the expelled negro members. The Governor refused, apparently not desiring to anticipate the action of Congress in the case. The attempt of the conservatives to help themselves thus came to naught, and the unhappy community drifted on toward anarchy and violence, according to the report now made by

The case of White and Clements.

General Terry to the President, who declared it to be his opinion that the United States Government must intervene anew in order to preserve it against that fate.

It was then with a good deal of irritation that Congress came to consider the subject of Reconstruction in Georgia again in the session of 1869–70, and the determination soon became manifest to impose additional and harder conditions upon this community than upon the others. Moreover, as matters appeared at that juncture, the ratification of the Fifteenth Amendment by the legislature of Georgia would be necessary to make out the required three-fourths majority. It was in this temper, and under the pressure of this supposed necessity, that Congress, acting promptly upon the general suggestion in the President's Message, passed a bill which provided that the Governor of Georgia should forthwith summon the persons declared by the proclamation of General Meade, of the date of June 25th, 1868, to be members-elect of the legislature, to assemble at Atlanta; that every such person should take an oath or affirmation that he had never, after having been a member of Congress or of a " State " legislature, or an officer of the United States or of a " State " "engaged in insurrection or rebellion against the United States, or given any aid or comfort to its enemies, or rendered, except in consequence of direct physical compulsion, any support or aid to any insurrection, or rebellion against the United States, or held any office under, or given any support to, any government of any kind acting in hostility to the United States, or levying war against the United States," or should make oath or affirmation that, if he had so acted, he had been relieved by Congress from any disability attaching to such act in the manner provided in the Fourteenth Amendment to the Constitution; that in case any person claiming to be a member of the legislature should fail to make such an oath or affirmation he should be excluded from a seat in the body; that no member-elect should be excluded on account of race, color or previous condition of servitude; that, on application of the Governor, the President should employ the military power of the United States to enforce the provisions of the Act; and that the legislature of Georgia should ratify the proposed Fifteenth Amendment to the Constitution of the United States before Senators and Representatives from Georgia should be admitted to seats in Congress. This bill was approved by the President on the 22d of December, 1869.

So great was the opposition to Reconstruction, under these hard conditions, on the part of the white people in Georgia, that the Governor was obliged to call for the military of the United States to aid him, and finally to step aside for General Terry, who by an order from the President, dated January 4th, 1870, was authorized to resume the powers in Georgia of the commander of a military district, as provided under the Reconstruction Act of March 2d, 1867. The General found a number of members in the legislature recognized by General Meade's proclamation who could not take either of the oaths or affirmations prescribed. These he caused to be removed from their seats in very arbitrary ways. This procedure put the Republicans in the legislature in majority, and they filled these vacancies by admitting persons who had received the next highest number of votes to those cast for the expelled members in the election, and who could take one or the other of the oaths or affirmations prescribed in the Act of the 22d of December, 1869.

Resumption of military government in Georgia.

The legislature as thus reconstructed was approved by the military authorities, and it now proceeded to fulfil the final condition required of Georgia, viz., the ratification of the proposed Fifteenth Amendment to the Constitution of the United States. It also ratified the Fourteenth Amendment. This was, from a legal point of view, entirely superfluous, since the Fourteenth Amendment was, at the moment, already a part of the Constitution, as much so as any other Article, and in resuming the status of a "State" in the Union, Georgia was, of course, subject to all parts of the Constitution alike. The legislature might, with equal reason, have ratified specially any other part of the Constitution. The idea seems to have been to correct any possible defects in the ratification of this amendment which the Georgia legislature had voted on July 21st, 1868.

Ratification of the Fifteenth Amendment by the Georgia legislature.

This purified legislature now elected United States Senators, both of them Republicans, of course. All these things were done in the latter part of January and the early part of February of 1870, and as the Congress was in session, there was reason to expect that Georgia would be, at once, fully restored as a "State" of the Union. A bill was reported in the House of Representatives on the 25th of February from the Committee on Reconstruction for this purpose. It was nearly identical in its provisions and language with the Virginia and Mississippi bills, but it dragged along through nearly five months of debate and partisan wrangling before it became law. The reason of this delay was that, on March 4th, General Butler proposed an amendment to the bill which provided: "That the power granted by the constitution of Georgia to the general assembly to change the time of holding elections, and prescribe the

Further delay in the admission of representatives from Georgia.

day of meeting of the general assembly, shall not be so exercised as to postpone the election of the next general assembly beyond the Tuesday after the first Monday in November in the year 1872, nor shall such power ever be by any future legislature so exercised as to extend the term of any office beyond the regular period named in said constitution; and the said general assembly shall by joint resolution consent to this condition before this Act shall take effect."

This language was at once taken to mean that Congress would undertake to empower the legislature of Georgia to extend the terms of the members of the Georgia legislature and of the Governor, elected in April of 1868, by two years, on the ground that the "State" government of Georgia was still provisional, and would so remain until the passage of this Act, and that these terms would, therefore, not really begin until the passage of this Act. The conservative Republicans as well as the Democrats repudiated this interpretation of the powers of Congress to extend, or to authorize the "State" legislature to extend, the terms of the members of the legislature and of "State" officers as an unprecedented usurpation. Some of them repudiated the idea that there could be a provisional "State" government, and declared that any further legislation in regard to the reconstruction of Georgia was unnecessary, since the Act of June 25th, 1868, had restored Georgia to her position as a "State" of the Union, along with North Carolina, South Carolina, Louisiana, Alabama, and Florida, upon certain conditions, all of which Georgia had fulfilled, just as the others had done, and since all the others had been admitted to the enjoyment of all of their rights and privileges as "States" of the Union without any further legislation than the Act of June 25th, 1868.

There is no doubt that the Butler amendment meant, and was intended by its author to mean, just what was charged by the conservatives. General Butler at last acknowledged and avowed it, and attempted to justify it. But he was unable to rally a majority to sustain it, and he withdrew it in the face of an amendment offered by Mr. Bingham on the 7th, which provided that nothing contained in the bill should be construed either to vacate any of the "State" offices in Georgia, or to extend the terms of the present holders of them beyond the time provided in the "State" constitution, or deprive the people of Georgia of the right under their "State" constitution of electing members of their legislature in the year 1870.

This amendment was passed on the 8th of March, and the bill as thus amended was passed by the House of Representatives, and sent to the Senate on the same day. It was immediately referred to the Judiciary Committee of that body and on the next day, the 9th, it was reported back to the Senate by this committee, without amendment. The Senate now considered it in committee of the whole from this time to April 19th, and when it was reported to the Senate it had been changed to a bill which declared the existing government of Georgia to be provisional and subject to the provisions of the Reconstruction Acts of 1867; ordered an election in Georgia on the 15th day of November, 1870, for members of the "State" legislature as provided for in the "State" constitution of 1868; ordered the assembly of this legislature on the 13th of December, 1870, and its organization preparatory to the admission of the "State" to representation in Congress; declared that the powers and functions of the members of the existing legislature should cease on the 13th day of December, 1870; and made it the duty of the President of the United States, in case of domestic violence in any municipality in the "State," reported to him by the legislature or Governor of the State, to suppress by military power such domestic violence, and "to exercise all such powers and inflict such punishments as may by the laws, or the rules and articles of war be exercised or inflicted in case of insurrection or invasion." The Senate concurred in the recommendations of the committee of the whole, and added a provision repealing that part of the Act of March 2d, 1867, which prohibited the organizing of any militia force in Georgia.

In this form and with this content the bill was returned to the House. Here it was again debated, off and on, until June 24th, when it was finally agreed upon with the following contents: "That the State of Georgia having complied with the Reconstruction Acts, and the Fourteenth and Fifteenth Articles of Amendment to the Constitution of the United States having been ratified in good faith by a legal legislature of said State, it is hereby declared that the State of Georgia is entitled to representation in the Congress of the United States. But nothing in this act contained shall be construed to deprive the people of Georgia of the right to an election for members of the general assembly of said State, as provided for in the constitution thereof," and "That so much of the Act of March 2d, 1867, as prohibits the organization, arming, or calling into service of the militia forces in the States of Georgia, Mississippi, Texas and Virginia be, and the same is, hereby repealed." *The final restoration of Georgia to her Federal relations.*

The Senate disagreed to the bill in this form and with these contents, and asked for a conference committee. The House agreed and appointed members. The conference committee agreed upon the bill as perfected by the House with the addition to the second section of these words: "And nothing in this or any other Act of Congress shall be construed to affect the term to which any officer has been appointed or any member of the general assembly elected, as prescribed by the constitution of the State of Georgia." Both the Senate and the House accepted and concurred in the recommendations of the committee, and the bill, as thus perfected, became law on the 15th day of July, 1870. This bill terminated the era of Reconstruction legislation by Congress, and at the next session of Congress, the session of 1870–71, the Senators and Representatives from Georgia were admitted to their seats, the Senate admitting those chosen to that body in July of 1868, Messrs. Hill and Miller. The attempt of Governor Bullock to prolong the terms of the members of the legislature and of the officers of the "State" government was decidedly disapproved of by President Grant's Administration, and an election was held for members and county officers and for Representatives in Congress in December of 1870. The white residents of the "State" stood well together, and carried the election by a large majority against the Republicans. So soon as the result was known Governor Bullock, whose term had still two more years to run, abandoned his office and left the "State," and Georgia was thus early rescued from negro domination, or rather "carpet-bag" domination through negro suffrage. Her harder experiences during the years from 1868 to 1870 had worked out to her advantage, in that it brought the respectable and capable portion of her white citizens together earlier than was the case in the other reconstructed Commonwealths similarly situated.

From the point of view of a sound political science the imposition of universal negro suffrage upon the

Southern communities, in some of which the negroes were in large majority, was one of the "blunder-crimes" of the century. There is something natural in the subordination of an inferior race to a superior race, even to the point of the enslavement of the inferior race, but there is nothing natural in the opposite. It is entirely unnatural, ruinous, and utterly demoralizing and barbarizing to both races. It is difficult to believe that the creation of such a relation between the blacks and whites of the South was at all within the intentions of the framers of the Reconstruction Acts. They were irritated because these communities would not accord civil equality to the freedmen, would not accept the proposed Fourteenth Amendment, and had passed acts which created a new species of slavery or quasi-slavery of the blacks. They thought they were placed between the alternative of continuing military government in the South indefinitely, or giving the negro the political power with which to maintain his civil rights.

Negro rule in the South from the point of view of political science and ethnical principle.

Opposition to military government in time of peace was an ingrained principle of the American people, and there was a large part of people of the North, nearly all adhering to the Republican party, who believed that manhood suffrage was the true principle of a sound political science. And it was thought that the only way of creating "States" in the South which would sustain the Republican party was by giving the negro the suffrage. It is not surprising, then, that they adopted the course which they did. There was a third alternative, as has already been pointed out, viz., the placing of these communities under Territorial civil government and keeping them there until the spirit of loyalty to the Nation was established and the principle and practice of civil equality among all citizens was made thoroughly secure.

But, as has been said, the idea that these communities were "States" of the Union, notwithstanding their rebellion against the United States and their attempted secession from the Union, seemed to prohibit the following of this course, the only true and sound course. And so these unhappy communities were given over, as sham "States" of the Union, to the rule of the ignorant and vicious part of their population, to be sustained therein by the military power of the Nation, under the excuse that that part alone was loyal.

A period of darkness now settled down upon these unhappy communities blacker and more hopeless than the worst experiences of the war. The conduct of the men who now appeared upon the scene as the creators of the new South was so tyrannic, corrupt, mean and vulgar as to repel the historian from attempting any detailed account of their doings, and incline him to the vaguest outline. Moreover it is most difficult to fix upon reliable facts in this period of confusion and political night, illuminated only by the lurid gleams of passion and hatred. It is best for the North, best for the South, best for the whole country, and best for the world that this terrible mistake of the North and this terrible degradation of the South should be dealt with briefly and impersonally, and that lessons of warning should be drawn from these experiences, instead of multiplying criminations and recriminations in regard to them.

CHAPTER XII

"CARPET-BAG" AND NEGRO DOMINATION IN THE SOUTHERN STATES BETWEEN 1868 AND 1876

Escape of Virginia, Georgia and Texas from Negro Rule—North Carolina's Rapid Recovery from Negro Rule—The Loyal League—Origin of the K. K. K.'s—Methods of the Ku-Klux—Periods in the History of Negro Rule—The Act for the Enforcement of the New Amendments—The Corruption in the New "State" Governments—The Supplemental Enforcement Act—The President's Proclamation of March 23d, 1871—The Ku-Klux Act of April 20, 1871—Interference of the United States Military Power in the Affairs of South Carolina—The President's Proclamation of May 3d, 1871—The President's Proclamation to the People of South Carolina—The Ku-Klux Trials—Corruption in the State Governments of the South—The Revolt in the Republican Party—The Liberal Republican Convention of 1872—Acceptance of the Liberal Republican Candidates by the Democrats—Division in the Democratic Party—The Republican Platform and Nominees—The Republican Triumph—Events in Alabama—Events in Louisiana—The Downward Course between 1872 and 1874—The Election of 1874—The Change in Alabama, Arkansas and Texas—The Status in South Carolina in 1874—The Day of Complete Deliverance—The Status in Mississippi in 1875—Fiat Money and the Resumption of Specie Payments—The Inflation Bill of 1874 and the Veto of it by the President.

VIRGINIA, Texas and Georgia had been in no great hurry, as we have seen, to exchange military government exercised by the white officers of the United States army for "State" government under the electorate proposed in the Reconstruction Acts. In this they were wise. The army officers did not, as a rule, sympathize with the radical

Escape of Virginia, Georgia and Texas from negro rule.

movements of the Republicans in Congress, and they so executed the duties imposed upon them as to cause the least suffering and inconvenience. [Their rule, though exercised under a repellent title, was in fact far milder than, and far preferable to, the civil government of the adventurer and the negro.] They mingled socially with the old families, and, in many cases, married their fair daughters. The common soldiers from the Northern " States " also fraternized with their race relatives in the South. They did not fancy the black soldiers either of the regular army or the "State" militia, and many were the cases in which they intervened between the defenceless ex-Confederates and the brutal blacks in blue. It is even said by men who have every opportunity to know that many of them doffed their uniforms on election day, went to the polls, and voted the Democratic ticket.

In spite of the threats of Congress, and the ever-increasing conditions imposed by that body upon the permission to resume the "State" status, these three communities held out under military rule until so many of their leading citizens had been amnestied by Congress and made again eligible to office and mandate, and until so much better provisions concerning the enfranchisement of the ex-Confederates had been secured, as to put them in a far better position to resume "State" government than was the case two years before. Moreover, these communities had larger white than black populations. After their full restoration, consequently, Virginia and Georgia escaped largely the suffering experienced by most of the others, and Texas also managed to pull through the years from 1870 to 1874 with only about a four-fold increase of taxation, and the creation of a debt of only about 5,000,000 of dollars, when she reached the period of union of almost all her best citizens in the Democratic party, which, in the election of Richard Coke as Governor in 1874, and of a majority of the legislative members, permanently triumphed in Texas. Mississippi also had held back in 1868 and 1869, as we have seen, in order to secure better terms for the ex-Confederates in the enfranchising and disfranchising provisions of the "State" constitution, and by doing so had accomplished this result. But Mississippi was one of the three Southern communities in which the negro population far outnumbered the white. Mississippi was not, for this reason chiefly, so fortunate as Virginia, Texas and Georgia. She was obliged, with South Carolina and Louisiana, to pass through the fiery furnace in order to fuse the respectable white elements in her population into a single political party with a well-understood and a well-determined purpose.

Of all the "States" included in the Congressional Act of June 25th, 1868, only North Carolina had been fortunate enough to rid herself, before 1872, of the rule of the adventurers and their ignorant negro support. This happened because matters were driven to a crisis sooner here than elsewhere. The legislature of 1868 had proceeded promptly to authorize the issue of $25,000,000 of bonds, when the whole taxable property of the "State" was not over $125,000,000. From the first moment the people were threatened with confiscation, and when to this was added the legislative act, known as the Schaffner law, authorizing the Governor to suspend civil government, and institute martial law in any part of the "State," and when he actually undertook to do so in three counties of the "State," the whites came together in the election of 1870, captured the legislature and redeemed the "State" from the hideous tyranny with which it was threatened.

North Carolina's rapid recovery from negro rule.

Already before the Reconstruction Acts were passed, the political adventurers in the South had begun organ-

The Loyal League. izing the negroes into secret bodies, known later as the Union or Loyal League. The members of these bodies were sworn to obey the decisions of the organization and to execute them. The original idea seems to have been a combination for protection against bands of lawless white people, and for mutual aid and assistance in the hard struggle for existence to which the freedmen were now exposed. The League soon took on, however, a political character, and became a sort of Republican party organization in the South.

It is difficult to determine whether the Ku-Klux organization preceded that of the Loyal League and pro-

Origin of the K. K. K.'s. voked it or not. So far as we know, both of them were first heard of in the year 1866. It is probable that the Ku-Klux had its origin a little farther north than the Loyal League. It is said by those who profess to know most about it, that the first appearance of this body was in one of the southern counties of Tennessee, Giles County; that it was first organized by a lot of young loafers, probably ex-Confederate soldiers, who lived in the town of Pulaski, the county town of that county; and that their first purpose was the playing of practical jokes upon the ignorant and superstitious negroes of the neighborhood. They operated in the night-time, went disguised, travelled on horseback, their horses being also disguised, and were oath-bound to execute the decisions of the organization, and to protect each other. Whatever may have been its origin, this body also soon found its political usefulness. It soon proved to be a powerful means for intimidating and terrorizing the negroes, and also white men acting with the negroes.

After the Reconstruction Acts were passed and put into operation, and especially after the Southern communities were reorganized as "States" under them, and the military governments gave way to the "State" governments, this organization spread all over the South, and contributed much by its violent and unlawful methods toward wringing finally the new "State" governments of the South from the hands of the negroes and the "carpet-baggers." As it extended, its methods became more lawless and violent. Its members whipped, plundered, burned, abducted, imprisoned, tortured and murdered, for the prime purpose of keeping the negroes from exercising suffrage and holding office. They were protected by many respectable people who would not have participated personally in their nefarious work. And they had confederates everywhere, who, upon the witness stand and in the jury box, would perjure themselves to prevent their conviction and punishment. It was even said that there were many cases where members of these Klans were able to have themselves subpœnaed as witnesses, or summoned as jurors, in the trials of their comrades, and that they were sworn to perjure themselves, if necessary, to clear each other. The respectable people of the South tried to make it appear that these lawless bands were simply freebooters, such as generally infest a country for a time after a period of war, and had no political meaning or purpose whatsoever; and it is probably true that the Klans never went beyond county organization, any wider bond than the county organization, or Klan, being rather the moral bond of a common purpose; but it cannot be well questioned now that they had one purpose at least in common, and that that was a chief purpose with them all, viz., to terrorize the negro out of the exercise of his newly-granted privileges of suffrage and office-holding, and keep him in his place as a menial.

The appearance of both the Loyal Leagues and the Ku-Klux Klans in the manner in which they appeared, and at the time when they appeared, ought not to cause any surprise to the student of history. Under the reconstruction of the Southern communities as pursued before March of 1867 it seemed as if the freedmen were to be left to the tender mercies of their former masters, irritated against them by the act of the North in emancipating them, and by failure in war to prevent it. It was entirely natural, not to say praiseworthy, for them to combine for the defence of their newly found rights, and for mutual assistance in the hard battle against want which they were now obliged to wage. And it was no less natural that they should look for the intellectual power necessary for forming such combinations to the white men from the North who had helped them out of their bondage, and had given them food and clothes in their hunger and nakedness.

The naturalness of these organizations.

And, again, when by the Reconstruction Acts and the restoration of martial law in the South under them, Congress turned the tables upon the Southern white people, and placed the ignorant barbarians in political control of them, and made every open attempt to resist this control a penal offence, it was also rather natural, though not praiseworthy, that men should have bound themselves together by secret oaths to do anything and everything in their power to defeat this blunder-crime against civilization. Whether natural or not, it always happens when such attempts are made, and it is always to be expected.

But to return to the order of the narrative. The formation of the Union Leagues in 1867 and 1868 enabled

"CARPET-BAG" AND NEGRO DOMINATION

the negroes to vote in these years for delegates to the constitutional conventions required under the Reconstruction Acts, and to vote upon the ratification of the constitutions framed by them, and to participate in the election for the "State" officers and legislative members under those constitutions, with the help and under the direction of these organizations, and to operate the newly established "State" governments under the same direction. This opened the way for the "carpet-bag" governments in the Southern "States," whose deeds may be now briefly narrated.

The opportunity for political adventurers.

The landing places in this story may be placed at the years 1872, 1874, and 1876. The year 1872 is the date of the national revolt against the policy of the Washington government in the affairs of the reconstructed "States." The year 1874 is the date when some of the reconstructed "States" succeeded in overthrowing carpet-bag and negro rule, and the Democrats succeeded in electing a majority of members in the lower House of Congress. And the year 1876 is the date of the complete overthrow of that rule and the complete establishment of the "solid South" under white Democratic government.

Periods in the history of negro rule.

Before all of the Southern communities had been admitted to representation in Congress, and before any of them except Tennessee had gotten fairly under way with their new "State" governments, a bill was presented in Congress to provide for the enforcement of the Fourteenth and Fifteenth Amendments to the Constitution of the United States. It will be remembered that these Amendments authorized the exercise of power by the United States Government against "State" action only. They read: "No *State* shall make or enforce any law which shall abridge the privileges or immunities of a citizen of

The Act for the enforcement of the new Amendments.

the United States; nor shall any *State* deprive any person of life, liberty, or property, without due process of law; nor deny to any person within its jurisdiction the equal protection of the laws"; and " the right of citizens of the United States to vote shall not be denied or abridged by the United States or by any *State* on account of race, color or previous condition of servitude."

It is entirely clear from this language that, in the enforcement of these new provisions of the Constitution, the United States Government must direct its powers against the action of the "States," respectively, through their legislators and officials, and against that only. But in this bill which became law on the 31st of May, 1870, Congress enacted penalties not only against "State" officers and agents for the violation of the Fourteenth and Fifteenth Amendments, but severe penalties against any *person* within the "States," as well as the Territories, who should undertake to deprive by unlawful means any other person of his right to qualify and vote at any election, and against any *person* who under color of any law, statute or ordinance, regulation or custom, should undertake to deprive any other person of his civil rights and civil equality. Congress also, in this Act, vested the jurisdiction over such cases in the United States courts and authorized the President of the United States to enforce their decisions by the aid of the United States army and navy if necessary. Now, while it may probably be rightly claimed that the *Thirteenth* Amendment to the Constitution, which reads: " Neither slavery nor involuntary servitude, except as a punishment for crime whereof the party shall have been duly convicted, shall exist in the United States, or in any place subject to their jurisdiction," empowers Congress to make laws protecting the civil rights and civil equality of persons within the "States" against infringement by other *persons*, and to invest the officers of the United States, both judicial and executive, with the power to enforce these laws, since in this Amendment the prohibition of slavery or involuntary servitude is not directed against "State" action solely, but against any attempt made by anybody to create an involuntary servitude, it cannot on the other hand be claimed, with any show of correct interpretation, that the *Fourteenth* Amendment warrants the exercise of any such power by the United States Government, and it is entirely out of the question to claim that the Fifteenth Amendment protects the right of a person, within a State, to vote against the attempt of another person or of other persons to infringe the same, or even against the "State" itself to do so, except it be on account of race, color or previous condition of servitude.

There is not the slightest doubt in the mind of any good constitutional lawyer, at the present time, that Congress overstepped its constitutional powers in that part of the Enforcement Act of May 31st, 1870, which related to the exercise of the suffrage, and trenched upon the reserved powers of the "States." The excuse for it was that lawless bands of white men, the Ku-Klux Klans and the like, were intimidating the blacks, and in the approaching elections of the autumn of 1870 would prevent them from voting. But that was a matter for the "State" governments to look out for, and the "State" governments in the South were, at the time of the passage of this Act, with the exception of Tennessee, in the hands of the Republicans.

Criticism of the Act.

Meanwhile the new "State" governments had well begun their career of corruption, shame and vulgarity. They were plundering the treasury, increasing the taxes, selling franchises, issuing bonds, and celebrating high carnival everywhere and all the time. The gentlemen and political leaders of the old school, and the old political class, of the South looked on aghast, with mingled feelings of bitter degradation and anger, and the hotspurs and desperadoes were stirred to deeds of intimidation and violence. There is little doubt that some negroes were terrified out of exercising the suffrage in the election of 1870. Not yet, however, had enough of the disqualified whites been amnestied, or enough intimidation been exercised, or sufficient unity among the whites been attained, to work the overthrow of "carpet-bag," negro rule. Enough, however, was threatened to influence the Republican Congress to proceed to more complete, if not more extreme, measures for the protection of the negro in his civil and political rights, and to move the President to garrison the principal points in the Southern "States" with United States soldiers.

The corruption in the new "State" governments.

The Congress passed the Act of the 28th of February, 1871, which so supplemented the Act of May 31st, 1870, as to place the whole control of the registrations and elections when and where Representatives to Congress should be chosen, in the hands of United States officers, the supervisors, and the deputy marshals, commissioners and judges of the United States courts. It may be claimed that Congress, under the power to regulate the manner of holding Congressional elections vested in it by Article I., section 4, of the Constitution, was authorized to pass this law, provided it confined the action of it to the Congressional registration and election. But since the "State" elections were held at the same time and place, and under the same control and direction as the Congressional, it was inevitable that the control of the United States officers would be exercised, either directly

The supplemental enforcement Act.

"CARPET-BAG" AND NEGRO DOMINATION 257

or indirectly, over those also. And this was unquestionably the chief purpose of the Act, so far as its execution in the Southern "States" was concerned.

But this was not yet enough in the views of the Administration. In the two years of his incumbency of the Presidential office, General Grant had fallen into the arms of the radical Republicans, who appeared to be in large majority, and the usual manœuvering had begun for the second term. Upon the basis of information, which turned out to be very insufficient and unreliable, the President, on the 23d of March, 1871, addressed a message to Congress, in which he affirmed that life and property were insecure in some of the "States," and the carrying of the mails and the collection of the revenue dangerous; that the power to correct these evils was not possessed by the "State" governments; and that it was doubtful if the Executive of the United States, under existing laws, had the power to meet these exigencies; and asked Congress to pass such laws as would enable him to cope with the situation. *The President's Message of March 23d, 1871.*

Congress answered this appeal with the noted, not to say notorious, Ku-Klux Act of April 20th, 1871, in which Congress simply threw to the winds the constitutional distribution of powers between the "States" and the United States Government in respect to civil liberty, crime and punishment, and assumed to legislate freely and without limitation for the preservation of civil and political rights within the "States," and for the punishment of the infraction of the same by individual persons conspiring together for that end, and for the punishment of the conspiracy alone, whether the infraction or the conspiracy was executed upon, or directed against, officers of the Government or merely private persons; and *The Ku-Klux Act of April 20th, 1871.*

in which the act of a combination of private individuals defying successfully the constituted authorities of the United States in a given "State," or those of the "State" concerned, was declared to be rebellion against the United States, upon the happening, and during the continuance, of which the President might suspend the privileges of the writ of Habeas Corpus within such districts as he, by proclamation, might designate.

The first part of this Act was, unquestionably, an unconstitutional encroachment upon the powers of the "States," in so far as it is related to the protection of political rights against infraction, or against conspiracy for the purpose of infraction, by private persons. The second part was probably within the powers of Congress, but it was a most extreme use of its powers. The "State" governments in the South were in the hands of the Republican "carpet-baggers" and Republican negroes, and there is no question that the governors and legislatures of these "States" were quick enough to call in the aid of United States troops long before it was necessary to do so. Moreover, the militia of these "States" was composed almost entirely of negroes, and the whites were forbidden to keep arms. Under such circumstances this Act of Congress empowering the President to establish martial law upon his own motion in time of peace within a "State" when combinations of private persons had successfully defied, in any instance, the laws of the "State" was a very stiff measure, and unwarranted by the facts of the situation.

The unconstitutionality of the Act.

As a matter of fact, the Governor of South Carolina had asked the President to give him United States soldiers for the protection of the "State" and its citizens against domestic violence, and the President had, on the 24th of March just preceding the passage of this act, issued his proclamation commanding the persons composing the unlawful combinations to disperse and retire to their abodes within twenty days. This was the method prescribed by the Constitution for bringing the military power of the United States to the assistance of a "State" government whenever the "State" government might not be able to maintain itself against domestic violence. There is no doubt that General Scott of Ohio, whilom officer in the Union army and in the Freedmen's Bureau, the "carpet-bag," radical Republican Governor of South Carolina, attributed the most traitorous character possible to these combinations, exaggerated the strength and extent of them to the highest possible degree, and called for United States troops to suppress them at the earliest possible moment. [The most trustworthy men in South Carolina affirmed then, and have continued to affirm to this day, that those combinations had no traitorous intent whatsoever, but were simply defensive in their nature; that the wholesale pardoning of criminals by the Governor and the vagrancy of the negroes had filled the country with desperadoes who made life, property, and female honor insecure; and that, as the militia was composed of the friends of these fiends, and the "State" government itself would not protect the white citizens, it was absolutely necessary for the white people to create some means of united action in self-defence and take the law into their own hands.] Statements to this effect were made by one Judge Carpenter, a Republican "State" official of South Carolina, before the investigating committee of Congress in 1871.

Interference of the United States military power in the affairs of South Carolina.

On the 3d day of May following the passage of the Ku-Klux Act, the President issued his general proclamation warning the people that the law applied to the whole country, but particularly exhorting the people in the newly reconstructed "States" to suppress all unlawful combinations by their own voluntary efforts, and declaring, that while he was reluctant to make use of the extraordinary powers conferred on him by the Act, he would nevertheless do so if it should be found necessary for securing all the citizens of the United States in "the peaceful enjoyment of the rights guaranteed to them by the Constitution and the laws."

The President's proclamation of May 3d, 1871.

On the 12th of the following October, the President directed his proclamation to the people of South Carolina alone, declaring that hostile combinations of persons making armed resistance to the civil authorities of the "State" and the United States, in their attempt to secure the people in their rights guaranteed by the Constitution of the United States and the Congressional Act of April 20th, 1871, too strong to be overcome by these authorities, existed in the counties of York, Marion, Chester, Laurens, Newberry, Fairfield, Lancaster and Chesterfield, and commanding the members of these combinations to deliver their arms and accoutrements into the hands of the United States officers in those districts, and disperse to their abodes within five days.

The President's proclamation to the people of South Carolina.

At the end of the five days of grace, the President issued a third proclamation, declaring that the members of these unlawful combinations in the places mentioned in his former proclamation had not dispersed and had not delivered up their arms and accoutrements as ordered, and suspending the privileges of the writ of Habeas Corpus in the counties of South Carolina above designated.

Suspension of the privileges of the writ of Habeas Corpus by the President in certain counties of South Carolina.

On the 3d day of the following November a fourth proclamation was published, in which the President acknowledged his error in including the county of Marion in the list of counties in which the privileges of the writ were suspended, but declared that the situation in Union county was such as to warrant the suspension of those privileges in that county also, and warned the insurgents in that county to deliver up their arms and accoutrements and disperse to their abodes within five days. This warning not having been obeyed, according to the views of the President, a final proclamation was issued by him on the the 10th day of November suspending the privileges of the writ of Habeas Corpus in Union county.

In execution of the Act of April 20th, and in pursuance of these proclamations, the President now sent a strong force of United States troops into the district composed of the nine counties mentioned, the commanders of which arrested some five or six hundred persons, kept them in confinement so long as they pleased, and procured the arraignment of some of them before the United States courts, where a number of them were convicted and sentenced to fine or imprisonment or to both. Whether there was any necessity for the exercise of such harshness as this is a grave question. It was felt at the South to be an abominable outrage, and the Democrats of the North held the same opinion. More ominous than all this, however, was the fact that many leading Republicans raised their voices in disapproval of it, and of the law which authorized it. *The Ku-Klux trials.*

During the year 1872, in addition to all this, there came to the knowledge of Congress and of the people of the North the frightful and scandalous corruption of the "State" governments in the South. It is very difficult to get at distinct and reliable facts upon a subject which officials undertake to cover up and keep shrouded in darkness. *Corruption in the "State" governments of the South.*

But the record of these doings in South Carolina was something as follows. The House of Representatives, the majority of the members of which were negroes, and the presiding officer of which was the notorious F. J. Moses, spent ninety-five thousand dollars to refurnish its assembly hall, where the aristocrats of South Carolina had never spent over five thousand. Clocks costing six hundred dollars each, sofas two hundred dollars each, chairs at sixty dollars each, desks at a hundred and twenty-five dollars each, mirrors at six hundred dollars each, cuspidors at eight dollars each—such were the items of the bill. In the four years from 1868 to 1872, two hundred thousand dollars were expended for furniture for the legislative chambers alone. Then came the bills of supplies, sundries and incidentals, amounting in one session to three hundred and fifty thousand dollars, one hundred and twenty-five thousand of it for a free restaurant, lunch counter and bar, at which the members and their friends fared most royally, eating, drinking and smoking, and paying not a penny therefor directly, nor indirectly, since many, if not most, of the members of that legislature paid no stiver of the taxes. Then came the printing bills, averaging more than one hundred and fifty thousand dollars a year where ten thousand dollars would have been more than enough to pay every legitimate expense of that kind.

Then came the sale of franchises of all kinds, and the pledging of the credit of the "State" in the form of bonds to aid all sorts of enterprises pretended to be set on foot, or promoted as is now said, by combinations of legislators or officials or their friends. In 1868 the "State" debt was about five millions of dollars, with almost enough assets to pay it. In 1872 the assets had disappeared and the debt was more than eighteen millions, and nothing worth mentioning to show for it. And all this when the "State" taxes had been raised from less than a half million of dollars a year on a valuation of over four hundred millions to two millions of dollars a year on a valuation of less than two hundred millions of property.

In Louisiana, under the leadership of the brilliant young adventurer, Henry C. Warmoth of Illinois, the financial history of the "State" was even more scandalous. During the four years of Warmoth's governorship, from 1868 to 1872, the average annual expenditure of the "State" government was about six millions of dollars, when, measured by the previous experiences of the "State," six hundred thousand dollars would have been ample to defray all legitimate expenses. At the beginning of Warmoth's administration the debt of the "State" was between six and seven millions of dollars, with more than enough assets to extinguish it. At the end of the four years of his power, in 1872, the debt was nearly fifty millions of dollars, the assets had all disappeared, and there was nothing worth mentioning to show for the one or the other.

In Louisiana.

[In the counties and municipalities of both "States" the corruption was equally rampant, shameless, and vulgar.] It is impossible to obtain exact figures in regard to it, or to estimate with any degree of exactness, or even probability, the amounts stolen and made away with. [In the other reconstructed "States" where the adventurers and the negroes held sway, the "State" governments worked along the same lines, though not to the same appalling extent.

It was the most soul-sickening spectacle that Americans had ever been called upon to behold. Every principle of the old American polity was here reversed. In place of government by the most intelligent and virtuous part of the people for the benefit of the governed, here was government by the most ignorant and vicious part of the population for the benefit, the vulgar, materialistic, brutal benefit of the governing set.⟩

It is no subject of surprise or wonder that, confronted with these frightful results of radical Republican policy and administration in the South, such Republicans as Horace Greeley, Charles Francis Adams, Lyman Trumbull, David Davis, Carl Schurz, Gratz Brown, Stanley Matthews, George Hoadly, J. R. Spaulding, George W. Julian, Horace White, David A. Wells, and the like, turned with disgust from the nauseating transactions and resolved to do what was in their power to put an end to it all. Even the radical, but honest, Sumner gave his adherence to the movement for a change of the Administration, as the only way to check the terrible corruption which was creeping over the land. Sumner, it is true, had been made to feel personally the heavy hand of the Administration. He had been dropped, the preceding year, from the chairmanship of the Committee on Foreign Relations at the requirement of the Administration, because he had so strongly and successfully opposed the Santo Domingo policy of the President and his "aide-de-camp." But he had opposed that because he saw in it corruption, robbery and bloodshed.

The revolt in the Republican party.

The Liberal Republicans were bolters, of course, from the regular organization, and there was no sufficient opportunity for them to construct a party organization for themselves in time for the Presidential election of 1872. A general call for the leaders among them to meet in mass convention was issued from a "State" convention of Liberal

The Liberal Republican convention of 1872.

"CARPET-BAG" AND NEGRO DOMINATION

Republicans in Missouri, and the meeting took place at Cincinnati on the 1st day of May, 1872.

The platform which it presented to the people demanded the removal, at once, of all political disabilities from the white men of the South, the maintenance of impartial suffrage and of equal civil rights, the cessation of military rule in the South and the supremacy of civil over military power, the reform of the civil service, and a speedy return to specie payments. Many of the Liberal Republicans were inclined toward a much more moderate tariff policy, but out of respect for the opinions of those among them who were strong protectionists, they abandoned their attempt to insert any doctrine on this subject in the platform. The protectionists were equally considerate, and so the new party went to the country uncommitted upon this very important question.

Their platform.

It was at first supposed that the choice of the convention for the Presidency would lay between Judge David Davis of Illinois, Charles Francis Adams of Massachusetts and Senator Lyman Trumbull of Illinois. But an unexpected hostility of a very bitter nature soon developed between the supporters of Davis and Adams, and rendered the nomination of either of them impossible. This was evident on the first ballot, on which Mr. Greeley, Senator Trumbull and Gratz Brown each received more votes than Judge Davis, and together more votes than Mr. Adams. It was thus manifest that the Western men would not take Mr. Adams and the Eastern men would not take Judge Davis. The compromise was quickly made upon Greeley, and Gratz Brown was put with him upon the ticket. It was an unfortunate selection. The country did not want any brilliant experiments at the moment. It wanted to settle down to business. And it was to be

Their nominees.

foreseen that it would not be willing to make a newspaper man President at such a juncture.

But stranger than the fact that the prince of protectionists was now running for the presidency on a platform which ignored protection, was the fact that the Democratic party, strengthened again by its Southern wing, now accepted the platform of the Liberal Republicans, and in convention at Baltimore, in July following the Cincinnati meeting, nominated the Liberal Republican candidates for the presidency and the vice-presidency as its own candidates. The action of the Democrats, both as to the platform and the candidates, was almost unanimous, and it would be ungracious to express any suspicion of its sincerity. The change of profession on the part of the Southern Democrats was very great, indeed, so great as to be surprising, but they had evidently come to the conclusion that it was useless to contend with the North any longer against the civil and political rights of the freedmen, and that it was best for all concerned to accept the inevitable, and try to put themselves in the most advantageous position possible for adjusting the relations of their section to it.

Acceptance of the Liberal Republican candidates by the Democrats.

Mr. Greeley was, indeed, in strange company, but the company had come to him. He had not gone to them. He welcomed their support, and became contaminated by it in the eyes of a vast majority of the people of the North. His own great ambition to be President also caused him to say and to do some imprudent and undignified things. More than all, the time had not yet come for the great change. The country was fast approaching a financial crisis, and any shock would bring it on with such sudden violence as to make it widespread and disastrous.

Mr. Greeley and the Democrats.

"CARPET-BAG" AND NEGRO DOMINATION 267

As the last move, the "straight-out" Democrats bolted the ticket in September, and at a convention held in Louisville, Kentucky, nominated Charles O'Conor of New York for President, and John Quincy Adams of Massachusetts for Vice-President. *Division in the Democratic Party.*

The September and October elections in Vermont, Maine, Pennsylvania, Ohio, and Indiana demonstrated the hopelessness of the opposition to the radical Republicans. They had held their convention in Philadelphia in the early part of June, had issued a platform which simply asserted the righteousness of what they had done and the determination to persist in the course heretofore followed, and had nominated General Grant for re-election to the presidency with Senator Henry Wilson, of Massachusetts, for his running mate. *The Republican platform and nominees.*

In the election, they swept all of the Northern "States" by heavy popular majorities, and with their election machinery in the Southern "States" they captured a majority of these also. In those Southern "States" which were free from carpet-bag negro rule the Greeley electors were chosen, that is in Maryland, Kentucky, Missouri, Tennessee, Georgia and Texas. In the North, a very large number of Democrats had failed to go to the polls. They could hardly have elected Greeley, however, had they all voted for him. They were pretty sure of this, and they took the opportunity of administering a rebuke to their chiefs for not nominating candidates who were members of their own party. *The Republican triumph.*

While there is no doubt that the re-election of General Grant, and the election of a strong Republican majority in Congress, quieted the mind of the North, there is also no doubt that they caused great discouragement among the white people of the South, since they operated as an encouragement to the adventurers and the negroes to persevere in their corrupt and conscienceless management of the "State" governments.

<small>The effect of the triumph of the Republicans.</small>

In several of the reconstructed "States" the Democrats had made strong efforts to secure control of the "State" governments. The Amnesty Act of May 22d, 1872, had removed the disqualifications of the Fourteenth Amendment from all the Southern leaders, except such as had been members of the Thirty-sixth and Thirty-seventh Congresses, or had held judicial, military, naval, or diplomatic office under the United States, or had been heads of departments in ministerial office. A large number of these leaders had thus been placed in a position to participate as candidates for office and legislative position in the election, and to aid greatly in the work of rescuing their "States" from negro Republican rule. In Alabama and Louisiana they had very nearly succeeded. In Alabama they had elected the Governor and a majority of the members to the lower house of the legislature in the autumn of 1870, and in 1872 they claimed to have elected a majority of the members to both houses.

In Alabama, the Democratic members-elect of the legislature convened in the capitol, and the Republican members-elect in the court-house. The Democratic Governor, Lindsay, recognized the Democratic legislature, and the Democratic legislature then canvassed the votes for Governor and declared the Republican candidate, D. P. Lewis, elected. Lewis then recognized the Republican legislature, and telegraphed to Opelika for United States soldiers to come to Montgomery. They arrived by the next train, and, backed by these, the Governor and his friends, in and

<small>Events in Alabama.</small>

out of the legislature, succeeded in constituting a legislature with a small Republican majority in both houses; and the whites fell back again under black rule, discouraged and exhausted by the exertions and the failure to escape from it.

In Louisiana the events were far more extraordinary and violent. Warmoth's rule was approaching its end, and his Republican enemies, what was known as the Custom House faction, the United States officials, were fairly panting to get at him. *Events in Louisiana.* To foil them, he went over to the Democrats and promised to give them a fair chance to elect their candidate for Governor and their candidates for the legislature. For this he expected protection from them against the Custom House gang, to whom he had denied what they had conceived to be their proper share of the public plunder, and who, if in possession of the "State" government, would make him answer for it. Warmoth supposed he was able with his election machinery to give the "State" to the Democrats whether the voters should do so or not. The election took place at the same time as the presidential election, November 4th, 1872. The returns were sent by the supervisors and commissioners of elections to Warmoth, and he delivered them to his Returning Board, consisting of himself, the Secretary of State, F. J. Herron, and one John Lynch; the other two members of the Board as constituted by the legislature, by the act of 1870, viz., Lieutenant-Governor Pinchback and one Anderson, being disqualified from serving, since both of them were candidates for office at this election. The Governor had his suspicions aroused about the loyalty of both Herron and Lynch to him before the count took place, and having the legal power to remove Herron, he did so at once and appointed one John Wharton, a friend upon whom he could rely, in

Herron's place. Lynch now refused to act with them, and Herron denied the power of the Governor to dismiss him from the Secretaryship of State, and from his *ex officio* membership in the Returning Board. Warmoth and Wharton proceeded, however, to supply the place of Lynch, as they might do under the law, and Herron and Lynch proceeded to supply the place of Warmoth.

The Warmoth Board had the returns, and it was also generally felt that the Democratic candidate for Governor, John McEnery, had been chosen by the voters. Moreover, the right of Herron to retain the office of Secretary of State was immediately brought before the supreme court of the "State," and the court gave its decision against Herron's contention. It seemed now certain that the Warmoth Returning Board would declare McEnery to have been elected Governor. But the Republican candidate, W. P. Kellogg, then a Senator from Louisiana in Congress, was watchful and resourceful. He secured from United States District Judge Durell an injunction which forbade the Warmoth Board to do anything except in the presence of the Lynch Board, and forbade McEnery from claiming his election under the returns which might be given out by the Warmoth Board.

Warmoth met this by a move which was equally a *coup de surprise*. The legislature had at its last session passed a law vesting the power to select the members of the Returning Board in the senate. The Governor had not signed this bill, and probably never intended to sign it, since it proposed to take the control of the Board out of his hands, but it now seemed to furnish him a way of escape from Durell's order. He hastily signed the bill and promulgated it as law, and as the senate was not in session, proceeded to appoint the members of the new Board himself, under the power of the Governor to make temporary appointments

<small>Warmoth and Durell.</small>

to office when the senate was not in session. He appointed one Dr. Feriet chairman of the Board, and put the election returns in his hands. This Board declared that McEnery had been elected Governor and that the Greeley electors had been chosen. The Governor published these decisions officially on the 5th day of December, and the affair seemed to have been closed. But to the surprise of everyone concerned, and of the whole country, in the middle of the night following, Judge Durell issued an order to the United States Marshal, S. B. Packard, to take possession of the capitol and hold it at the pleasure of the Judge against all unlawful bodies attempting to convene therein. The Judge claimed that Warmoth had committed a contempt against his court in the Returning Board proceeding, and he declared that the Lynch Board was the legal body. His order furthermore required the commander of the United States troops to furnish a detachment of soldiers to sustain the United States marshal in taking possession of the capitol, and in enforcing the Lynch Board's canvass and decision.

A more palpable outrage upon the lawful powers of a "State" could hardly have been conceived. The Judge had not a scintilla of authority upon which to rest his proceeding. It is claimed that he was drunk when he made the order. But this can hardly have been true, that is he could not have been any more than ordinarily drunk, since the order was not withdrawn when he became ostensibly sober again, but was made the basis of a proceeding which lasted through many days, and the results of which were the counting in of Kellogg and of a Republican legislature by the Lynch Board, the immediate instalment of the Lynch Board legislature, the almost immediate impeachment of Warmoth by it and his removal from the governorship, the installation of the

Lieutenant-Governor, the negro Pinchback, in his seat, the recognition of the Lynch Board legislature and of Pinchback by the President of the United States as the lawful legislature and executive of Louisiana, and the inauguration of Kellogg as Governor at the end of the Warmoth-Pinchback term. If this was all the work of a drunken spree, it must have been a very long one, and there must have been many participants in it besides the Judge.

The Warmoth Board Governor and legislature undertook to set up government also, sustained as they undoubtedly were both by the law, and by public opinion in Louisiana and probably throughout the country, and partially organized a militia force. It was the fighting between this militia and the metropolitan police in the streets of New Orleans which occasioned the suppression of the McEnery government at last by United States soldiers.

For two years more now the government of the adventurers, based on negro support, continued in the "States" south of the Tennessee line, except Georgia. Property was decreasing in amount and value; taxes were being doubled; and new bond issues were being made, and the bonds sold at a great reduction upon their face value, or stolen outright. But the day of deliverance was coming. The conscience of the Nation had been aroused, and in the elections of 1874 the voters throughout the country delivered a stunning rebuke to the party responsible for the hideous situation in the South. It is true that other issues were influential in producing the *bouleversement* of 1874, especially the financial panic of 1873 and the corruption in the circles of the Federal Administration itself, the Whiskey ring frauds, and the Indian agent peculations. We must also remem-

"CARPET-BAG" AND NEGRO DOMINATION 273

ber that at this very election several of the Southern "States" relieved themselves of Republican rule and sent solid, or almost solid, Democratic delegations to Congress. But with all proper allowance for the effect of these things, there still remained, as the chief cause of the change of view in the North, the revolt of the popular conscience against being any longer dragooned into the support of the policy of the Republican party in the Southern "States," and the popular disgust at the everlasting "waving of the bloody shirt" whenever the dominance of that party seemed anywhere threatened. At any rate, it was a clean sweep, and from a majority of two-thirds in the Forty-third Congress, the Republicans found themselves in possession of only about one-third of the seats in the Lower House of the Forty-fourth Congress.

Moreover, three more of the Southern "States" freed themselves, at this time, from "Black Republican" rule. In Alabama, the respectable whites had now about all gone into the Democratic ranks, and with the election of George S. Houston as Governor, and a legislature in large majority Democratic, the "State" won at last its self-government. Likewise by a similar fusion of all the respectable whites into the Democratic party, A. H. Garland was elected Governor of Arkansas and a legislature with a large Democratic majority was chosen, and from that time forward the "State" government has been in the hands of its own citizens. The same result was reached in Texas, where the union of the respectables of all parties upon the Democratic candidates elected Richard Coke Governor and a legislature of reputable white men. *The change in Alabama, Arkansas and Texas.*

Even South Carolina very nearly escaped her thraldom, and came near to electing a white Democrat Governor. As it was, she got a moderate Republican for

Governor, Mr. D. H. Chamberlain, a Northerner indeed, but a man of great ability and undoubted honesty, who did everything in his power to redeem the "State" from the miserable condition into which the errors and crimes of his predecessors had brought it. He naturally soon found himself in conflict with some of the leaders of his own party in the "State" and at Washington, and was greatly impeded by them in carrying out his own purposes. At last, in 1875, the break between him and the members of his party in the legislature was completed by the act of the legislature in electing the notorious F. J. Moses, Jr., and the negro, W. J. Whipper, "State" judges. The Governor was so incensed at this act of downright depravity that he refused to commission the two judges-elect to the judicial offices to which they had been chosen. Whipper threatened to use force to gain possession of the office, and the Governor issued his proclamation threatening to arrest every person who should give Whipper any aid or support in this attempt as disturbers of the public peace. The Governor triumphed and protected the "State" against the terrible degradation which impended over it, but his brave attitude ruined him with the radical and base elements of his party.

The status in South Carolina in 1874.

Governor Chamberlain.

The day of complete deliverance was now, however, rapidly approaching. The election of 1875 in Mississippi showed that the domination of the "Black Republicans" in the Southern "State" governments could last no longer. Here was a "State" in which the negro population exceeded the white very largely, but in the election of 1875 the whites finally got together and what they could not accomplish in one way they did in another. The whites organized themselves into rifle clubs, attended the Republican

The day of complete deliverance.

meetings and insisted upon a division of the time between their own speakers and the Republican speakers at these meetings. A great deal of fraud and intimidation was practised, and some violence was exercised, but always in such a manner as not to provoke the calling of United States troops to the scene. The immediate occasion of these desperate movements on the part of the whites was the treatment accorded the petition made by the taxpayers' convention of the "State" to the legislature for relief from the intolerable burdens under which the taxpayers were suffering. This petition of the 4th of January, 1875, recited that between the years 1869 and 1874 the rate of "State" taxation had been raised from ten cents on the hundred dollars of assessed value of lands to one dollar and forty cents, and that in many cases the increase in the rate of the county levies had been even greater, so that the whole product of the soil was hardly sufficient to pay the taxes. The negro legislature laughed at these representations, and did not deign to consider them, much less to do anything to satisfy the frightful grievances complained of. It was now a choice between complete destruction and the employment of any means necessary to escape from it. There was no use in talking about observing the letter of the law at such a moment. The law was iniquitous and it was rapidly destroying all that was left of prosperity, civilization, morality and decency. If it would not yield, it had to be broken. The movement was successful. It was really a revolution. It resulted in the election of a Democratic legislature in November of 1875, the disruption of the Republican party in the "State," the framing of an impeachment against the Republican Governor, Ames, his resignation and departure from the "State," and the accession of the

<small>The status in Mississippi in 1875.</small>

Democrat, John M. Stone, to the gubernatorial office.

It was thus that the eventful year 1876 was introduced, and it was an earnest of the relief which was now to come to the remaining "States" of the South suffering under the rule of the adventurers and their negro allies.

While the Republican party had step by step, and almost unconsciously, involved itself in the support of dishonest and oppressive government at the South, it was, on the other hand, fighting the battle for financial honesty in the Nation at large against the fiat money heresy and the schemes of repudiation invented and supported by the national Democracy. Its Congressional majority had passed the Refunding Acts of July 14th, 1870, and January 20th, 1871, for refunding the debt of the United States in coin bonds bearing five, four and one-half and four per centum interest. These acts authorized the issue of eighteen hundred millions of dollars in these new bonds, five hundred millions payable after ten years, and bearing five per centum interest, three hundred millions payable after fifteen years and bearing four and one-half per centum interest, and one thousand millions payable after thirty years and bearing four per centum interest. By the Act of March 18th, 1869, the Republican Congress had declared that all of the obligations of the United States should be paid in coin or its equivalent, unless otherwise specifically stipulated in the law authorizing the obligation. This Act was made applicable to past, as well as future, obligations. It rested on the principle that debts must be paid in the best money of the country unless otherwise agreed to in the contract. This is, of course, the sound principle both of morals and finance, and no act of Congress pronouncing

Fiat money, and the resumption of specie payments.

it would have been considered necessary, except for the great fact that the Democratic party, in its campaign of 1868, had espoused the opposite doctrine and had fought the campaign largely under that issue. The Act, however, might of course be repealed, and in that case the question as to whether the principal sum of the greater part of the national indebtedness should be paid in coin would be again opened, since the laws authorizing the incurring of these obligations provided only for the payment of the interest upon them in coin. It was in order to forestall the possibility of a repeal of the Act of March 18th, 1869, as well as in order to make a large saving in the interest charge, that these Refunding Acts were passed.

After the panic of 1873 had resulted in such a depression of business and depreciation of values throughout the country as to create greater discontent with the existing political management, and this discontent had manifested itself so distinctly in the elections of 1874, announcing to the Republican party that after March 5th, 1875, a Democratic majority would prevail in the House of Representatives, it was manifest to the Republican leaders, in Congress and out of Congress, that if anything was to be done in regard to the resumption of specie payment, anything for bringing the paper currency of the United States up to a coin value, it must be done speedily, and on the 21st of December, 1874, Mr. Sherman reported a bill from the Finance Committee to the Senate for this purpose, which became a law on the 14th day of January following, and which provided for the redemption of the fractional currency with silver coins of the value of ten, twenty-five and fifty cents, so rapidly as these coins could be minted; abolished the charge of one-fifth of one per centum on the coinage of gold, making the coinage of gold at the mints of the

United States free; repealed the law limiting the aggregate amount of the circulating notes of the national banking associations, and the law for the withdrawal of national-bank currency from, and its redistribution among, the several "States" and Territories; ordered the Secretary of the Treasury in issuing new circulating notes to the national banking associations to retire United States legal tender notes to the amount of eighty per centum of such issues, until the United States legal tender notes should be reduced to three hundred millions of dollars, and after January 1st, 1879, to redeem these legal tender notes in coin on their presentation at the office of the Assistant Treasurer of the United States in the city of New York, in sums of not less than fifty dollars; and, to enable the Secretary of the Treasury to do this, authorized him to use any unappropriated surplus revenue which might be, from time to time, in the Treasury, and to sell bonds of the description mentioned in the Act of July 14th, 1870, in such amounts as he should find necessary to accomplish the purpose.

It is true that the Republican majority in Congress had not taken this high ground concerning the public credit and sound money without some wavering. The President himself had become frightened by the panic of the autumn of 1873, and in his annual message of December 1st following had made recommendations that might be regarded as favorable to an inflation of the existing body of paper money. His party friends in Congress very soon produced a bill which, among other things, provided for the increase of the United States notes and the national bank notes to the extent of about one hundred millions of dollars, and passed it. But the President had either thought the question out more fully, or had been in receipt of some very sound advice, after he wrote the message of December 1st, 1873. On the 22d of April, 1874, he sent a special message to Congress vetoing the bill. This stand of the President recalled the Republicans in Congress from their economic aberrations, and set them again upon the course which led to the Act of the 14th of January, 1875.

The inflation bill of 1874 and the veto of it by the President.

While at the moment this law for the resumption of specie payments in the short period of four years, or rather less, from the time of its enactment seemed a rather hazardous, not to say desperate, move on the part of the Republicans, it soon became manifest that they could have done nothing so calculated to strengthen the hold of the party upon the solid and conservative men of the country as just this very thing. Many of these men who had usually voted with the Republicans disapproved of the Southern policy of the party, and were on the point of turning against it. With the Resumption Act the financial policy of the Republican party, and of the country, was dragged to the front, and the Southern policy was forced backward, and made to constitute a less prominent issue in the campaign of 1876. This was not only wise party management, but it was also a fortunate thing for the entire country. The country was not yet in a position to endure a Democratic administration, and, on the other hand, it was surfeited with reconstruction Republican administrations. It wanted a sound money Republican administration, which would devote itself to the development of the economic interests of the whole people, and would let the "State" governments in the South have a chance to work out their own salvation. And this was just what it got in the election of 1876, and in the administration of President Rutherford B. Hayes.

CHAPTER XIII

THE PRESIDENTIAL ELECTION OF 1876 AND ITS CONSEQUENCES

The Republican National Convention of 1876—The Platform—The Nominees—The National Democratic Convention of 1876—The Platform—The Nominees—The Campaign and the Election—The Count and the Twenty-second Joint Rule—Views in Regard to the Power to Count the Electoral Vote—The Republicans in Advantage in the Count of the Vote—The Electoral Commission Bill—The Passage of the Bill—The Members of the Commission—The Fifth Justice—Justice David Davis—The Counting of the Electoral Vote by Congress—The Double Returns from South Carolina, Florida, Louisiana and Oregon—The Counsel before the Commission—The Republican Position—The Democratic Position—The Decisions of the Commission—Mr. Hayes Declared President—The Truth in Regard to the Election—Mr. Hayes's Southern Policy—The Result of His Policy—Reconciliation between the North and the South.

WHEN the managers of the Republican party met in National nominating convention at Cincinnati, on the 14th of June, 1876, they rightly divined the policy which alone could lead them to victory in the elections of the following autumn. They constructed their platform in such a way as to place the financial issue in the foreground, with the pledges of the party to uphold the public credit, and to place the currency of the country on a coin basis. They also declared the pacification of the South to be a sacred duty, and pledged the

The Republican National Convention of 1876.

The platform.

party to a thoroughgoing reform of the civil service. Connected therewith were, of course, the usual platitudes about the civil and political liberty and equality of every American citizen and of everybody else.

While there was no name before the convention commanding universal popular assent, as had been the case at the second nomination of Lincoln and the two nominations of Grant, still there was one which, in so far as its possessor was known, inspired strong, if not enthusiastic, confidence. It was not pronounced in the first balloting so loudly as that of the brilliant Blaine, or the stolid Morton, or the arrogant Conkling, but, as the voting continued, more and more of the ballots contained it, and at last on the seventh round, it received a majority of the votes. The choice was a wise one. Mr. Hayes had been a good soldier, a valuable member of the National legislature, and an excellent Governor of his native "State," in which office he was serving for a third term at the time of his nomination for the Presidency. He was a man of sound sense, unimpeachable character, generous feeling, pleasing manners, and resolute will. There was a tendency at first on the part of the friends of some of the disappointed aspirants to belittle his qualities, and to represent him as a weak man, and his conciliatory methods were often mistaken for weakness by those who were not his rivals or his enemies, or the friends of his rivals or his enemies; but as history sets his character and his work in their proper perspective they both stand out more and more strongly, and make his Administration appear to be one of the most important in American annals. Especially does it honor him for his earnest, faithful and successful battle for sound money and the maintenance of the public faith, and for his determination to put an end to the support by Federal bayonets of the "carpet-bag," negro "State" governments of the South.

A fortnight after the nomination by the Republican convention of Rutherford B. Hayes for President and William A. Wheeler for Vice-President, the Democratic leaders met at St. Louis for the purpose of issuing the campaign creed of their party and choosing its candidate for the chief magistracy of the Nation. The platform put forward by them was remarkable for its length, its language of fierce vituperation, and its loud calls for reform. Its specific propositions were the reduction of the duties on foreign imports to a revenue basis, and the repeal of the Resumption Act of 1875, on the strange ground that it obstructed the return to specie payments.

The National Democratic Convention of 1876.

The platform.

Their candidate had virtually been determined on before they met. It could be nobody else than the popular Governor of New York, Samuel J. Tilden, shrewd in business, rich, the most successful political manager New York had produced since Van Buren, greatly heralded as the very archpriest of reform, the hope of the young men in politics; but not a statesman in the highest sense of the word, nor a demagogue in the lowest sense of that word—a genuine American politician of the first order. He was nominated on the second ballot, and by a unanimous vote. With him was placed as candidate for the second place the popular Mr. Hendricks of Indiana. It was a strong ticket, and it was generally believed that it would win. Mr. Tilden himself felt sure of the electoral votes of all the Southern "States" and of New York, Indiana, New Jersey and Connecticut.

The nominees.

Mr. Tilden quietly managed his own campaign, while Mr. Hayes left his political interests in the hands of the

ELECTION OF 1876 AND ITS CONSEQUENCES 283

very astute chairman of the National committee of the Republican party, Senator Chandler of Michigan. There was not much doubt on the morning following the election, the morning of the 8th November, that the Democrats had triumphed. Almost all of the Republican newspapers conceded it. But the Republican managers knew that they could do what they pleased with the electoral votes of South Carolina, Florida and Louisiana, through their canvassing boards in these "States," with the power in these boards to throw out the returns from any place where, in their opinion, there had been any violence, intimidation, fraud or bribery exercised or attempted; and when the managers found that they were pretty sure of the electoral votes of all of the Northern Commonwealths, except Connecticut, New York, New Jersey and Indiana, they simply added to the one hundred and sixty-six electoral votes of which they were practically sure the nineteen votes of Louisiana, Florida and South Carolina, of which they were absolutely sure, if needed, and sent out from their head-quarters the positive announcement that Hayes and Wheeler had been elected by a majority of one electoral vote.

The campaign and the election.

But the final count of the electoral vote must be in the presence of the two Houses of Congress assembled in one place, and the Democrats were in majority in one of the Houses, and the twenty-second joint rule, as it was called, which had been applied since the count of the electoral vote of 1864 for the ascertainment of the result of the returns to Congress, ordained that the electoral vote of any "State" might be thrown out by either House. If this rule should be considered as still in force, and be applied in the impending count, the Democratic House of Representatives could reject the returns of the Repub-

The count and the twenty-second joint rule.

lican authorities in South Carolina, Florida and Louisiana, and thus secure the election of Mr. Tilden. This rule, however, was not necessarily binding upon this Congress, as it had not been re-enacted by the Houses composing it. That is, either House could lawfully refuse to acquiesce in its further application. The Republicans now repudiated it, although it was their predecessors who had created it.

Some of the Republicans now claimed that the Constitution vested the Vice-President, or rather the President of the Senate, with the power to count the electoral votes. The language of the Constitution was, and still is, "the President of the Senate shall, in the presence of the Senate and House of Representatives, open all the certificates and the votes shall then be counted." No President of the Senate had, however, ever ventured to determine whether a disputed return, in case any such had been received by him, was to be counted, and Mr. Ferry, the President of the Senate, gave his Republican friends to understand that he did not feel like assuming any such responsibility.

Views in regard to the power to count the electoral vote.

Nevertheless, the Republicans were in decided advantage. They had the President of the United States to execute by force whatever they might resolve upon, and they had the President of the Senate, whose scruples the Democrats had not discovered, and, of course, they had one House of the Congress, the Senate.

The Republicans in advantage in the count of the vote.

The Democrats felt that they must make an effort to change the situation. They, therefore, quickly seized upon a suggestion made by a Republican member of the Judiciary Committee of the House of Representatives, Mr. G. W. McCrary, and voted a measure in the House for the appointment of

The Electoral Commission Bill.

members to a joint committee of the two Houses, which committee should immediately report a proposition for counting the electoral votes. This was the 14th of December, 1876. The Senate agreed to this measure on the next day. Three Republicans and four Democrats were appointed by the House, and four Republicans and three Democrats by the Senate, and the committee so constituted reported, on the 18th of January, 1877, the famous Electoral Commission bill.

The essential provisions of the bill were, first, the creation of a Commission composed of five members of the House of Representatives, five members of the Senate, and five Justices of the Supreme Court of the United States, the members from the House to be chosen by the House, the members from the Senate to be chosen by the Senate, while the Justices of the Supreme Court from the first, third, eighth and ninth circuits were designated in the bill, and they were authorized to select a fifth from among the other members of the Court; second, the fixing of the rule that the electoral vote of any "State" from which only a single return had been received should be counted unless *both* Houses should decide otherwise, and of the other rule that when more than one return had been received from any "State," the Commission should forthwith decide which return should be counted, and this return should be counted unless *both* Houses should reject the decision, or order otherwise; and third, the reservation of any right existing under the Constitution and laws to question before the courts of the United States the titles of the persons who should be declared elected President and Vice-President to these respective offices. The bill was subjected to a most thorough discussion in *both* Houses. It passed the Senate on the 24th of January by a vote of forty-seven to seventeen. Twenty-one Repub-

The passage of the Bill.

licans and twenty-six Democrats voted in favor of it, and sixteen Republicans and one Democrat voted against it. It passed the House on the 26th by a vote of one hundred and ninety-one to eighty-six. Thirty-three Republicans and one hundred and fifty-eight Democrats voted for it, and sixty-eight Republicans and eighteen Democrats voted against it. It is certainly fair, therefore, to call it a Democratic measure. The President signed the bill, nevertheless, on the 29th.

The Senate immediately chose Messrs. Edmunds, Frelinghuysen and Morton, Republicans, and Messrs. Bayard and Thurman, Democrats, to represent it upon the Commission, and the House chose Messrs. Garfield and Hoar, Republicans, and Messrs. Abbott, Hunton and Payne, Democrats. The Justices of the Supreme Court designated by the bill as members of the Commission were Messrs. Clifford, Strong, Miller and Field. Strong and Miller were understood to be Republicans, and Clifford and Field Democrats. Upon these four the duty was imposed to select the fifth Justice.

The members of the Commission.

Since without the fifth Justice the Commission would consist of seven Republicans and seven Democrats, it was evident that this Justice would be the umpire in every question of disputed returns which the two Houses could not themselves settle by concurrent agreement. The responsibility which this Justice would have to bear would be one of the most onerous and solemn duties ever imposed upon any mortal. It could be no less than the making of a President, and it might be the determination of the question whether there should be another civil war. It was not a responsibility to be courted, but no man upon whom it might fall could, with honor, refuse to accept it.

The fifth Justice.

It was the general feeling throughout the discus-

ELECTION OF 1876 AND ITS CONSEQUENCES

sion of the bill that the man who would be chosen was Judge David Davis. He had been a Republican and a close personal friend of Lincoln, but had latterly inclined toward the Democracy, and, it was thought, had favored the election of Mr. Tilden. He was regarded as the man of least political prejudice among a set of men of very little political prejudice. The Democrats, however, were entirely willing to risk their cause in his hands, because they believed it was strong enough on its merits to convince any unprejudiced mind, and there is little question that the Republicans were afraid to risk their cause in his hands, because they knew that they must win on every point or lose altogether, and they hesitated to take such desperate chances unless whatever political prejudice might exist in the mind of the umpire should be on their side.

But to the apparent surprise of everybody and to the consternation of the Democrats, Justice Davis was chosen by the Illinois legislature, on the 25th of January, the day after the bill passed the Senate, and the day before it passed the House, United States Senator, and a few days after the bill passed the House, he accepted the position, which act involved his resignation at an early day of his judicial office; and as he was now to leave the bench and go into the political branch of the Government, as a Democratic Senator, elected by the Democrats of the Illinois legislature, there appeared to him an evident impropriety in his acting on the Commission as a representative of the unpolitical branch of the Government, and especially as that member upon whom the weightiest responsibility would fall, and who would, therefore, be expected to act with greatest political impartiality, and with an eye single to public justice. Whether Justice Davis sought this election to the senatorship at this juncture or not,

Justice David Davis.

in order to escape the great responsibility that was about to fall upon him, we do not know. He was not a particularly brave man. He was a big, fat man, a good liver, and loved his ease. Ordinarily men will not exchange the high and life-long office of a Justice of the Supreme Court of the United States for a seat in the Senate. Unless he had his eye upon the Presidency of the United States, it would be very hard to explain his action in exchanging his high judicial position for the senatorship on any other ground than his desire to escape the terrible responsibility of deciding whether Tilden or Hayes should be President. It is even more difficult to account for the action of the Democrats in the legislature of Illinois. They certainly did not intend to harm the chances of Mr. Tilden by this act. The Republicans might have invented such a scheme for disposing of the Justice, but for Democrats to have been concerned in any such movement is incredible. It is probable that it was simply a blunder on their part. They did not appreciate the incompatibility between the position of a Democratic Senator-elect and membership on the Electoral Commission as a judicial representative. They thought that as the Justice would not take his seat in the Senate until after the 4th of March he would remain a member of the Supreme Court until then, and as such would be fully qualified for the place on the Commission. The legislature at Springfield had no such delicate and discriminating sense of official proprieties as obtained in Washington, and throughout the more fastidious East.

The Democrats in the House of Representatives learned of the election of Justice Davis to the Senate on the morning of the day they were to vote on the passage of the Electoral Commission bill. Even they did not fully realize that it meant that the Justice would not serve on the Commission. Moreover, they had gone to such lengths with the bill that it was too late to turn back. So far as is known the Justice did not inform them or anybody else of his intention to accept the senatorship, or of his scruples about being a member of the Commission, until after the bill became law. When he did do so, the correctness of his position was so clear that the four Justices named in the Act immediately selected Justice Joseph P. Bradley as the fifth judicial member of the Commission. Bradley was a Republican, as were the other three members of the court, Waite, Hunt and Swayne. That is, after Justice Davis was disposed of there remained only Republicans to choose from, and Bradley being regarded as the least partisan, and the most learned in the law, was selected. He fully realized the vast responsibility which had been thus unexpectedly thrust upon him, but he accepted it bravely and without flinching, and discharged it with honor and success.

The Houses of Congress, and also the Electoral Commission, met on the 1st day of February to count the electoral vote. The Democrats still felt sure of success, since they would win the election, if successful upon a single point, while the Republicans, to be successful, must win upon every point. On the other hand, the hopes of the Republicans had been raised by gaining the majority of the Commission. *The counting of the electoral vote by Congress.*

When the returns were opened by the President of the Senate two sets of returns were found from each of the four "States," Florida, Louisiana, South Carolina, and Oregon. In the case of Florida the electors voting for Hayes and Wheeler sent with their votes the certification of the "State" Canvassing Board and of the Governor to their election. The case of South Carolina was the same. *The double returns from South Carolina, Florida, Louisiana and Oregon.*

In the case of Louisiana the electors voting for Hayes and Wheeler sent with their votes the certification of Governor Kellogg and of the "State" Canvassing Board acting with him to their election, and the electors voting for Tilden and Hendricks sent the certification of John McEnery, claiming to be Governor, and the Canvassing Board acting with him, to their election.

The Oregon case was more complicated. The three Republican electors received the highest number of votes, as reported by the Secretary of State, who by the laws of Oregon was the "State" canvassing officer, to the Governor. But one of them, Watts, held the office of postmaster in a small place at the time of his election, and the Constitution of the United States provides that "no Senator or Representative, or person holding any office of trust or profit under the United States, shall be appointed an elector." The Democratic Governor of Oregon decided in his own mind that Watts was not eligible, and made out his certification to include, beside the two Republican electors who were eligible, one Cronin, the Democrat receiving the highest number of votes for elector, although the number received by him was a minority of all the votes cast for the electoral tickets. This certificate was attested by the Secretary of State, and was given to Cronin. When the day for the meeting of the electors came around Cronin presented himself holding the Governor's certificate, the only certificate which had been issued to the electors by Governor Grover. But in spite of the fact that he had this technical advantage, the two Republican electors, whose names were included in the Governor's certificate, refused to act with him, and he refused to let them have the certificate to attach to their return of the electoral vote to the President of the Senate of the United States unless they should so act. Both parties persisted in their refusals. Whereupon Cronin selected one J. N. Y. Miller and one John Parker to fill up the electoral college of Oregon and these three cast two electoral votes for Hayes and Wheeler and one for Tilden and Hendricks, and, after attaching the Governor's certification to the record of their vote in due form, sent this return to the President of the Senate of the United States, as required by the Constitution. At the same time the two Republican electors, Odell and Cartwright, met to cast the electoral vote of the Commonwealth. Watts was also present. He had resigned his office of postmaster, and now he resigned his position as elector. The other two accepted his resignation, and immediately chose him an elector. The three then cast the electoral vote of the Commonwealth for Hayes and Wheeler. As we have seen, they did not have the certification of their election by the Governor to attach to their votes, as required by the law of the United States, but they procured from the Secretary of State a certified copy of the canvass of the votes for the electors, which showed the election of the three Republican candidates, and sent this, and also a copy of their proceedings in accepting the resignation of Watts, and then electing him an elector, along with their report of the vote of the electors for President and Vice-President, to the President of the Senate.

Both the Republicans and the Democrats were represented by most able counsel before the Electoral Commission. William M. Evarts, Stanley Matthews, E. W. Stoughton, and Samuel Shellabarger were pitted against a formidable array both as to ability and numbers on the other side, Judge J. S. Black, Matthew H. Carpenter, Charles O'Conor, J. A. Campbell, Lyman Trumbull, Ashbel Green, Montgomery Blair, George Hoadly, William C. Whitney, R. T. Merrick and A. P. Morse. *The counsel before the Commission.*

The Republicans took their stand at the outset upon the principle that Congress could not go behind the returns of the "State" Canvassing Board or officer, in counting the electoral vote from any "State." They contended that in the election of the President and Vice-President, the Constitution had separated the procedure into two distinct parts, and had assigned the first part to the control of the several "States" exclusively, and the second part to the control of Congress exclusively; that up to the completion of the election of the electors the exclusive control of the "States" respectively extended, but that all control after that point had been reached was in Congress, and that Congress had no power whatever, under the Constitution, to revise, interfere with, or examine into, that part assigned by the Constitution to the "States" respectively, and, on the other hand, that Congress was bound to disregard any act of the "States," or of any of the officers or agents of the "States," in that part assigned exclusively by the Constitution to its own control. There is no question that this was all sound constitutional law and that the Democrats would have to abandon entirely their old "States'" rights doctrine and go over to the most extreme nationalism in order to combat it.

The Republican position.

It did not appear to them necessary to do this in order to win their case. One single electoral vote from any one of the four "States," from which double returns had been received, would elect Tilden and Hendricks. It did not seem to them that the line between the powers of the "States" and those of Congress over the election of the President and Vice-President could under the existing facts be drawn anywhere without giving them at least this one vote. If the returns as certified to by the Governors and the "State" canvassing officer, officers, or boards, of these four

The Democratic position.

"States" should be received and counted they would have this one vote from Oregon. If, on the other hand, the popular vote for the electors as it came into the hands of the "State" canvassing officers or boards was to be received and counted, then they would have the electoral votes of at least Louisiana, Florida, or South Carolina, and perhaps of all of them. But the Republicans contended that the line between "State" control and Congressional control was to be drawn between the Governor's certification and the report of the "State" canvassing officer, officers, or board to the Governor of the result of the vote for the electors. The certification issued by the Governor, they held, was ordered by Congressional law and was under Congressional control, even when the "State" canvassing officer, officers, or board should join with the Governor in the certification of the persons chosen electors. The report of the vote for the electors by the "State" canvassing officer, officers, or board to the Governor was thus the final act under "State" control, was the final act in the election of the electors. This was unquestionably sound constitutional law. But it would give all the electoral votes from all four of the "States," from which double returns had been received, to Hayes and Wheeler, and would elect them by one vote.

The view of the counsel for the Republican candidates prevailed with a majority of the Commission. By a majority of a single vote the Commission gave all the electoral votes of the four "States" from which double returns had been received to Hayes and Wheeler, and since the decisions of the Commission were final unless negatived by both Houses of Congress, and the Republican Senate, of course, sustained the decisions of the Commission, there was nothing for the Democrats to do but submit or have recourse to violence. Threats were freely expressed of having

The decisions of the Commission.

Mr. Tilden take the oath of office, and then conducting him, under the support of a large armed body, to the White House and installing him there. But it was observed that the Southern Democrats did not participate in these menacing declarations, and it was soon learned that Mr. Tilden himself would not lend himself to any such desperate movement. Moreover, the existing President had, with his usual promptness and decision, prepared himself to meet all exigencies, and had let it be known that he would uphold the decisions to which Congress and its Commission might come by any power necessary to accomplish the result.

In the early morning of March 2d, the count was completed, and Hayes and Wheeler were proclaimed by the presiding officer of the Senate, Mr. Terry, *Mr. Hayes declared President.* elected President and Vice-President of the United States by a majority of one electoral vote. The popular vote for the electors was about eight millions three hundred thousand. Of this vast number the Tilden electors had received the majority by about two hundred and fifty thousand, according to the Republican count, and by about three hundred thousand, according to the Democratic count. It must be remembered, however, that it is quite possible for the candidate of one party to receive a popular majority throughout the whole country, and the candidate of the other to receive a majority of the electoral votes, simply because the popular vote is counted, in electing the electors, by "States" and not in the aggregate.

The truth in regard to the whole transaction of the election probably is that the Democrats did in some places in the South intimidate voters; that the Republican "State" canvassing officers, making this a justification, or an excuse, did throw out votes that ought to have been counted; and that the existing law of elections, administered by Republicans, was capable of being so interpreted as to give legal warrant to all that was done by them. A perfectly fair election in the "States" of Louisiana, Florida, and South Carolina, with the law of suffrage then obtaining, would probably have resulted in a popular majority for the Republican candidates for electors. Accepting the law of suffrage as then existing for the basis of our reasoning, it will have to be conceded that the Republicans were in the right both morally and legally, and that the title of Hayes and Wheeler to the offices of President and Vice-President was entirely sound and unimpeachable. They were inaugurated on the 5th day of March, 1877, without any attempt at resistance or disturbance from any quarter.

The truth in regard to the election.

During the counting of the electoral vote it was suspected that the friends of Mr. Hayes were giving some assurances to the Southerners in Congress in regard to what the policy of his Administration would be concerning the "State" governments in the South. The unwillingness of the Southern Democrats to join with their party associates of the North in any revolutionary projects was attributed partly to this. While there is no evidence that Mr. Hayes ever pledged himself to the Southerners in regard to anything, still it is probably true that his views concerning the unwisdom of the employment of the military power of the United States in upholding the negro-Republican "State" governments in the South were imparted to them by his friends. At any rate, he announced in his inaugural address that he considered the re-establishment of local self-government in these "States" to be one of the prime objects of his Administration, and he speedily withdrew the support of the military power of the United States from the three

Mr. Hayes's Southern policy.

negro-Republican "State" governments, and left them to their own resources.

The result was that, although the Republican candidates for Governor and for the members of the legislature in these three "States" received about the same vote as the Republican presidential electors, and in January of 1877 actually assumed power, the Democratic candidates ousted them from the offices, and in sufficient number from the legislative seats, and established at last Democratic white rule in all the "States" of the South. In Florida the Republican, M. L. Stearns, gave way to the Democrat, George F. Drew, in the gubernatorial office; in South Carolina D. H. Chamberlain gave way to Wade Hampton, and in Louisiana, S. B. Packard gave way to Francis T. Nicholls.

<small>The result of his policy.</small>

Order and peace were quickly established everywhere, and the plundered and impoverished South could at last take hope and feel courage to make a new effort to recover some degree of prosperity and some measure of domestic content. For ten years the dark night of domination by the negro and adventurer had rested upon the unhappy section, until it had been reduced to the very abomination of desolation. Broken in health and fortune, sick at heart, conscious of the terrible degradation which had been imposed upon them, and politically ostracized, the better part of the white population of the South had staggered and groped through the hideous experiences of this period, and such of them as had not perished during the awful passage had now at last been relieved of the frightful scourge, and half dazed, as if just recovering from a terrible nightmare, found themselves again in the places of power and responsibility. But they brought with them, as their dominant passion, undying hatred of the Republican party as the author of all their woes, and as their dominant policy, the stern and unbending resolve to stand together as one man against every movement which had even the slightest tendency toward a restoration of the hated conditions from which they had escaped. [No sane mind can wonder at "the solid South," or at the Democratic South. Life, property, happiness, honor, civilization, everything which makes existence endurable demanded that the decent white men of the South should stand shoulder to shoulder in defending their families, their homes and their communities from any return of the vile plague under which they had suffered so long and so cruelly; and human instinct determined that this should be done in connection with that party which was hostile to the Republican party. The differences which lead to a fair fight and the wounds which are received in it are easily healed, but indignities heaped upon a fallen foe create a bitterness of heart that lasts so long as life endures.

[Slavery was a great wrong, and secession was an error and a terrible blunder, but Reconstruction was a punishment so far in excess of the crime that it extinguished every sense of culpability upon the part of those whom it was sought to convict and convert. More than a quarter of a century has now passed since the blunder-crime of Reconstruction played its baleful part in alienating the two sections of the country. Until four years ago little progress had been made in reconciling them. It is said now that the recent war with Spain, in which men from the North and men from the South marched under the same banner to battle and to victory, has buried the hatchet forever between them. But they had done this many times before, and yet it did not prevent the attempt to destroy the Union. It cannot be in this alone that the South feels increased security against the doctrines and the poli-

<small>Reconcilia-
tion between
the North and
the South.</small>

cies and interferences of the Republican party with regard to the negro question, the great question which has made and kept the South solidly Democratic. It is something far more significant and substantial than this. It is to some the pleasing, though to others startling, fact, that the Republican party, in its work of imposing the sovereignty of the United States upon eight millions of Asiatics, has changed its views in regard to the political relation of races and has at last virtually accepted the ideas of the South upon that subject. The white men of the South need now have no further fear that the Republican party, or Republican Administrations, will ever again give themselves over to the vain imagination of the political equality of man. It is this change of mind and heart on the part of the North in regard to this vital question of Southern "State" polity which has caused the now much-talked-of reconciliation.

CHAPTER XIV

INTERNATIONAL RELATIONS OF THE UNITED STATES BETWEEN 1867 AND 1877

The Purchase of Alaska—The Contention of the House of Representatives in Regard to its Power over Treaties—The Senate's Position and the Compromise—Irritation of the American People against Great Britain—The Johnson-Clarendon Treaty — President Grant's Statements in His First Annual Message and in His Second Annual Address—Sir John Rose's Mission to the United States—The Joint High Commission—The Treaty of Washington—The Alabama Claims and the Geneva Convention—Triumph of the Diplomacy of the United States—Organization of the Tribunal and Filing of the Cases—The Controversy between Mr. Fish and Lord Granville—The Filing of the Counter Cases and the Argument—Obstacles—Decision of the Tribunal in Regard to National and Indirect Damages—The Decision of the Tribunal in the Case of the *Florida*—The Decision in the Case of the *Alabama*—The Decision in the Case of the *Shenandoah*, and other Vessels—International Principles Settled by the Geneva Tribunal—The Northwest Boundary Question—The Fisheries Question—The Halifax Commission and Award — The Burlingame Treaty with China—The Attempt to Annex the Dominican Republic to the United States—The Treaty—The Treaty before the Senate—Its Rejection—The President's Attempt to Renew Negotiations—The Committee of Inquiry—The Report of the Committee—The Abandonment of the Scheme.

THE two chief products of American diplomacy in the decade between 1867 and 1877 were the purchase of Alaska, and the treaty of Washington with Great Britain.

The purchase of Alaska, the northwest corner of the North American continent, together with the islands adjacent thereto, a vast region of some five hundred thousand square miles in extent, inhabited chiefly by a few savage tribes, was effected by a treaty, negotiated by Mr. Seward and the Russian diplomatist, Baron Stoeckl, and ratified by the Senate of the United States on the 30th of March, 1867.

The purchase of Alaska.

The proposition came from the side of Russia, and it appeared that Russia was more eager to sell than the United States was to buy. The price agreed on was seven millions two hundred thousand dollars in gold, and most people in the United States thought, at the time, that this great sum was being paid for nothing but a barren area of snow and ice. The country was declared to be utterly worthless by some of the best informed men in Congress, and a man of no less ability and influence than Mr. Shellabarger opposed the purchase on the ground that it involved an extension of territory dangerous to the existence of the Republic.

The reasons for and against the purchase.

On the other hand, such men as General Banks and Mr. Stevens contended that from the point of view of a business transaction alone it was worth the money; and Mr. Higby, of California, told his colleagues that they were mistaken in regard to the climate of the region. The consideration, however, which seems to have had most weight was gratitude toward Russia, whose government had manifested the most friendly feeling for the Union in the struggle against the giant rebellion, and had even threatened interference in behalf of the Union against interference in behalf of the Confederacy by any other European state. That acute observer of political opinion, Mr. Blaine, affirmed that a like offer from any other European government would most probably have been declined.

INTERNATIONAL RELATIONS 301

It is, however, almost certain that Mr. Seward had another very profound reason for making the purchase, one which he could not very well proclaim from the housetops, especially as the feeling on his part, and on the part of the Government and of the people of the North, was most kindly toward Russia. It was this: The United States would in this way and at a comparatively small cost rid herself forever of any danger of Russian colonization on the North American continent, and of the danger of any complications between Russia and Great Britain upon this continent. This was a most important political consideration, one which much overbalanced the price paid for the territory and the cost of its administration. *A real political reason for the purchase.*

When the bill for making the appropriation to pay for Alaska came before the House of Representatives, that body raised the question of the power of the House over treaties involving the payment of money by the United States, by asserting in the preamble of the bill that its consent was necessary to the validity of such treaties. It did so on the ground that as an independent legislative body it could refuse any appropriation at its own discretion, and that as all foreign countries were bound to know this from the wording of the Constitution, no foreign country could consider a treaty with the United States, involving financial obligations by the United States, as completed until the House of Representatives should have voted the appropriation of the amount stipulated in the agreement. *The contention of the House of Representatives in regard to its power over treaties involving the payment of money by the United States.*

The Senate, on the other hand, repudiated this doctrine, and rejected the bill with the preamble containing it as it came from the House of Representatives.

The bill then went to a conference committee of the two Houses, and this committee invented a preamble which The Senate's position and the compromise. read: "Whereas the President has entered into a treaty with the Emperor of Russia, and the Senate thereafter gave its advice and consent to said treaty, and whereas said stipulations cannot be carried into full force and effect, except by legislation to which the consent of both Houses of Congress is necessary; therefore be it resolved," etc. Both Houses adopted the bill in this form and it became law July 27th, 1868.

The contention of the House was good political science, but it is still doubtful whether it is the constitutional law of the United States or not. The more recent constitutions of even the European states, such as those of Germany and France, make the consent of both houses of the legislature necessary to the validity of all treaties involving the appropriation of money, or the assumption of any financial obligation. This is as it should be; and the Constitution of the United States ought to be so amended as to establish clearly the same principle.

We have, in the preceding volume of this series, followed the history of the relations of the United States Irritation of the American people against Great Britain. with Great Britain down to the close of the rebellion, and have referred to the general irritation on the part of the loyal people of the United States against the British government for its attitude in regard to the acts of its subjects in furnishing warships and munitions to the Confederates. There were many who favored turning the great military power with which the United States emerged from the Civil War against Great Britain, and forcing a settlement of those difficulties by the trial of arms; but Seward remained in the direction of the foreign affairs of the Union, and he had had enough of war. Moreover, he foresaw a change of government in Great Britain, and with it he hoped for a change of sentiment on the part of the new government on the international question. This event happened in consequence of the parliamentary election of 1867. The Minister of Foreign Affairs in Mr. Gladstone's cabinet was first Lord Stanley, and then the Earl of Clarendon, both of them very different in character from Lord John Russell. From the outset each of them manifested a sincere desire to reach an amicable settlement of all differences with the United States. The trouble at this juncture seems to have been the extravagance of the claims of the United States. Mr. Adams, whose patience had become much worn, talked about private damages, national damages and an apology. The British Ministers thought this too preposterous to be seriously meant. *Change of Ministry and Parliamentary majority in 1867.*

Before, however, the discussion had fairly begun Mr. Adams returned to the United States, and Mr. Reverdy Johnson was sent out to the British Court. Mr. Johnson yielded much of the ground assumed by Mr. Adams in reference to claims for national injury, and in January of 1869 concluded an agreement with the Earl of Clarendon for submitting to arbitration the claims for direct damage to property rights. *The Johnson-Clarendon treaty.*

The Senate of the United States promptly rejected the treaty with much feeling, because it did not contain proper provision, in its view, for the reparation of wrongs to the Nation. The feeling among the people of both countries ran so high that the Governments deemed it wise to cease, for a time, negotiations upon the subject. The new President, Grant, in his Message of December 6th, 1869, described the situation in the following language :

"Toward the close of the last Administration a convention was signed in London for the settlement of all outstanding claims between Great Britain and the United States, which failed to receive the advice and consent of the Senate to its ratification. The time and the circumstances attending the negotiation of that treaty were unfavorable to its acceptance by the people of the United States, and its provisions were wholly inadequate for the settlement of the grave wrongs that had been sustained by this Government, as well as by its citizens. The injuries resulting to the United States by reason of the course adopted by Great Britain during our late Civil War in the increased rates of insurance, in the diminution of exports and imports and other obstructions to domestic industry and production, in its effect upon the foreign commerce of the country, in the decrease and transfer to Great Britain of our commercial marine, in the prolongation of the war and the increased cost, both in treasure and lives, of its suppression, could not be adjusted and satisfied as ordinary commercial claims which continually arise among commercial nations; and yet the convention treated them as such ordinary claims, from which they differ more widely in the gravity of their character than in the magnitude of their amount, great even as is that difference. Not a word was found in the treaty, and not an inference could be drawn from it, to remove the sense of the unfriendliness of the course of Great Britain in our struggle for existence, which had so deeply and universally impressed itself upon the people of this country. Believing that a convention thus misconceived in its scope and inadequate in its provisions would not have produced the hearty, cordial settlement of pending questions, which alone is consistent with the relations which I desire to have firmly established be-

[President Grant's statement in his first Annual Message.]

tween the United States and Great Britain, I regarded the action of the Senate in rejecting the treaty to have been wisely taken in the interests of peace and as a necessary step in the direction of a perfect and cordial friendship between the two countries. A sensitive people, conscious of their power, are more at ease under a great wrong wholly unatoned than under the restraint of a settlement which satisfies neither their ideas of justice nor their grave sense of the grievance they have sustained. The rejection of the treaty was followed by a state of public feeling on both sides which I thought not favorable to an immediate attempt at renewed negotiations. I accordingly so instructed the Minister of the United States to Great Britain, and found that my views in this regard were shared by Her Majesty's Ministers. I hope that the time may soon arrive when the two Governments can approach the solution of this momentous question with an appreciation of what is due to the rights, dignity and honor of each, and with the determination not only to remove the causes of complaint in the past, but to lay the foundation of a broad principle of public law which will prevent future differences and tend to firm and continued peace and friendship."

For another year things drifted, and the views of the two Governments seemed to be getting wider apart, when President Grant wrote in his Message of December 5th, 1870:

"I regret to say that no conclusion has been reached for the adjustment of the claims against Great Britain growing out of the course adopted by that Government during the Rebellion. The Cabinet of London, so far as its views have been expressed, does not appear to be willing to concede that Her Majesty's Government was guilty of any negligence, or did or permitted any act during the War

The President's statement in his second annual message.

by which the United States has just cause of complaint. Our firm and unalterable convictions are directly the reverse. I therefore recommend to Congress to authorize the appointment of a commission to take proof of the amount and the ownership of these several claims, on notice to the representative of Her Majesty at Washington, and that authority be given for the settlement of these claims by the United States, so that the Government shall have the ownership of the private claims, as well as the responsible control of all the demands against Great Britain. It cannot be necessary to add that whenever Her Majesty's Government shall entertain a desire for a full and friendly adjustment of these claims the United States will enter upon their consideration with an earnest desire for a conclusion consistent with the honor and dignity of both nations."

This was what is now called "a twist of the lion's tail." It was something of a twist, although it was accompanied with the offer of the olive branch, instead of the sword. It was effective, even more effective for the conciliatory tone of the final paragraph. Moreover, with the German armies encamped around Paris and throughout France, the affairs of Continental Europe were too unsettled and precarious for Great Britain to run the risk of any serious complications with the United States.

Accepting the President's message as an invitation to renew negotiations, the British Government, at the beginning of the next year (1871), sent Sir John Rose to Washington to sound the President in regard to the matter. The President greeted his advances with great cordiality, and on the 26th of the month (January), Sir Edward Thornton, the British Minister to the United States, formally proposed to the Hon. Hamilton Fish, the Secretary of State, the appointment of a Joint High

Sir John Rose's mission to the United States.

Commission, to consist of five persons representing each Government, to sit at Washington, for the purpose of settling the questions between the two Governments relative to Great Britain's North American possessions. Mr. Fish immediately expressed the willingness of his Government to enter upon the negotiation, provided the differences growing out of the events of the Civil War should be included among the subjects to be considered. The British Government accepted Mr. Fish's proviso, and the respective Governments proceeded to appoint the members of the Commission. President Grant designated Hamilton Fish, Ebenezer R. Hoar, Justice Samuel Nelson, Robert C. Schenck and George H. Williams. Her Majesty selected Earl de Grey and Ripon, Sir John Macdonald, Sir Stafford Northcote, Sir Edward Thornton and Professor Montague Bernard. These eminent gentlemen proceeded immediately upon their momentous undertaking, and on the 8th of May (1871) concluded the treaty between the two Governments, known as the Treaty of Washington, which was duly ratified, and on the 4th of July proclaimed to the world. *The Joint High Commission.*

The first eleven articles of this agreement relate to the claims for damages arising from the incidents of the Civil War, known as the Alabama Claims. This was the subject of transcendent importance in the Treaty; this was the subject which was, by these articles, referred to the Court of Arbitration to sit at Geneva. *The Treaty of Washington.*

They contain, in the first place, an expression of regret for the escape of the Confederate vessels from British ports and for the depredations committed by them.

They provide, secondly, for a tribunal of arbitration, composed of five members, one of whom should be named by the President of the United States, one by Her Britannic Majesty, one by the King of Italy, one by the President of the Swiss Confederation, and one by the Emperor of Brazil; and, in case either of these last three mentioned should fail to name an arbitrator, they provide that one should be named by the King of Sweden and Norway; and finally, that one agent should be named by each of the high contracting-parties to represent it generally in all matters connected with the arbitration.

They provide, in the third place, that "the Arbitrators shall meet at Geneva, in Switzerland, at the earliest convenient day after they shall have been named, and shall proceed impartially and carefully to examine and decide all questions that shall be laid before them on the part of the Governments of the United States and Her Britannic Majesty respectively," and that "all questions considered by the Tribunal, including the final award, shall be decided by a majority of all the arbitrators."

<small>The Alabama claims and the Geneva convention.</small>

They provide, in the fourth place, that each of the two high contracting parties should deliver his written or printed case, together with all the evidence in support of it, to each of the arbitrators and to the agent of the other party, as soon as possible after the organization of the Tribunal, and within a period not exceeding six months from the 17th of June, 1871; that within four months after the delivery on both sides of the case, each party might put in a counter case, with additional evidence, in reply to the case of the other party; that the arbitrators might extend the time, under certain circumstances, for delivering the counter case; that "within two months after the expiration of the time limited for the delivery of the counter case on both sides," the agent of each party should deliver to each of the arbitrators "and to the agent of the other party a written or printed argument showing the points and referring to the evidence upon which his Government relies"; and that the arbitrators might require further argument by counsel, giving to each party an equal chance to be heard.

They provide, in the fifth place, that the Tribunal should consider the case of each vessel separately; that it might, however, award a gross sum, or that in case it did not award a sum in gross, the high contracting parties should appoint two members of a board of assessors, and request the Italian Minister at Washington to appoint a third, which board should determine the amounts due in the cases in which the arbitrators had pronounced responsibility.

They provide, in the sixth place, that in deciding the matters submitted the arbitrators should be governed by the following rules:

"A neutral government is bound, first, to use diligence to prevent the fitting out, arming, or equipping, within its jurisdiction, of any vessel which it has reasonable ground to believe is intended to cruise or to carry on war against a Power with which it is at peace; and also to use like diligence to prevent the departure from its jurisdiction of any vessel intended to cruise or carry on war as above, such vessel having been specially adapted, in whole or in part, within such jurisdiction, to warlike use. Secondly, not to permit or suffer either belligerent to make use of its ports or waters as the base of naval operations against the other, or for the purpose of the renewal or augmentation of military supplies or arms, or the recruitment of men. Thirdly, to exercise due diligence in its own ports and waters, and, as to all persons within its jurisdiction, to prevent any violation of the foregoing obligations and duties."

They provide, in the seventh place, that the high contracting parties would "agree to observe these rules as between themselves in the future, and to bring them to the knowledge of other maritime powers, and to invite them to accede to them."

And they provide, finally, that the result of the proceedings of the Tribunal and the Board of Assessors, in case such board should be appointed, should be accepted as a final settlement of all the claims known as the Alabama Claims, and should be a bar to any further proceedings in regard to them.

It will be seen that the Government of the United States had in this Treaty substantially won all of the points for which it had contended. The Queen's Government had apologized. It had agreed that the general principles of international law in regard to the duties of neutrals toward belligerents should take precedence over municipal statutes, and should not be limited by municipal statutes. And it had agreed that the Tribunal of Arbitration should decide *all questions* laid before it by the Governments of the United States and of Her Britannic Majesty respectively.

<small>Triumph of the diplomacy of the United States.</small>

It is true that Her Majesty's Government qualified its acceptance of the rules to be applied in determining its responsibility by inserting an explanation in the Treaty of the following tenor: "Her Britannic Majesty has commanded her High Commissioners and Plenipotentiaries to declare that Her Majesty's Government cannot assent to the foregoing rules as a statement of principles of international law which were in force at the time when the claims mentioned in Article I. arose, but that Her Majesty's Government, in order to evince its desire of strengthening the friendly relations between the two countries and of making satisfactory provision for the future, agrees that, in deciding the questions between the two countries arising out of those claims, the Arbitrators should assume that Her Majesty's Government had undertaken to act upon the principles set forth in these rules."

And it is also true that, while, according to the letter of the Treaty, the United States Government was left unfettered as to the character of the claims which it might lay before the Arbitrators, Her Majesty's Government had been led to expect more moderation in this respect than the popular sentiment in the United States seemed to indicate.

The two Governments and the high personages invited by them proceeded in due time to appoint the Arbitrators. The President of the United States appointed Mr. Charles Francis Adams; Her Majesty named Chief Justice Alexander Cockburn; the Italian King designated Count Frederic Sclopis; the President of the Swiss Confederation designated Mr. Jacob Staempfli, and the Emperor of Brazil named the Baron d'Itajubá. _{The arbitrators, agents and counsel.}

The President of the United States also appointed Mr. J. C. Bancroft Davis as the agent of the United States before the Tribunal, and Mr. Caleb Cushing, Mr. William M. Evarts and Mr. Morrison R. Waite as counsel.

Her Majesty's Government also appointed Lord Tenterden as the agent of Great Britain before the Tribunal, and Sir Roundell Palmer as chief counsel.

On the 15th of December, 1871, the Arbitrators organized the Tribunal at Geneva with Count Frederic Sclopis in the chair as presiding officer, and with Mr. Alexander Favrot as secretary. The printed case of each of the high contracting parties was filed immediately by the agent of each, and the Tribunal ordered the counter cases to be filed _{Organization of the Tribunal and filing of the cases.}

on or before the 15th day of the following April. The Tribunal then adjourned to June 15th following, unless sooner called together by the secretary.

The contents of the case of the United States became immediately known to the British Ministers, but not for some weeks to the British people. The Ministers were not apparently disturbed in mind about it, although they discovered at once that it contained claims for national damages and indirect damages as well as for direct damages to individuals; but as soon as the newspapers got hold of this fact, they raised a tremendous hue and cry, and accused those who had prepared the case of taking an unfair advantage of the wording of the treaty. The Minister of the United States in London, General Schenck, informed Mr. Fish by cable of the agitation in London over the subject and of the demand of the newspapers that the claim for national and indirect damages should be withdrawn. Mr. Fish replied firmly that "there must be no withdrawal of any part of the claim presented." At this moment the session of Parliament opened and the Queen's speech contained a criticism of the extravagance of the claims of the United States in the case submitted to the Tribunal. The matter was warmly debated in Parliament, and on February 3d the British Foreign Minister, Lord Granville, opened a diplomatic discussion with Mr. Fish upon the subject. Mr. Fish, however, held his ground with great courage and ability, insisting that the claims of every character should be disposed of by the Tribunal in order to remove them from the domain of further controversy and in order to establish perfect harmony in the relations of the two countries.

The controversy between Mr. Fish and Lord Granville.

Before this discussion terminated the day arrived for the filing of the counter cases. They were both promptly filed with a reservation of all rights by each of the high contracting parties. The diplomatic discussion culminated in an attempt to make a supplemental treaty, which should provide that the Government of the United States should withdraw its claims for national losses and indirect losses, on the condition that no such losses should be claimed by either Government in the future. But the day arrived for the filing of the arguments before anything was effected. The agent of the United States filed his argument on the day fixed, the 15th of June, but the British agent only filed a statement setting forth the differences between the two Governments in the interpretation of the Treaty in respect to claims for national and indirect damages, and the late negotiations and discussions between the two Governments concerning these differences. The British agent also expressed the hope that, if time were given, these negotiations would prove fruitful, and asked the Arbitrators to adjourn for eight months. *The filing of the counter cases and the argument.*

It looked as if the work of the commissioners, who had framed the Treaty, and of the Arbitrators, who had now given six months of their time to its execution, would go for naught, and that the Governments and the people of the two countries would be thrown back into the relations existing during the years 1869 and 1870, with intensified feelings of hostility. The Arbitrators realized the seriousness of the situation and did not yield to the request of the British agent. They adjourned to the 19th of the month, that is for four days only, in order to deliberate upon the proposition. When they reassembled on the 19th the President of the Tribunal announced that the Arbitrators had decided to inform the two high contracting parties, at that *Obstacles.* *Decision of the Tribunal in regard to national and indirect damages.*

juncture, that the Arbitrators did not consider the claims for national and indirect damages to be a good foundation in international law "for an award of compensation or computation of damages between nations;" but were unanimously of the opinion that such claims should "be wholly excluded from the consideration of the Tribunal in making its award, even if there were no disagreement between the two Governments as to the competency of the Tribunal to decide them." The President said further, that the Arbitrators made this announcement in order that the Government of the United States might consider if it would adopt some course in reference to these claims, which would relieve the Tribunal from deciding upon the request of the British agent for an adjournment.

The President of the United States was duly informed of this announcement by the Tribunal, and, upon the advice of the learned counsel for the United States, he instructed the agent of the United States to make the following reply to the Tribunal:

"The declaration made by the Tribunal, individually and collectively, respecting the claims presented by the United States for the award of the Tribunal for, first, the losses in the transfer of the American commercial marine to the British flag, second, the enhanced payment of insurance, and, third, the prolongation of the war and the addition of a large sum to the cost of the war and the suppression of the Rebellion, is accepted by the President of the United States as determinative of their judgment upon the important question of public law involved."

This reply was read to the Tribunal on the 25th of June, and on the 27th the British agent, under instructions from his Government, withdrew his request for an adjournment and filed his argument.

It was supposed by the Americans that the whole case on both sides was now in, and that, unless the Arbitrators should require further argument or statement in reference to specific points, the Tribunal would now proceed to make its decisions. But the British counsel and the British agent immediately petitioned the Tribunal to be allowed to prepare and present another argument, and to have six weeks' time in which to do it, and even the member of the Tribunal appointed by the British Government exerted himself to secure this delay and this new opportunity for the British agent and his counsel. The Tribunal felt, however, that it was in possession of the evidence and the argument necessary for determining the question before it, and refused the request.

The Tribunal now adjourned to the 15th of July, in order to give its members time and opportunity to study the cases. On the 15th, the arbitrators reassembled and invited the agent and counsel of each of the high contracting parties to sit with them in their conferences. To all others, however, the doors were closed. They spent some two days discussing the order of the procedure which they should follow, and finally adopted the order proposed by Mr. Staempfli, and also indicated in the Treaty itself, which was to take up the case of each vessel separately, and allow each Arbitrator to express a provisional opinion upon it, which opinion, however, should not be conclusive even on the Arbitrator himself who gave it.

On the 17th of the month (July), the Tribunal proceeded to take up the case of the *Florida* and to hear the opinions of the Arbitrators upon it. Four of the five Arbitrators were of the opinion that the British Government had failed to exercise due diligence in the discharge of its neutral duties toward the United States in this case. Sir Alexander Cock- *The decision of the Tribunal in the case of the Florida.*

burn alone disagreed with this view. The four also held that the tenders of the *Florida* should follow the lot of their principal. The reading of the opinion in the case of the *Florida* was finished on the 22d, and the Tribunal adjourned to the 25th.

Upon the reassembly of the arbitrators, Baron d'Itajubá called on the British counsel for a statement or an argument on the questions of due diligence, and of the effect of commissions held by Confederate war vessels which had entered British ports, and of the legitimacy of coal supplies to Confederate vessels in British ports. Of course the counsel of the United States would be permitted to reply.

The Tribunal approved the proposition, and then proceeded to the case of the *Alabama*. The Arbitrators The decision in the case of the *Alabama*. agreed unanimously in their views of this case, holding the Government of Great Britain guilty of a lack of due diligence. The case of the tender to the *Alabama* was viewed in the same light.

The Tribunal then took up the case of the *Shenandoah*. The Arbitrators were unanimously of the opinion The decision in the case of the *Shenandoah*, and other vessels. in this case that the British Government had not failed in due diligence anterior to the time when the vessel entered the port of Melbourne. On the other hand, three of the Arbitrators, Count Sclopis, Mr. Adams and Mr. Staempfli, held that the British Government was responsible for all the acts of this vessel committed after leaving Melbourne.

In regard to all the other vessels mentioned in the case of the United States, excepting only the *Retribution*, the Arbitrators were unanimous in the opinion that the British Government had not failed in due diligence in the discharge of its duties as a neutral, and in regard to the *Retribution* three of the five Arbitrators held the like opinion. After hearing the additional arguments called for, the Tribunal closed the doors on the 26th of August, and, without the presence even of agents or counsel, deliberated upon the momentous questions submitted to it. On the 9th of September the decision was adopted. The Tribunal then adjourned to the 14th, upon which day the decision was to be proclaimed to the world.

The public session of the Tribunal on the 14th was a solemn and an imposing affair with nothing to mar the satisfaction of those who participated in it, except the discourtesy of Sir Alexander Cockburn, who not only kept the assembly waiting for his appearance long past the appointed hour, but departed with unseemly haste at the close of the valedictory pronounced by the president, Count Sclopis.

The award followed the line of the opinions already recited. It convicted the British Government of a lack of due diligence in the discharge of its neutral duties in the cases of the *Alabama* and the *Florida* and their respective tenders, and also in the case of the *Shenandoah* from the time she left the port of Melbourne, but exonerated it in all other cases.

The award also repeated the decision announced by Count Sclopis, on the 19th of June, excluding the claims for national and indirect damages, and then fixed the amount due to the United States from Great Britain in the gross sum of "fifteen millions five hundred thousand dollars in gold, as the indemnity to be paid by Great Britain to the United States for the satisfaction of all the claims referred to the consideration of the Tribunal." Sir Alexander Cockburn refused to sign the award, and filed a statement of his reasons for his dissent. The other four members of the Tribunal signed it, and as the majority rule had been provided for in the Treaty, both of the high contracting parties were duly bound, and so regarded themselves.

As to principles decided by the entire procedure of the commissioners and of their Governments in the forma-

<small>International principles settled by the Geneva Tribunal.</small>

tion of the Treaty, and of the Arbitrators in making the award, we may say, first, that all questions of damages resulting from the lack of due diligence on the part of a neutral in the fulfilment of the duties of neutrality were regarded as proper subjects for arbitration, and that the determination of the question whether the claims presented, or any of them, are a good foundation for an award of compensation was also regarded as a proper question for arbitration; second, that due diligence to be exercised by neutral governments is diligence "in exact proportion to the risks to which either of the belligerents may be exposed from a failure to fulfil the obligations of neutrality on their part"; third, that the fact that a commission was only subsequently given by a belligerent to a vessel constructed, equipped or armed for the belligerent in the port of the neutral does not heal the violation of the duties of neutrality by the neutral in not using due diligence to prevent such construction, equipment or armament in its ports ; fourth, that the privilege of ex-territoriality accorded to vessels of war can never be appealed to for the protection of acts done in violation of neutrality; fifth, that no neutral can excuse itself from the due discharge of the duties of neutrality on account of imperfections in its own laws and government; and sixth, that the cost to the belligerent of pursuing vessels, which have been enabled to operate against the belligerent on account of the dereliction of the neutral, and all indirect loss resulting therefrom, do not constitute a " good foundation for an award of compensation or computation of damages between nations."

Two other questions of great importance were placed in course of solution by the Treaty of Washington. One was the contention between the two high contracting parties concerning the boundary line between the United States and British Columbia from the point where the forty-ninth parallel of north latitude intersects the middle of the channel which separates the continent from Vancouver's Island to the Pacific Ocean. The contention on the part of Great Britain was that this line should run, according to the stipulations of the Treaty of June 15th, 1846, through the Rosario Straits, and on the part of the United States that it should run through the Canal de Haro. The high contracting parties agreed, in the thirty-fourth article of the Treaty of Washington, to submit this question to the arbitration and award of His Majesty the German Emperor, whose decision thereon should be final and without appeal. The German Emperor, William I., accepted this duty; and on the 21st of October, 1872, announced his award, upholding the contention of the United States. *The Northwest boundary question.*

The other question was that which related to the common rights of fishing to be enjoyed by the citizens and subjects of the two high contracting parties along the Atlantic coast. The eighteenth article of the Treaty provided that the inhabitants of the United States should have for the term of twelve years, in common with the subjects of Her Britannic Majesty, the right to take sea fish "of every kind, except shell-fish, on the sea-coasts and shores, and in the bays, harbors, and creeks, of the Provinces of Quebec, Nova Scotia, and New Brunswick, and the colony of Prince Edward's Island, and of the several islands *The Fisheries question.*

thereunto adjacent, without being restricted to any distance from the shore, with permission to land upon the said coasts and shores and islands, and also upon the Magdalen Islands, for the purpose of drying their nets and curing their fish." By article nineteenth the same right was accorded to British subjects, in common with the citizens of the United States, along "the eastern sea-coasts and shores of the United States north of the thirty-ninth parallel of north latitude, and on the shores of the several islands adjacent thereunto, and in the bays, harbors and creeks of the said sea-coasts and shores of the United States and of the said islands." Finally, by article twenty-first free trade between Canada and Prince Edward's Island and the United States in the produce of their respective sea-fisheries was established.

The contention on the part of Great Britain in regard to this subject was that the rights and privileges accorded to the citizens of the United States by these articles were more valuable than those conceded to the subjects of Great Britain by the United States, and that a sum of money should be paid to Great Britain by the United States in offset thereof. The United States denied the British assumption, and the two high contracting parties agreed, in the twenty-third article of the Treaty, to leave this matter to the arbitration and award of three commissioners, one to be appointed by the President of the United States, one by Her Britannic Majesty, and a third by the President and the Queen conjointly, provided they could agree upon a person within three months from the date when the Treaty should take effect and, if not, then by the Austro-Hungarian Ambassador at the Court of St. James.

The Halifax commission and award.

The President named, as the representative of the United States, the Hon. Ensign H. Kellogg. The Queen appointed, as her representative, Sir Alexander T. Galt. And the two high contracting parties not being able to agree upon the third member of the commission, the Austro-Hungarian Ambassador to the Queen named Maurice Delfosse, the Belgian Minister Plenipotentiary to the United States. Delfosse had been proposed by the British Government to the Government of the United States as the third commissioner, and the President had objected to him as being the representative of a country whose interests were too nearly allied with those of Great Britain. It was naturally understood by the President that this had disposed of Delfosse, and the Government at Washington was taken by surprise when the Austro-Hungarian Ambassador at London, Count Beust, made it manifest that he should name Mr. Delfosse. Mr. Fish, the Secretary of State, with true diplomatic instinct, immediately accommodated himself, however, to the situation, and congratulated Delfosse upon his appointment. Count Beust announced the choice of Delfosse on the 2d of March, 1877, nearly six years after the Washington Treaty was negotiated and signed, during which period the fisheries of Newfoundland were brought under the same agreements as those of Canada, Prince Edward's Island, and the United States above the thirty-ninth parallel. The Commission finally met at Halifax in the latter half of the year 1877 and on November 23d, 1877, made its award, sustaining by a vote of two to one the contention of Great Britain, and adjudging that the United States Government should pay the Government of Great Britain the sum of five millions five hundred thousand dollars in gold.

The representative of the United States, Mr. Kellogg, dissented from the decision ; and it was felt in the United States that the Government had been overreached in the matter. Considerable delay in the payment of the amount thus resulted, and some controversy over it with Great Britain occurred. But finally, on November 21st, 1878, the draft for the amount was delivered to the British Government by Mr. Welsh, the Minister of the United States at the Court of St. James.

Two other events of an international character happened within the decade between 1867 and 1877 to which brief reference should be made, viz., the Chinese Treaty of 1868, and the strong and persistent attempt of President Grant to bring Santo Domingo under the sovereignty of the United States.

In 1861 Anson Burlingame, a citizen of the United States and a resident of Massachusetts, was sent as Minister of the United States to China. He was a diplomatist of much skill, and he succeeded in making such a deep impression upon the Emperor of China that the latter, on his resignation as Minister of the United States to China in 1867, made him Envoy Extraordinary from China to the United States and the European states for the purpose of securing treaties of amity and commerce between China and the states of the civilized world. He came immediately to the United States and negotiated with Mr. Seward, the Secretary of State of the United States, the Treaty of July 28th, 1868, whereby freedom of emigration and immigration between China and the United States was established, upon the principle of the "inherent and inalienable right of man to change his home and allegiance" expressly subscribed to by the United States and China in the Treaty; the residence of Chinese consuls in the ports of the United States, with the same privileges and immunities as the British and Russian consuls enjoyed in said ports, was agreed to; and freedom of religion for citizens of

The Burlingame Treaty with China.

the United States in China, and Chinese converts to the Christian religion in China, and for Chinese subjects in the United States, was mutually pledged. This Treaty was heralded at the time as being an immense advance in bringing China into close sympathy with modern civilization. But very soon the "labor element," as it assumes to call itself, in the United States, began to find fault with the liberal provisions upon the subject of emigration and immigration, and has succeeded in forcing the Government of the United States back from its ideal position to the old ground of national exclusiveness. The example set by the United States has been accepted by the Chinese Government as a justification of its old methods, and as an excuse for dropping back into them in great measure.

At the moment of General Grant's accession to the presidency there was civil commotion in the Dominican Republic. Buenaventura Baez was the legal President of the Republic, but he had lost the support of a very large proportion of the population, who were following a leader named Cabral. *The attempt to annex the Dominican Republic to the United States.* Cabral and his party were so strong that Baez feared the overthrow of his government, and sought to avert it by proposing annexation to the United States.

In July of 1869, President Grant sent General Orville E. Babcock to Santo Domingo with written instructions from the Secretary of State, Mr. Fish, to inquire into the political situation there and into the value and resources of the country. Babcock, terming himself aide-de-camp to the President of the United States, succeeded somehow or other in so impressing his importance and authority upon the willing Baez and his confederates as to move them to sign a treaty *The Treaty.* for the annexation of the Dominican Republic to the United States. It appears that he pledged the President of the United States to use privately all his influence with the members of Congress for the ratification of the Treaty.

On the 10th of January, 1870, President Grant sent this proposed Treaty to the Senate for ratification. He must have thought that there would be no difficulty in securing for it the approval of that body, for his message was only three lines in length and contained no argument. It was referred to the Committee on Foreign Affairs, and it soon became manifest that a serious opposition to ratification was developing itself. The President now procured from the Dominican representative at Washington an agreement to an extension of the time for ratification, and in communicating this to the Senate on May 31st he went into an argument in support of the proposed treaty. He said, among other things, that the acquisition of this country would cut off one hundred millions of dollars' worth of the imports of the United States and largely increase its exports, and would thus enable the United States to extinguish its large debt abroad; that it would give the United States military command of the entrance to the Caribbean Sea and "the Isthmus transit of commerce"; and that it was necessary in order to maintain the Monroe Doctrine. He declared that the inhabitants of Santo Domingo yearned "for the protection of our free institutions and laws, and our progress and civilization." And he affirmed that he had information that a European Power was standing ready to offer two millions of dollars for the possession of Samana Bay alone. It would be difficult to find another message of a President of the United States which contained an equal amount of such extravagant nonsense.

The Treaty before the Senate.

The Committee on Foreign Affairs thoroughly sifted the subject, and recommended that the proposed Treaty be not ratified, and the Senate, despite the influence of the Administration, sustained the Committee. This action of the Senate occurred on the 30th of June. The President was surprised, mortified and indignant. He was especially angry with the chairman of the Committee on Foreign Affairs, Senator Sumner, and was from that moment determined to oust Sumner from that position.

<small>Its rejection.</small>

In his next annual message, that of December 5th, 1870, he took up the matter again, went over all of his old arguments expressed in even more extravagant language than before, and added the prophecy that if the United States did not take Santo Domingo, European nations would acquire the Bay of Samana and create there a great commercial city to which the United States would become tributary without receiving corresponding benefits, and that then the folly of the rejection of so great a prize by the United States would be recognized. He then asked Congress to authorize him to appoint a commission to negotiate a treaty with the authorities of Santo Domingo for its annexation to the United States, and suggested that the treaty so negotiated might be ratified by a joint resolution of the two Houses of Congress, instead of by the Senate alone.

<small>The President's attempt to renew negotiations.</small>

These recommendations and suggestions and the language in which they were expressed were felt to be most exasperating by those Senators and Representatives who opposed the President's scheme, and the President's supporters saw quickly that Congress would not sanction any such measure as he proposed. In place of it, Senator Morton, of Indiana, offered in the Senate a resolution to empower the President to appoint a commission, composed of three persons, to go to Santo Domingo and inquire into the politi-

<small>The Committee of Inquiry.</small>

cal situation and the resources of the country. This resolution finally passed under strong opposition, and the House of Representatives concurred in it with the proviso, which the Senate accepted, that the resolution should not be construed as committing Congress in any manner or degree to the policy of annexing Santo Domingo to the United States.

The report of the commissioners. The President appointed as commissioners Benjamin F. Wade, Andrew D. White and Samuel G. Howe. These gentlemen proceeded to Santo Domingo, made their inquiries, and furnished the President with a report sustaining his views and recommendations.

On the 5th of April, 1871, the President submitted this report to Congress, accompanied by a message which contained a justification of his own conduct in the whole matter, and an attack upon those who opposed his policy of annexation, especially upon Senator Sumner. It was a very undignified, not to say puerile, document, and *The abandonment of the scheme.* ought never to have been written, much less sent. It revealed, however, the fact that the President understood at last that he must abandon his pet scheme. He did it, however, with a very bad grace, and in his last annual message he repeated for the third time his old arguments in favor of his miserable project, "not," he said, "as a recommendation for a renewal of the subject of annexation," but in vindication of his conduct in regard to it. It is needless to add that none of his fearful predictions about European occupation of Santo Domingo, in case the United States should fail to seize it, and the destruction of the Monroe Doctrine, have come to pass. On the other hand, the Monroe Doctrine has attained an almost monstrous growth which at times appears as likely to threaten as to preserve the peace of the two Americas, and the poor little Dominican Republic, which was incapable of self-government, still exists and seems to be bettering its condition by its own efforts, while the great European city in the Bay of Samana, to which the United States was to become tributary, has not even the substance of a mirage in the waters upon which the vast marines of the world were to ride in approaching its docks and landings. Such has been the fulfilment of the prophecy upon which was based the supposed necessity of expansion beyond the seas!

INDEX

ABBOTT, JOSIAH G., on electoral commission, 286
Adams, Charles Francis, joins liberal republicans, 264; candidate for presidential nomination, 265; returns from England, 303; at Geneva arbitration, 311, 316
Adams, John Q., nominated for vice-presidency, 267
Alabama, in Lincoln's proclamation, 11; electoral vote of 1864 rejected, 22; reconstruction in, 37; convention and election in, 38; vote on thirteenth amendment, 55; in the reconstruction bill, 112; registration in, 146; election in, 149; disfranchisements in, 150; voting on constitution, 151, 153, 197; act on admission of members from, 198; reconstruction declared complete, 202; ratifies fourteenth amendment, 203, 204; republicans get control in, 268, 269; change in character of government, 273
Alabama, the, case of, 316, 317
Alabama claims, 307, 308, 316, 317
Alaska, purchase of, 297–302
Alexandria, Va., Pierpont government at, 13, 224
Alta Vela, matter of claim to, 177, 178
Ames, Adelbert, resigns as governor of Mississippi, 275
Anderson, T. C., in Louisiana politics, 269
Arkansas, in Lincoln's proclamation, 11; Lincoln's acts toward, 12; presidential reconstruction in, 15; congressmen refused seats, 15; in Lincoln's message, 19; electoral vote of 1864 rejected, 22; attitude of Johnson to, 38; vote on thirteenth amendment, 55; in the reconstruction bill, 112; registration in, 147; election in, 149; disfranchisements in, 150; ratifies constitution, 155, 197; ratifies fourteenth amendment, 197; act of June, 1868, as to, 198, 199, 201; reconstruction declared complete, 202; ratifies fourteenth amendment, 203, 204; change in character of government, 273

Ashburn, George W., in convention of 1866, 100
Ashley, James M., action on thirteenth amendment, 29
Austin, Tex., convention at, 229

BABCOCK, ORVILLE E., mission to Santo Domingo, 323
Baez, Buenaventura, in Dominican politics, 323
Baird, Absalom, New Orleans riot, 94–97
Baltimore, Md., republican convention at, 20; democratic convention at, 266
Banks, Nathaniel P., appoints election in Louisiana, 14; views on purchase of Alaska, 300
Bayard, Thomas F., on electoral commission, 286
Bell, John, desertion of the Union cause, 221
Benton, Thomas H., in convention of 1866, 100
Bernard, Mountague, on Joint High Commission, 307
Beust, Count, names Delfosse for Halifax commission, 321
Bingham, John A., on joint committee on reconstruction, 57; on impeachment committee, 174; impeachment manager, 175; approves letter on Alta Vela claims, 177; offers amendment as to Georgia, 242
Black, Jeremiah S., counsel for Johnson, 176; his withdrawal, 177, 178; counsel before electoral commission, 291

329

Blaine, James G., proposes amendment to reconstruction bill, 115, 116; approves letter on Alta Vela claims, 177; in convention of 1876, 261; views on purchase of Alaska, 300
Blair, Francis P., nominated for vice-presidency, 211; conduct in the campaign, 211, 212
Blair, Montgomery, in convention of 1866, 99; counsel before electoral commission, 291
Blow, Henry T., on joint committee on reconstruction, 57
Borie, Adolph E., becomes secretary of the navy, 231; resigns, 232
Botta, John Minor, in convention of 1866, 100
Boutwell, George S., on joint committee on reconstruction, 57; on impeachment committee, 174; impeachment manager, 175; becomes secretary of the treasury, 232
Bradley, Joseph P., on electoral commission, 289
Brodhead, James O., letter from F. P. Blair, 211
Brown, B. Gratz, joins liberal republicans, 264; nominated for vice-presidency, 265, 296
Browning, Orville H., enters cabinet, 90; in convention of 1866, 99
Brownlow, William G., elected governor of Tennessee, 25; in convention of 1866, 100
Bullock, Rufus B., share in reconstruction of Georgia, 237-239, 241, 244
Burlingame, Anson, treaty with China, 322
Butler, Benjamin F., impeachment manager, 175; signs letter on Alta Vela claim, 177; attack on Johnson, 181; proposes bill as to Georgia, 240; withdraws his amendment, 242

CABRAL, in Dominican politics, 323
Cameron, Simon, in convention of 1866, 100
Campbell, James, in convention of 1866, 99
Campbell, John A., counsel before electoral commission, 291
Canada, the fisheries question, 320-322

Canby, Edward R. S., supersedes Sickles, 143
Carpenter, Matthew H., counsel before electoral commission, 291
Carpenter, testimony as to Ku-Klux, 259
Cartter, David K., action in case against Thomas, 171, 172, 174
Cartwright, J. C., Oregon elector of 1876, 291
Chamberlain, Daniel H., as governor of South Carolina, 274; retires from the office, 296
Chandler, Zachariah, in convention of 1866, 100; manages campaign for Hayes, 268
Chase, Salmon P., presides at impeachment of Johnson, 176; rulings, 181; puts final question, 191; candidate for presidential nomination, 210
Cherokee Nation vs. Georgia (5 Peters 1), 144
Chicago, Ill., democratic convention at, 207; republican convention of 1868, 207
China, the Burlingame treaty, 322
Cincinnati, O., liberal republican convention at, 265; republican convention of 1876, 280
Civil Rights, state legislation on, 45-52, 62; bill on, in Congress, 68-70; the bill criticised, 71; bill passed over veto, 73
Clarendon, Earl of, treaty negotiated with Johnson, 303
Clements, White vs., 237
Cleveland, O., radical republican convention at, 20; soldier convention at, 101
Clifford, Nathan, on electoral commission, 286
Cochrane, John, nominated for vice-presidency, 20; withdraws, 21
Cockburn, Alexander, at Geneva arbitration, 311, 315, 317
Coke, Richard, elected governor of Texas, 249, 273
Colfax, Schuyler, elected Speaker, 42; appoints committee on impeachment, 174; nominated for vice-presidency, 207; character of acceptance, 208
Columbia, S. C., made head-quarters of second military district, 135

INDEX

Committee of the House on Elections, Georgia case referred to, 223

Committee of the House on Impeachment, appointed, 174; proceedings, 175 *et seq.*

Committee of the House on Reconstruction, reports bill, 112; bill passed, 117; Covode resolution referred to, 171; reports impeachment resolution, 173; reports bill as to Georgia, 240

Committee of the House on the Judiciary, action as to thirteenth amendment, 28; Blaine moves reference to, 116

Committee of the House on the Rebellious States, 15

Committee of the Senate on Elections, Georgia case referred to, 223

Committee of the Senate on Finance, bill reported from, 277

Committee of the Senate on Foreign Relations, Sumner loses chairmanship of, 264; opposes Dominican treaty, 324, 325

Committee of the Senate on the Judiciary, action as to thirteenth amendment, 26–28; proposes Freedmen's Bureau bill, 64; reports a civil rights bill, 68; action on bill repealing Tenure-of-Office Act, 233

Committee of the Senate on the Rebellious States, 15

Congress of the United States, power vested in, 3; action on State perdurance, 5; power over territories, 6; relation of its acts to Reconstruction, 12; legislation on Reconstruction, 15; action as to electoral vote of 1864, 21, 22; twenty-second joint rule, 24, 25; attitude to Tennessee, 26; meeting of December, 1865, 40; Johnson's views of powers of, 41; demand of southerners for seats, 56; joint committee on reconstruction, 57, 58; passes Freedmen's Bureau bill, 66; passes civil rights bill, 70, 73; the fourteenth amendment, 74–79; proposal of committee on reconstruction, 80; reports to, on reconstruction, 84–86; passage of Freedmen's Bureau bill, 87–90; relation to campaign of 1866, 98; attacked by Johnson, 102; effect of election of 1866, 104; effect of Johnson's message on, 105; passes bill for negro suffrage in District of Columbia, 107, 108; bill vetoed, 107, 108; bill passed over veto, 109; vetoes sent to, 126; encroachment on President's power, 128; passes supplemental reconstruction bill, 129; opening of fortieth Congress, 132; passes bill interpreting Reconstruction Acts, 140; passes bill over veto, 142; as to powers of, 147; attitude of southern whites to acts of, 149; additional bill as to reconstructed States, 152, 153; comment on the act, 154; message to, of December, 1867, 158–160; admission of Southern members, 198, 202; action on proclamation of fourteenth amendment, 204; friction with Johnson, 214; annual message to, 214; action on fifteenth amendment, 217; question as to southern members, 223, 225; admits members from Virginia, 228; passes modification of Tenure-of-Office Act, 234; readmission of Georgia, 235–244; attitude to the South, 248; bill to enforce the amendments, 253–255; control of elections to, 256; statute on the Ku-Klux, 257, 258; legislation on finance, 276–279; electoral count of 1877, 283, 284; bill for electoral commission, 284, 285; action as to Santo Domingo, 326. *See* House of Representatives; Senate; Statutes of the United States

Conkling, Roscoe, on joint committee on reconstruction, 57; in convention of 1876, 281

Connecticut ratifies fourteenth amendment, 203, 204

Constitution of the United States, government provided by the, 2–4; relation of State government to, 5, 6; powers of Congress over elections, 22; eligibility to vice-presidency, 23, 24; adoption of the thirteenth amendment, 26–30, 55; the fourteenth amendment, 73–80, 82, 83; fourteenth amendment in the campaign of 1866, 98; fourteenth amendment rejected in South, 106, 109; fourteenth amendment with reference to re-

vival of State functions, 110; tests of, applied to reconstruction bill, 113; in reconstruction bill, 120, 121; interpreted by the Supreme Court, 144; fourteenth amendment ratified in Arkansas, 197; ratification of fourteenth amendment completed, 202-205; action on fifteenth amendment, 217; fifteenth amendment ratified by Georgia, 240; provision for enforcement of amendments, 253-255
Covode, John, resolutions on Johnson, 171
Cowan, Edgar, action on the Stevens resolution, 57; in convention of 1866, 99
Cox, Jacob D., in Pittsburg convention, 102; becomes secretary of the interior, 231
Creswell, John A J., in convention of 1866, 100; becomes postmaster-general, 231
Cronin, E. A., Oregon elector in 1876, 290, 291
Curtin, A. G., in convention of 1866, 100
Curtis, Benjamin R., counsel for Johnson, 176; argument, 182, 183
Cushing, Caleb, at Geneva arbitration, 311
Custer, George A., in Cleveland convention, 101

DAVIS, DAVID, joins liberal republicans, 264; candidate for presidential nomination, 265; elected Senator, 287; relation to electoral commission, 288
Davis, Henry Winter, bill on reconstruction, 15-18; protest against Lincoln's proclamation, 19
Davis, J. C. Bancroft, at Geneva arbitration, 311
Delaware, in election of 1866, 104; votes for Seymour, 212
Delfosse, Maurice, on Halifax commission, 321
Dennison, William, resignation, 90, 142
District of Columbia, bill for negro suffrage in, 107; bill vetoed, 108; bill passed over veto, 109; bill on colored schools in, 216
Dix, John A., in convention of 1866, 99

Dixon, James, action on the Stevens resolution, 57; vote on impeachment, 191
Doolittle, James R., action on the Stevens resolution, 57; in convention of 1866, 99; view of the Stanton case, 189; vote on impeachment, 191
Drew, George F., becomes governor of Florida, 296
Durant, Thomas J., in convention of 1866, 100
Durell, E. H., in Louisiana politics, 270, 271

EDMUNDS, GEORGE F., on electoral commission, 286
Electoral Commission, creation, 284, 285; membership, 286-289; proceedings, 290-293
Emory, W. H., relations with Johnson, 175, 179, 181
English, James E., in convention of 1866, 99
Evarts, William M., counsel for Johnson, 176; counsel before electoral commission, 291; at Geneva arbitration, 311
Ewing, Thomas, in Cleveland convention, 101; nominated as secretary of war, 173

FARRAGUT, DAVID D., accompanies Johnson to the West, 102
Favrot, Alexander, at Geneva arbitration, 311
Federal government, system of, 1, 2
Ferry, Thomas W., announces result of 1876 election, 294
Fessenden, William P., on joint committee on reconstruction, 57; theory of reconstruction, 60; opinion on impeachment, 184; view of the Stanton case, 189; vote on impeachment, 191
Field, Stephen J., on electoral commission, 286
Fish, Hamilton, becomes secretary of state, 232; negotiations with Great Britain, 306, 307; controversy with Granville, 312; congratulates Delfosse, 321
Fisheries Question, the, 320-322
Flanders, Benjamin F., elected to House of Representatives, 14

Florida, in Lincoln's proclamation, 11; electoral vote of 1864 rejected, 22; reconstruction in, 37; convention in, 38; adopts thirteenth amendment, 39; in the reconstruction bill, 112; registration in, 147; election in, 149; ratifies constitution, 155, 197; act on admission of members from, 198; reconstruction declared complete, 202; ratifies fourteenth amendment, 203, 204; contest as to election returns of 1876, 283, 289; change of administration, 296

Florida, the, case of, 315–317

Fowler, Joseph S., vote on impeachment, 191

Freedmen's Bureau, created, 44, 45; Grant's opinion of its officers, 63; bill of 1866, 64–67; bill passed over veto, 87–90. *See* Statutes of the United States

Frelinghuysen, Frederick T., on electoral commission, 286

Frémont, John C., nominated for presidency, 20; withdraws, 21

GALT, ALEXANDER T., on Halifax commission, 321

Garfield, James A., approves letter on Alta Vela claims, 177; on electoral commission, 286

Garland, Augustus H., elected governor of Arkansas, 273

Geneva Arbitration, 307, 308, 311–318

Georgia, in Lincoln's proclamation, 11; electoral vote of 1864 rejected, 22; reconstruction in, 37; convention and election in, 38; vote on thirteenth amendment, 55; in the reconstruction bill, 112; case of Georgia vs. Stanton, 146, 195; registration in, 147; election in, 148; election in, 149; ratifies constitution, 155, 197; controversy in, 155; act on admission of members from, 198, 199; reconstruction declared complete, 202; ratification of fourteenth amendment, 205; votes for Seymour, 212; question in Congress as to representation of, 224; question of representation of, 235–237; military government in, 238, 239; fifteenth amendment ratified, 240; admission delayed,

241, 242; finally restored to federal relations, 243, 244; escape from negro rule, 247, 248; election of 1872 in, 267

Gerry, Elbridge, in convention of, 1866, 100

Gillem, A. C., arrest of McCardle, 196

Granger, Gordon, in Cleveland convention, 101

Grant, Ulysses S., report on conditions at the South, 63; accompanies Johnson to the West, 102, acting Secretary of War, 143, 158; injunction against sought, 146; appointed acting secretary of war, 163; his action thereon, 164, 165; relations with Johnson, 166–168; nominated for presidency, 207; character of acceptance, 208; attitude to reconstruction, 223; proclamation as to Virginia, 227; orders as to Mississippi and Texas, 229, 230; policy characterized, 230, 231; attitude to Tenure-of-Office Act, 231–234; first annual message, 234; suggestion as to Georgia, 235; message of March, 1871, 257; proclamation of March, 1871, 258; proclamation of May, 1871, 259, 260; proclamations of April and November, 1871, 260, 261; relations with Sumner, 264; nominated for second term, 267; elected, 267; veto of inflation bill, 279; messages on relations with Great Britain, 303–306; policy as to Santo Domingo, 323–326

Granville, Lord, controversy with Fish, 312

Great Britain, change in ministry, 303; Grant's messages on relations with, 304–306; the Geneva arbitration, 307–318; the British Columbia boundary, 319; the fisheries question, 320–322

Greeley, Horace, in convention of 1866, 100; joins liberal republicans, 264; nominated for presidency, 265, 266; defeated, 267

Green, Ashbel, counsel before electoral commission, 291

Grey and Ripon, Earl de, on Joint High Commission, 307

Grider, Henry, on joint committee on reconstruction, 57

334 INDEX

Grimes, James W., on joint committee on reconstruction, 57; view of the Stanton case, 189; vote on impeachment, 191
Groesbeck, William S., counsel for Johnson, 177

HABEAS CORPUS, writ of, privileges suspended in District of Columbia, 39
Hahn, Michael, elected to House of Representatives, 14; elected Governor of Louisiana, 14
Halifax, N. S., fisheries commission at, 320, 321
Hamlin, Hannibal, count of electoral votes, 24
Hampton, Wade, in convention of 1868, 211; becomes governor of South Carolina, 206
Hancock, Winfield Scott, supersedes Sheridan, 143; in convention of 1868, 210
Harlan, James, resignation, 90, 142
Harris, Ira, on joint committee on reconstruction, 57
Hawley, Joseph R., in republican convention of 1866, 207
Hayes, Rutherford B., significance of his election, 279; nominated for presidency, 281, 282; the campaign, 283 et seq.; election formally declared, 294; policy toward the South, 295, 296
Henderson, John B., introduces amendment abolishing slavery, 26, 27; vote on impeachment, 191
Hendricks, Thomas A., candidate for presidential nomination, 210; nominated for vice-presidency, 282
Herron, Francis J., in Louisiana politics, 269, 270
Higby, William, views on purchase of Alaska, 300
Hill, Benjamin H., enters Senate from Georgia, 244
Hoadly, George, joins liberal republicans, 264; counsel before electoral commission, 291
Hoar, Ebenezer R., becomes attorney-general, 231; on Joint High Commission, 307
Hoar, George F., on electoral commission, 286
Hood, John B., near Nashville, 23

House of Representatives of the United States, admits members from Louisiana, 14; refuses seats to members from Arkansas, 15; action on thirteenth amendment, 28-30; elects Colfax Speaker, 42; the Stevens resolution, 42-44; speech by Stevens, 58; passes Freedmen's Bureau bill, 66; passes civil rights bill, 73; representation in, 74; election of 1866, 98; effect of election of 1866, 104; attempt to impeach Johnson, 109; bill on reconstruction before the, 112-118; resolution on confiscation act, 122; tenure-of-office bill in, 125; bill on reconstructed States, 153; action on dismissal of Stanton, 171; proceedings of impeachment against Johnson, 173 et seq.; passes bill repealing Tenure-of-Office Act, 232, 233; democrats secure control of, 253, 273; jurisdiction over treaties, 301, 302. See Congress of the United States; Statutes of the United States
Houston, George S., elected governor of Alabama, 273
Howard, Jacob M., on joint committee on reconstruction, 57; illness delays vote on impeachment, 190
Howe, Samuel G., commissioner to Santo Domingo, 326
Hunt, Ward, 289
Hunton, Eppa, on electoral commission, 286

ILLINOIS, ratifies fourteenth amendment, 203, 204; Davis elected Senator from, 287
Indiana, election of 1886 in, 103; ratifies fourteenth amendment, 203, 204; election of 1872 in, 267
Iowa, election of 1866 in, 103; ratifies fourteenth amendment, 203, 204
d'Itajubá, Baron, at Geneva arbitration, 311, 316

JENKINS, CHARLES J. institutes suit against Stanton, 145; removed by Meade, 155
Johnson, Andrew, elected vice-president, 21; calls Tennessee convention, 23; proclamation of Feb.

INDEX 335

25, 1865, 25; becomes president, 30; plan and acts as to reconstruction, 31-41; proclamation of May 29, 1865, 33, 34; identity of his plan with Lincoln's, 36; proclaims federal law in force in Virginia, 37; proclamations as to civil government, 39; message of Dec., 1865, 40; relation to congressional views of reconstruction, 61; sends Grant and Schurz through the South, 63; veto of Freedmen's Bureau bill, 66, 67; speech of Feb. 22, 1866, 67; veto of civil rights bill, 70, 71; effect of it, 72; veto overridden, 73; as to fourteenth amendment, 80; message as to Tennessee, 83; veto of Freedmen's Bureau bill overridden, 88-90; relations with Stanton, 90, 91; changes in cabinet, 90; relation to New Orleans riot, 95, 96; endorsed by convention of 1866, 99; criticized by conventions of 1866, 101, 162; takes part in campaign of 1866, 102; proclamation declaring war ended, 103; message of Dec., 1866, 104, 105; vetoes bill as to negro suffrage in District of Columbia, 107, 108; bill passed over his veto, 109; first attempt at impeachment, 109; vetoes resolution on confiscation act, 122; influence of Seward on, 124; vetoes reconstruction bill and tenure-of-office bill, 126; encroachment on his power, 128; veto of supplemental reconstruction bill, 132, 133; orders under the statutes, 135, 136, 138; vetoes bill interpreting reconstruction acts, 140, 141; distrust of Stanton, 140; veto overridden, 142; suspends Stanton, 142, 143; Mississippi vs. Johnson, 145, 195; supersedes Pope with Meade, 152; the attempt to impeach, 157-194; message on suspension of Stanton, 160-163; relations with Grant, 164-168; supersedes Stanton with Thomas, 169, 170; Covode resolution, 171; action of House on impeachment, 173 *et seq.*; vetoes overridden, 197, 199, 202; proclaims reconstruction completed, 202; conduct in campaign of 1868, 213; last annual message, 214; proclamation of Dec., 1868, 215; veto of colored school bill, 216; retirement, 218, 219; relations with republicans, 219-221; policy compared with Grant's, 230

Johnson, James, appointed governor of Georgia, 37

Johnson, Reverdy, on joint committee on reconstruction, 57; report on reconstruction, 86; in convention of 1866, 99; offers bill on reconstruction, 117; negotiates treaty with Clarendon, 303

Joint Committee on Reconstruction, 57, 58; recommendation on representation, 74; proposes bill, 80; its bill rejected, 82; final report of, 84-86

Joint High Commission, 307

Julian, George W., on impeachment committee, 174; joins liberal republicans, 264

KANSAS ratifies fourteenth amendment, 203, 204

Kellogg, Ensign H., on Halifax commission, 320, 321

Kellogg, William P., in Louisiana politics, 270-272; certificate in 1876 election, 290

Kendall vs. United States (12 Peters 524), 144

Kentucky, reconstruction in, 7, 13; in Lincoln's message, 20; in election of 1866, 104; votes for Seymour, 212; election of 1872 in, 267

Kenzie, Lewis M., in convention of 1866, 100

Kernan, Francis, in convention of 1868, 209

Koontz, William H., approves letter on Alta Vela claims, 177

Ku-Klux, the, 250-252, 255; act of April, 1871, 257, 258; trials, 261

LAWRENCE, WILLIAM B., in convention of 1866, 99

Lewis, D. P., elected governor of Alabama, 268

Liberal Republicans, convention of 1872, 264, 265; in campaign of 1872, 266

Lincoln, Abraham, views and acts as to reconstruction, 8-30; his proposed oath of allegiance, 10; attitude to the Pierpont government, 13; course toward Louisiana, 14, 15; proclamation of July 8, 1864, 18, 19; message of Dec. 6, 1864, 19, 20; renominated, 20; re-elected, 21; message of Feb. 8, 1865, 22; views of powers of Congress, 24; attitude to Brownlow's administration, 26; nature of acts as to abolition, 26; signs resolution on thirteenth amendment, 29; assassinated, 30; his cabinet retained by Johnson, 32; identity of plan of reconstruction with Johnson's, 36

Lindsay, Robert B., course as governor of Alabama, 268

Logan, John A., on impeachment committee, 174; impeachment manager, 175; approves letter on Alta Vela claim, 177

Louisiana, in Lincoln's proclamation, 11; Lincoln's acts toward, 12; presidential reconstruction in, 14, 15; in Lincoln's message, 19; electoral vote of 1864 rejected, 21, 22; attitude of Johnson to, 38; vote on thirteenth amendment, 55; contest for control of state government, 92-98; in the reconstruction bill, 112; registration in, 147; election in, 149; disfranchisements in, 150; ratifies constitution, 155, 197; act on admission of members from, 198; reconstruction declared complete, 202; ratifies fourteenth amendment, 203, 204; votes for Seymour, 212; corruption in, 263; contest for political control in, 269-272; contested electoral vote of 1876, 283, 289, 290; change of administration, 296

Louisville, Ky., democratic convention at, 267

Loyal League, the, 250, 252

Luther vs. Borden, (7 Howard 1), 144

Lynch, John, in Louisiana politics, 269-272

MACDONALD, JOHN, on Joint High Commission, 307

McCardle, William H., case of, 195, 196

McClellan, George B., nominated for presidency, 20; electoral votes, 21

McClernand, John A., in Cleveland convention, 101

McCrary, George W., suggests electoral commission, 284

McEnery, John, in Louisiana politics, 270-272; certificate in 1876 election, 290

Maine, election of 1866 in, 108; ratifies fourteenth amendment, 203, 204; election of 1872 in, 267

Marvin, William, appointed governor of Florida, 37

Maryland, in Lincoln's message, 20; in election of 1866, 104; votes for Seymour, 212; election of 1872 in, 267

Massachusetts ratifies fourteenth amendment, 203, 204

Matthews, Stanley, in convention of 1866, 100; joins liberal republicans, 264; counsel before electoral commission, 291

Meade, George G., supersedes Pope, 152; report on Alabama election, 153; removes Jenkins, 155; proclamation of June, 1868, 238, 239

Merrick, Richard T., counsel before electoral commission, 291

Michigan ratifies fourteenth amendment, 203, 204

Miller, J. N. Y., Oregon elector of 1876, 291

Miller, Samuel F., on electoral commission, 286

Miller enters Senate from Georgia, 244

Minnesota ratifies fourteenth amendment, 203, 204

Mississippi, in Lincoln's proclamation, 11; electoral vote of 1864 rejected, 22; reconstruction in, 37; convention in, 38; rejects thirteenth amendment, 39; law on vagrancy, etc., 46-52, 62; opinion of this legislation, 53; in the reconstruction bill, 112; Mississippi vs. Johnson, 145; registration in, 147; election in, 149; disfranchisements in, 151; constitution rejected in, 156; arrest of McCardle in, 196; martial law in, 202; no share in election of 1868, 212; ratification of constitution, 229; restored to federal relations, 229; negro rule in, 249; political conditions in 1875, 274, 275

INDEX 337

Mississippi vs. Johnson (4 Wallace 475), 145, 193, 195
Missouri, Reconstruction in, 7, 13; in Lincoln's message, 20; ratifies fourteenth amendment, 203, 204; liberal republicans in, 265; election of 1872 in, 267
Monroe, John T., as mayor of New Orleans, 94
Montgomery, Ala., made head-quarters of third military district, 135
Moorhead, James K., approves letter on Alta Vela claims, 177
Morgan, Edwin D., vote on Freedmen's Bureau bill, 67
Morrill, Justin S., on joint committee on reconstruction, 57
Morse, Alexander P., counsel before electoral commission, 291
Morton, Oliver P., in convention of 1866, 100; in convention of 1876, 281; on electoral commission, 286; resolution on Santo Domingo, 325
Moses, F. J., connection with South Carolina corruption, 262
Moses, F. J., Jr., judge-elect of South Carolina, 274

NASHVILLE, TENN., convention at, 236
National Nominating Conventions, radical republican of 1864, 20; democratic of 1864, 20; republican of 1864, 20; of 1866, 99-102; republican of 1868, 207; democratic of 1868, 208; liberal republican of 1872, 264, 265; democratic of 1872, 266; republican of 1868, 267; republican of 1876, 280, 281; democratic of 1876, 282
Nebraska ratifies fourteenth amendment, 203, 204
Nelson, Samuel, on Joint High Commission, 307
Nelson, Thomas A. R., counsel for Johnson, 176
Nevada ratifies fourteenth amendment, 203, 204
New Hampshire ratifies fourteenth amendment, 203, 204
New Jersey, ratifies fourteenth amendment, 203, 204; withdrawal of ratification, 203, 205, 206; votes for Seymour, 212

New Orleans, La., convention at, 14; riot at, 92-98; head-quarters of fifth military district, 135
New York, ratifies fourteenth amendment, 203, 204; votes for Seymour, 212
New York, N. Y., democratic convention of 1868 at, 208
New York *Tribune* prints protest of Wade and Davis, 19
Niblack, William E., motion in House, 43
Nicholls, Francis T., becomes governor of Louisiana, 296
North Carolina, in Lincoln's proclamation, 11; electoral vote of 1864 rejected, 22; reconstruction in, 35; convention in, 38; vote on thirteenth amendment, 55; in the reconstruction bill, 112; registration in, 147; election in, 149; ratifies constitution, 155, 197; act on admission of members from, 198; reconstruction declared complete, 202; ratifies fourteenth amendment, 203, 204; recovery from negro rule, 249
Northcote, Stafford, on Joint High Commission, 307
Northwest Ordinance, 27
Norton, Daniel S., action on the Stevens resolution, 57; vote on impeachment, 191

O'CONOR, CHARLES, nominated for presidency, 267; counsel before electoral commission, 291
Odell, W. H., Oregon elector of 1876, 291
Ohio, election of 1866 in, 103; vote on negro suffrage in, 148; ratifies fourteenth amendment, 203, 204; withdrawal of ratification, 203, 205, 206; election of 1872 in, 267
Ord, Edward O. C., in fourth military district, 135
Oregon, ratifies fourteenth amendment, 203, 204; votes for Seymour, 212; contested electoral returns of 1876, 289-291

PACKARD, S. B., takes possession of Louisiana capitol, 271; retires from office of governor, 296
Palmer, Roundell, at Geneva arbitration, 311

Parker, John, Oregon elector of 1876, 291
Parsons, Lewis E., appointed governor of Alabama, 37
Paschal, George W., in convention of 1866, 100
Patterson, David T., vote on impeachment, 191
Payne, Henry B., on electoral commission, 286
Pendleton, George H., nominated for vice-presidency, 21; candidate for presidential nomination, 208
Pennsylvania, election of 1866 in, 103; ratifies fourteenth amendment, 203, 204; election of 1872 in, 267
Perry, Benjamin F., appointed governor of South Carolina, 37
Philadelphia, Penn., conventions of 1866 at, 99, 100; republican convention of 1872 at, 267
Phillips, Wendell, characterised by Johnson, 67
Pierpont, Francis H., attitude of Lincoln to, 13; supported by Johnson, 37, 224
Pinchback, P. B. S., in Louisiana politics, 269, 272
Pittsburg, Penn., soldier convention at, 101
Poland, Luke P. connection with Thomas case, 174
Pope, John, in third military district, 136; injunction sought against, 146; election orders, 151; recalled, 152
Preston, William, in convention of 1868, 210
Pulaski, Tenn., place of origin of Ku-Klux, 250

RANDALL, ALEXANDER W., appointed postmaster-general, 90; accompanies Johnson to the West, 102
Rawlins, John A., becomes secretary of war, 232
Raymond, Henry J., views on reconstruction, 59; vote on fourteenth amendment, 87; in convention of 1866, 99
Reconstruction, theory of, 1-7; Lincoln's views and acts as to, 8-30; Seward's view of, 12; in Louisiana, 14; the Wade-Davis bill, 15-18; relation of party conventions to, 20; in Tennessee, 23, 25; Johnson's plan as to, 31-41; in North Carolina, 35; in the several States, 37, 38; views of House on, 43; attitude of republicans, 44; joint committee on, 57; views of Stevens, 58; views of Raymond and Shellabarger, 59; theory of Sumner, 60; reports of congressional committee, 84-86; as an issue in the campaign of 1866, 98; Johnson's defence of his policy as to, 102; bill in the House, 112-114; the Blaine amendment, 115, 116; the Sherman bill, 117; the bill as finally passed, 118-122; vetoed by Johnson, 126; republican motives in, 127; supplemental bill on, 129-131; vetoed, 132; acts on, criticised, 133, 134; application of acts on, 135-137; congressional interpretation of acts on, 138; bill interpreting the statutes on, 140; application of statutes on, 146 *et seq.*; process of, declared completed, 203; attitude of Grant toward, 223; end of legislation on, 244; reconstruction characterized, 297. *See* Statutes
Republican party, schism threatened in, 20; attitude to reconstruction, 44; attitude to southern legislation, 52, 54; feeling toward southern congressmen, 56; attitude to views of Stevens, Raymond and Shellabarger, 59; attitude to presidential reconstruction, 60, 61; position on civil rights, 62; attitude to Freedmen's Bureau bill, 89; attitude to Stanton, 90, 91; in campaign of 1866, 99, 101; convention of 1866, 104; in election of 1866, 104; views on reconstruction, 110, 111; motives in Reconstruction, 127; interpretation of Johnson's message, 160; action in vote on impeachment, 191; effect of McCardle case on, 197; convention of 1868, 207; criticism of views of, 217; relations with Johnson, 219-221; control of Grant, 257; revolt in the party, 264, 265; convention of 1872, 267; get control of Alabama legislature, 268, 269; lose control in Congress, 273; financial policy, 276; con-

vention of 1876, 280, 281; campaign of 1876, 283 *et seq.;* views as to powers of Congress, 292
Retribution, the, case of, 316
Rhode Island ratifies fourteenth amendment, 203, 204
Richmond, Va., made head-quarters of first military district, 135; convention at, 226, 227
Robeson, George M., becomes secretary of the navy, 232
Rogers, Andrew J., on joint committee on reconstruction, 57
Rose, John, mission of, 306
Ross, Edmund G., vote on impeachment, 191
Rousseau, Lovell H., in Cleveland convention, 101
Russia, purchase of Alaska from, 300–302

SAFFORD, M. J., in convention of 1866, 100
St. Louis, Mo., Johnson's speech at, 102
Samana Bay, 324, 327
Santo Domingo, Sumner's position as to, 264; attempt to annex to United States, 323–327
Schaffner law, the, 249
Schell, Augustus, in convention of 1868, 209
Schenck, Robert C., in convention of 1866, 100; on Joint High Commission, 307; at London, 312
Schofield, John M., assigned to first military district, 135, 226; nominated as secretary of war, 190; confirmed, 192; retained by Grant, 231; resigns, 232
Schriver, General, in Stanton-Thomas incident, 169, 170, 172, 173
Schurz, Carl, report on conditions at the South, 63; in convention of 1866, 100; joins liberal republicans, 264
Sclopis, Frederic, at Geneva arbitration, 311, 316, 317
Scott, R. K., views of Ku-Klux, etc., 259
Senate of the United States, refuses seats to members from Arkansas, 15; adopts thirteenth amendment, 26–28; the Stevens resolution, 43, 44, 57; passes Freedmen's Bureau bill, 66; passes civil rights bill, 70, 73; effect of election of 1866, 104; passes reconstruction bill, 118; tenure-of-office bill in, 122, 125; passes resolution on confiscation act, 122; bill on reconstructed States, 153; action on suspension of Stanton, 162, 163; action on dismissal of Stanton, 170; acts as court of impeachment, 176 *et seq.;* vote on impeachment, 190, 191; confirms Schofield, 192; resolution on the amnesty proclamation, 215, 216; confirms Grant's nominees, 232; admits members from Georgia, 244; currency bill in, 277; ratifies treaty with Russia, 300; rejects Johnson-Clarendon treaty, 303; rejects Dominican treaty, 324, 325. *See* Congress of the United States; Statutes of the United States
Seward, William H., views on reconstruction, 12; sends thirteenth amendment to states, 29; retained by Johnson, 32; calculation as to thirteenth amendment, 52, 55, 56; announces adoption of thirteenth amendment, 55; action on fourteenth amendment, 80; accompanies Johnson to the west, 102; influence on Johnson, 124; proclaims ratification of fourteenth amendment, 202; procedure as to the proclamation, 203–205; negotiates purchase of Alaska, 300–301; negotiates treaty with China, 322; instructions to Babcock, 323
Seymour, Horatio, nominated for presidency, 210; defeated, 212
Shaffer, J. W., secures letter on Alta Vela claims, 177
Sharkey, William L., appointed governor of Mississippi, 37; institutes suit against Johnson, 145
Shellabarger, Samuel, theory of reconstruction, 59–61; counsel before electoral commission, 291; opinion of purchase of Alaska, 300
Shenandoah, the, case of, 316, 317
Shepley, George F., military governor of Louisiana, 14
Sheridan, Philip H., New Orleans riot, 94, 97; in fifth military district, 135; superseded by Hancock, 143

Sherman, John, offers bill on reconstruction, 117; father-in-law of Ewing, 178; reports currency bill, 277
Sickles, Daniel E., in second military district, 135; superseded by Canby, 143
Sinclair, John G., in convention of 1866, 99
Skinner, J. B. L., postmaster-general *ad interim*, 186, 188
Slavery, adoption of the thirteenth amendment, 26-30
South Carolina, in Lincoln's proclamation, 11; electoral vote of 1864 rejected, 23; reconstruction in, 37; convention and election in, 38; law on vagrancy, 46; vote on thirteenth amendment, 55; in the reconstruction bill, 112; registration in, 147; election in, 149; character of convention in, 150; ratifies constitution, 155, 197; act on admission of members from, 196; reconstruction declared complete, 203; ratifies fourteenth amendment, 203, 204; request of governor for troops, 258; proclamations of president as to, 260, 261; corruption in, 262; conditions in 1874, 274; contested electoral returns of 1876, 283, 289; change of administration, 296
Spaulding, J. R., joins liberal republicans, 264
Speed, James, resignation, 90, 142; in convention of 1866, 100, 101
Staempfli, Jacob, at Geneva arbitration, 311, 315, 316
Stanbery, Henry, appointed attorney-general, 90; in case of Mississippi vs. Johnson, 145; in case of Georgia vs. Stanton, 146; arrest of Thomas, 172; counsel for Johnson, 176
Stanley, Lord, secretary for foreign affairs, 303
Stanton, Edwin M., attitude to Johnson, 90, 91; as to the New Orleans riot, 95, 96; dissents from instructions on reconstruction, 136; distrusted by Johnson, 140; suspended, 142, 143, 158; case of Georgia vs. Stanton, 146, 195; message on suspension of, 160-162; action of Senate as to, 162, 163; superseded by Thomas, 169-172; removal discussed before Senate, 178, 179; power to remove, 185; his violations of law, 189; abdication, 192
Statutes of the United States, of Aug. 7, 1789, 184; of May 8, 1792, 186, 187; of Feb. 13, 1795, 179, 186, 187; of July 31, 1861, 175; of Feb. 20, 1863, 187, 188; of Mar. 3, 1865, 44, 64, 65, 89; of April 9, 1866, 68-73; of July 16, 1866, 87-90; of Feb. 5, 1873, 197; of Mar. 2, 1867 (on reconstruction), 112-121, 126, 136, 159, 160, 175, 179, 193, 197, 215, 235, 239, 243, 245, 247, 250-253; of Mar. 2, 1867 (on tenure-of-office), 122-126, 160-163, 165, 166, 174, 178, 181, 184, 185, 188, 189, 214, 231-234; of Mar. 11, 1867, 155; of Mar. 23, 1867, 129-133, 136, 159, 160, 193, 197, 235, 245, 247, 250-253; of June 22, 1868, 198; of June 25, 1868, 202, 241, 249; of June 28, 1868, 198; of July 26, 1868, 302; of Mar. 18, 1869, 276, 277; of April 10, 1869, 229; of Dec. 22, 1869, 239; of May 31, 1870, 255, 256; of July 14, 1870, 276, 278; of July 15, 1870, 244; of Jan. 20, 1871, 276; of Feb. 28, 1871, 256; of April 20, 1871, 257, 260, 261; of May 22, 1872, 268; of Jan. 14, 1875, 279, 283
Stearns, M. L., retires as governor of Florida, 296
Stephens, Alexander H., seeks seat in Congress, 56
Stevens, Thaddeus, proposes substitute thirteenth amendment, 28; resolution on representation, 42-44, 57; view of Mississippi legislation, 53; on committee on reconstruction, 57; views of reconstruction, 58; characterized by Johnson, 67; view as to effect of secession, 81; introduces bill on reconstruction, 112; refuses to accept the Blaine amendment, 115, 116; on impeachment committee, 174; impeachment manager, 175; approves letter on Alta Vela claims, 177; views on purchase of Alaska, 300
Stewart, Alexander T., nominated for secretary of treasury, 231; declines, 232

INDEX 341

Stockton, John P., in convention of 1866, 99
Stoeckl, Baron, negotiates treaty for sale of Alaska, 300
Stone, John M., elected governor of Mississippi, 276
Stoughton, E. W., counsel before electoral commission, 291
Strong, William, on electoral commission, 286
Sumner, Charles, theory of reconstruction, 60, 61; characterized by Johnson, 67; joins liberal republicans, 264; relations with Grant, 264, 325
Supreme Court of the United States, relation of dicta to reconstruction, 12; decisions, 144–146, 179, 195, 196
Swayne, Noah H., 289

TENNESSEE, in Lincoln's proclamation, 11; in Lincoln's message, 20; electoral vote of 1864 rejected, 21, 22; Reconstruction in, 23, 25; civil government established in, 25; ratifies thirteenth amendment, 30; attitude of Johnson to, 38; vote on thirteenth amendment, 55; ratifies fourteenth amendment, 82, 83; ratifies fourteenth amendment, 203, 204; election of 1872 in, 267
Tenterden, Lord, at Geneva arbitration, 311
Tenure-of-Office Bill, the, introduced, 122, 123; contents, 124, 125; vetoed, 125; case of Stanton, 162 *et seq.* See Statutes
Terry, Alfred H., modifies Virginia vagrant act, 225, 226; resumes military control in Georgia, 239
Texas, in Lincoln's proclamation, 11; electoral vote of 1864 rejected, 22; war declared ended in, 103; in the reconstruction bill, 112; registration in, 147; election in, 149; martial law in, 202; no share in election of 1868, 212; restored to federal relations, 229, 230; escape from negro rule, 247–249; election of 1872 in, 267; change in character of government, 273
Thomas, George H., in third military district, 135; transferred, 136
Thomas, Lorenzo, appointed to supersede Stanton, 169–173; his position discussed before Senate, 179, 181; law as to appointment of, 186
Thornton, Edward, negotiations at Washington, 306, 307
Thurman, Allen G., on electoral commission, 286
Tilden, Samuel J., in convention of 1866, 99; in convention of 1868, 209; nominated for presidency, 282; the campaign, 283 *et seq.*
Townsend, E. D., orders from Stanton, 170; in temporary charge of war department, 192
Trumbull, Lyman, reports thirteenth amendment, 26; in convention of 1866, 100; opinion on impeachment, 184; view of the Stanton case, 189; vote on impeachment, 191; proposal as to Tenure-of-Office Act, 233; joins liberal republicans, 264; candidate for presidential nomination, 265; counsel before electoral commission, 291
Twenty-second joint rule of Congress, 24, 25

UNION LEAGUES, formation of, 250, 252

VALLANDIGHAM, CLEMENT L., in convention of 1866, 99
Van Winkle, Peter G., view of the Stanton case, 189; vote on impeachment, 191
Vermont, election of 1866 in, 103; ratifies fourteenth amendment, 203, 204; election of 1872 in, 267
Vicksburg, Miss., made head-quarters of fourth military district, 135
Virginia, reconstruction in, 7; omission from Lincoln's proclamation, 13; electoral vote of 1864 rejected, 22; reconstruction in, 37; vote on thirteenth amendment, 55; in the reconstruction bill, 112, 122; registration in, 147; election in, 149; disfranchisements in, 151; martial law in, 202; no share in election of 1868, 212; question in Congress as to representation, 224; partition of, 224; the vagrant act, 225, 226; a military district, 226, 227; restored to federal relations, 228; escape from negro rule, 247, 248

WADE, BENJAMIN F., bill on reconstruction, 15-18; protest against Lincoln's proclamation, 19; opinion of Johnson, 32; commissioner to Santo Domingo, 326
Waite, Morrison R., 289; at Geneva arbitration, 311
Walker, Robert J., in case of Mississippi vs. Johnson, 145
War Department, Freedmen's Bureau organized in, 44
Ward, Hamilton, on impeachment committee, 174
Warmoth, Henry C., connection with Louisiana corruption, 268; contest for control in Louisiana, 269-273
Washburne, Elihu B., on joint committee on reconstruction, 57; becomes secretary of state, 231; resigns, 232
Washington, treaty of, 299, 307-310, 319
Watts, John W., Oregon elector in 1876, 290, 291
Welles, Gideon, accompanies Johnson to the west, 102
Wells, David A., joins liberal republicans, 264
Wells, J. Madison, in contest for control of Louisiana, 93
Welsh pays Halifax award, 322
West Virginia ratifies fourteenth amendment, 203, 204
Wharton, John, in Louisiana politics, 269, 270
Wheeler, William A., nominated for vice-presidency, 282; election formally declared, 294
Wheeling, W. Va., government at, 224
Whipper, W. J., judge-elect of South Carolina, 274
Whiskey ring, 273
White, Andrew D., commissioner to Santo Domingo, 326
White, Horace, joins liberal republicans, 264
White vs. Clements, 237
Whitney, William C., counsel before electoral commission, 291
William I., Emperor, award as to northwest boundary, 319
Williams, George H., offers bill on reconstruction, 117; introduces tenure-of-office bill, 122; impeachment manager, 175; motions, 191; on Joint High Commission, 307
Wilson, Henry, theory of reconstruction, 60; on impeachment committee, 174; impeachment manager, 175; elected vice-president, 267
Windom, William, introduces thirteenth amendment in House, 28
Winthrop, Robert C., in convention of 1866, 99
Wisconsin ratifies fourteenth amendment, 203, 204
Wood, Fernando, in convention of 1866, 99
Wool, John E., in Cleveland convention, 101

Printed in the United States
137140LV00002BA/4/A